Jewish American Literature since 1945

An Introduction

Stephen Wade

Edinburgh University Press

With thanks to Ann Vinnicombe

© Stephen Wade, 1999

Edinburgh University Press
22 George Square, Edinburgh

Typeset in 10 on 12½ Stone Serif
by Hewer Text Limited, Edinburgh, and
printed and bound in Great Britain by
MPG Books Ltd, Bodmin

A CIP record for this book is available
from the British Library

ISBN 1 85331 226 6 (paperback)

Jewish American Literature
since 1945

To

Contents

Introduction:

Persistent Themes and Questions

Definitions and Boundaries

This study of Jewish-American literature begins with the emergence of specifically Jewish-American authors in the earlier years of the century, despite the date of 1945 as the official starting-point. Dominant voices such as Philip Roth and Saul Bellow shortly after the Second World War had precursors who had achieved a great deal, and any study of this literature must begin with Abraham Cahan and Henry Roth. But before any initial criticism is offered on particular writers, there are some fundamental questions to be asked, and some historical and social factors to summarise.

The first issue is to try to define what is meant by Jewish-American literature. There is the problem of language first of all; there is a tradition of writing in Yiddish in place of English. Isaac Bashevis Singer writes everything in Yiddish. Then there is the problem of what is meant by 'Jewish'. Since the first large-scale immigration of Eastern European Jews into the USA in the period 1880–1920 there have been various degrees of assimilation into American lifestyles and ideologies. Even before this, as early as the 1840s, there had been the emergence of Reform Judaism as opposed to Orthodox Judaism.

By 1945, a Jewish-American could be Conservative, Orthodox, Reform, assimilated or even what may be called 'a good Jew' yet being largely American in moral and intellectual outlook.

To make sense of this, it is profitable to insist that studies of this kind are concerned with that body of writing which is written in English by Jewish-American writers who take as their themes and preoccupations questions of Jewish life and identity within the social and ideological fabric of American society. It is difficult to be certain about recurring themes within this writing, just as it is hard to define Judaism itself. For example, Chaim Potok writes in detail about Hassidic Jews; Bellow is often concerned with the life of the intellectual and thinker; Roth uses popular culture and European contexts; Erica Jong relates Jewishness to femininity and feminism. In all this, is there a clearly perceived area which may be common subject-matter?

One answer to this is that there is. On the level of great universal literary discourse, there are these: the Holocaust, Zionism, European Jewry, assimilation and religious practice. In one of the most recent works dealt with in this study, Arthur Miller's 1994 play, *Broken Glass*, Miller explores the persistence of these huge issues by making his character Sylvia Gellburg suffer a paralysing illness which is attributable, in one sense, to her perception that the Nazi Final Solution, reported in the newspapers (the play is set in 1938), is indirectly responsible. Miller reiterates a question which runs through the texts in this book:

> *Gellburg*: But there are some days I feel like going and sitting in the Shul with the old men and pulling the *tallis* [prayer-shawl] over my head and be a full-time Jew the rest of my life. . . . And other times, I could almost kill them. They infuriate me. I am ashamed of them and that I look like them.[1]

Miller here is expressing something of the central duality that has been felt ever since the establishment of a schism in American Jewry in the Reform movements of the 1840s. In his 1972 film *A Stranger Among Us*, Sidney Lumet has his assimilated Jewish detective say of the Hassidim that 'they embarrass me'. The Hassidim maintain the traditional lifestyle and religious practices of Judaism and are the least American-ised. Yet, there is also a humorous side to these self-criticisms. The Jewish joke about the Jew who lands on a desert island to find another Jew who shows him around says much about this. The castaway shows off a synagogue proudly. They walk a little further and there is another synagogue. 'Why two synagogues?' the visitor asks.

'That's the one we don't go to.' This is not trivial; the attitudes expressed in Jewish jokes have had an impact on literature itself, and one aspect of this writing is that its serious aims and pretentions are always paralleled in the humour which undermines it in the general mediation of the subject. Much the same may be said of Irish literature, for instance.

In other words, the mediated statements about Jewishness in America have always been related to various conflicts – that is, until recent years, when the view has been expressed that there is no issue any more. The extensive fictional enquiries and intellectual excursions of the Bellow–Malamud–Roth novels of the 1960s and 1970s said so much about all these dualities of arrival and identity, that it might seem to some that there is nothing left of importance today in America when it comes to Jewish American writing. Irving Howe in 1977 said that 'Jewish fiction has probably moved past its highpoint.'² This is far from the truth. This is perhaps the most exciting and rewarding time to study the literature of the Jewish-Americans. As each generation of immigrants has moved further into assimilated American life, the more the deeper and wider religious and political meanings of being Jewish have been preserved and studied. Centres for Jewish Studies are mushrooming once more in the USA and the most urgently contemporary subjects of women's lives within Jewish communities, the re-teaching of the Holocaust, the reaction against materialism and, most of all, a new attempt to define and understand the art and literature of the first-and-second generation immigrants are not only notable but vibrant. Even established writers are still causing critics and readers to rethink the experience of Jews in urban and suburban America. In a review of Philip Roth's *American Pastoral*, Dale Peck says this:

> What it boils down to is this: Roth/Zuckerman has always been fascinated by the spin that immigrant Jews have put on the quintessentially American experience of assimilation

largely because he viewed it as not just impossible but undesirable. Now . . . Zuckerman is reconsidering that position. Maybe assimilation is . . . ordinariness – and is all a man should hope for.[3]

Behind this critique is a long and wordy tradition of writing that seeks to insist that the Jewish intellectual has a special sensitivity, a vestige of European cultural acquisition that sets him apart from materialist America. Can Roth really be saying this? That ordinariness is the destination of all this? Followers of Roth's hero Zuckerman will find Peck's comments hard to take but believable in the end.

Some Established Themes

One firmly entrenched feature of Jewish writing – there long before America became the main centre of Jewish population – is the idea of the 'little man'. In the stories of Isaac Bashevis Singer we have this, and it goes deep into the literary conventions of Yiddish. Singer himself commented, in an interview, that he didn't really follow this entirely:

> Well, the Yiddish writer was not really brought up with heroes. I mean there were very few heroes in the Jewish ghettos – very few knights and counts and people who fought duels. In my own case, I don't feel I write in the tradition of the 'little man' because their man is actually a *victim*.[4]

Nevertheless, this figure of the *nebbish* and *schlemiel* persists. He is to be found in the films of Woody Allen just as often as in the novels of Bellow or Roth. He is there in much comedy and film. Both Yiddish words convey failure and incompetence, referring to someone who is laughed at because of small stature and failure to succeed in life.

But this 'little man' is also a universal figure in modernist literature, so his appearance in Jewish-American writing is no surprise. Bloom in James Joyce's *Ulysses* is both Jewish and 'little'. Modernism in many ways created this non-entity who is

of abiding interest, using the microscope to study his insignificance. In the hands of a writer such as Saul Bellow or Philip
Roth, the *Kleinman* achieves another status – representative of a
multiplicity of values and universal aspirations. His failure is
magnificent and totally egalitarian. In the context of Jewish
social philosophy, though, he is always seen in contra-distinction to the man who succeeds, who gathers wealth and lives the
American Dream. The little man suffers too, and often sees this
as a trial which is, finally, both meaningful and beneficial in
some way.

Woody Allen comments on his character, Kleinman, in
Shadows and Fog, when asked about perpetuating a myth of
Jewish masochism:

It seems to me a completely accurate portrayal of standard
feelings Jews have about Jews. Maybe other people have
them too. But it's certainly a prevalent feeling that Jews have
about other Jews.[5]

Clearly, the 'little man' subject relates also to many familiar
themes in American literature. Arthur Miller's *Death of a Salesman* for instance, with its central character of Willy Loman,
seems to deal with the notions of social mobility, the achievement of the 'Dream', material wealth and the need for a
harmonious family life. Not only does Loman link well with
more clearly definable Jewish protagonists in American texts,
but he also defines the universality of the small man's aspirations and failures.

The following chapters will trace the development and notable metamorphoses of *Kleinman*, from his beginnings in the
dispossessed of the novels written in the period 1900 to 1945,
through the absurd comedy of Roth and Allen, emerging into
the depiction of specifically new versions of being American in,
for instance, the work of Erica Jong and Cynthia Ozick. But the
notion of Kleinman is only one perspective on the protagonists
of this fiction.

The Immigrant Experience

As with all literatures concerned with departure and arrival, the Jewish-American texts deal with shifting notions of identity. But the immigrants into the America of the early twentieth century were also moving from a largely peasant economy, with settled patterns of social and religious life, into the hub of modernity. As the sociologist J. L. Bau puts it:

> Internally, the discovery of the modern world has meant taking a fresh look – reinforced by the modern physical and social sciences . . . and . . . western notions of aesthetics and morality – at Jewish tradition itself. This is often referred to as a crisis of Jewish identity; but such a description makes the whole problem one of individual response. It suggests that now, as each American Jew lives the greater part of his life outside of the Jewish tradition, he must invariably question the remaining fragmentary relation that he has to the Jewish tradition.[6]

This explains a great deal of the fictional interest in Jewish-American fiction, and also forms the basis of much that the literature of the American Diaspora adds to the identity questions.

The fact remains that over two million Jews went to America between 1880 and 1920, and that succeeding generations have revised and redefined that immigrant experience. Naturally, the fact that these peoples had such a long history behind them in their former lives means that several interesting and creative dichotomies are set up on establishment in America. In the central concepts of religious practices and beliefs, it is difficult to see a clear pattern, largely because there is no central creed, no one primary formulated doctrine in Judaism that unites all shades of belief. Consequently, even on arrival in the New World, there were already differences in varieties of Jewish faith and social life in the immigrants.

But there is a concept of Jewishness that goes beyond all the establishment values, and this is often claimed as a changeless,

sustaining and ultimately definitive quality which all succeeding generations should hold on to. For instance, Isaac Bashevis
Singer says this of a Yiddish writer he knew:

He was brought up with the idea that one should get out of
Jewishness and become universal. And because he tried so
hard to become universal, he became very provincial. This is
the tragedy.[7]

So much of this literature of immigration and of changing into
an American is the pivotal subject-matter on which later writers
work and create. Arguably, the quintessential fictional statements on this are to be found in Abraham Cahan's novel, *The
Rise of David Levinsky* (1917). When David has just arrived, he is
on the streets, and he explains a new friend's interpretation of
the New World:

He went on to show how the New World turned things
upside down, transforming an immigrant shoemaker into
a man of substance, while a former man of leisure was forced
to work in a factory here.[8]

Understandably, the third-generation Jewish-Americans
needed to relocate the European past and also the shocks
involved in arrival and assimilation. Every detail of this social
upheaval has been written about, from changes in clothes and
fashion to concepts of morality, education and sexuality. In the
1990s it is clear that the newest generation is beginning to
compare its people's literature of ethnicity and difference with
that of Black American writing, and noting the differences in
self-esteem, defined uniqueness and linguistic distinctness.[9]

Conflicts

Historians have recounted the various splinter-groups and
divisions which have gradually fragmented whatever concept
was meant by the term 'American Jewry'. Any term such as this
one implies that there is some kind of monolithic ideology

embracing all versions of Jewishness. The truth is that there have been internal and external conflicts which have partly caused immensely productive creative impulses and partly brought about irreparable harm. In terms of this study, the two central conflicts affecting the literature of the period are:

1. Jews as an ethnic minority with specific identities to be preserved in a massively saturated popular cultural macro-society. In other words, a new version of cultural assimilation.
2 Internecine opposition, in which various versions of Orthodox and Reform Jews have maintained differences.

As a figure isolated as different, the archetypal Jew, created by Western culture at its centre, textualising peripheral concepts such as the Noble Savage or the Romantic Poet, has been constructed as either a victim – rootless and ostracised – or as a usurer, a winner in the capitalist game learned of his masters. Gore Vidal, writing in the 1970s, linked them with other minorities in America in this way:

> Jews, blacks and homosexuals are despised by the Christian and Communist majorities of East and West. Also, since the invention of Israel, Jews can count on the hatred of the Islamic world.[10]

It is enlightening to compare attitudes now, twenty years on from Vidal's well-publicised essay. To many, the stress of difference is hardly an issue any more. To others, it is a cultural acquisition, no more political and urgent than, say, morris dancing as an emblem of Englishness. But again, there has been diversity and conflict. The Lubervitcher Orthodoxy might label the assimilated Jews as 'Nice Irvings' and despise their acquired patina of American-ness, whatever that is.

Such conflicts are often made by an awareness of fundamental identity being erased. To extremists, total assimilation into Americans is tantamount to finishing what Hitler started in his Final Solution, and a leading rabbi has said this in an educational video.[11]

The inner conflicts, apparent in many of the texts covered in this book, are situated within such large-scale oppositions, but other factors complicate these existential questions still further. The central protagonists of the influential fictions and dramas of Bellow, Malamud, Roth, Miller and others often find themselves beset by problems of the uprooted, of the place of the intellect and creativity in American society and of the survival of cultural and aesthetic values in a consumer society. Those characters who remain adherents of Jewish religious practice have the added burden of clinging to the old world of *Shul* and *Shtetl* while being modern Americans.

Even in Britain, a recent argument about the establishment of an *eruv* (a demarcated area forming a Jewish community) in London had prompted one journalist to write:

> Religious Jews have been alarmed to discover that their prospects can disappear overnight once their faith becomes too visible.[12]

The recurrent imaginative interests of the Jewish-American writers have been balanced fruitfully between the perils of stagnation within Orthodoxy and the need to be utterly transformed, reborn without any vestige of Jewishness retained. But certain aspects of Jewish ideology and religious philosophy have persisted and are now inspiring a new generation of writers and artists.

Moralism and Voluntaryism

If citizens in a society whose forces absorb them still retain elements of their basic religious impulses, then a secular morality replaces the religious tenets. It has been argued that this has happened to Judaism since the first colonists. J. L. Bau puts it like this:

> Moralism is reflected by the insistence on the question 'Does N. lead a good life?' as a prevalent American substitution for the question 'Does N. lead a Christian life?' The distinction

between moralism and religion was well understood in colonial times.[13]

The notion of moralism involves a conception of religion as
being a life in which we behave rightly and fairly towards
others, allowing them freedom, being tolerant and so on.
Voluntaryism is the idea that 'the rights of the individual
always should take precedence over the rights of society'.[14]
Put these ideas together and we have that specific brand of
American individualism which rests on tolerance and on a
respect for spirituality which may align itself to no general
creed: the outcome is all.

These lines of thought obviously sit easily with the beliefs of
Judaism, which is, after all, a religion with flexibility, kindness
and openness to others, despite some of the images created by
extremists. 'Jewish stress has remained fixed for many centuries
. . . on its program for living a good life. Institutional arrange-
ments have been secondary to this purpose.'[15] In Isaac Bashevis
Singer's seminal story, 'Gimpel the Fool' for instance, the
village rabbi relents in imposing punishment on Gimpel's
erring wife when Gimpel himself pleads for her.

Finally, the literature covered here includes gentiles of
course. In a startlingly powerful essay, the poet John Berryman
describes a scene of anti-Semitism he witnessed:

The imaginary Jew I was was as real as the imaginary Jew
hunted down, on other nights and days, in a real Jew . . . the
real and the imaginary blood flow down together.[16]

How the gentiles are textualised in the literature of the period
before 1945, compared with recent decades, is enough for a
study in itself. But one example will show the potential interest:
that of the appeal of the WASP male (White Anglo-Saxon
Protestant). In the stories of Anzia Yezierska, he is adored as
a beautiful ideal. He embodies the aspirations of the immigrant
Jewish woman. But such constructions are impossible in later
decades; it took an impassioned innocence and a poetic vision
within traditionally conceived realistic fiction to include such
representations. A simple comparison of Yezierska's and Jong's

male characters will show this immeasurable change. The gentile world is, as this makes clear, an arena of increasing duality and doubt. The identities formed there are to be redefined as the enquiries initiated in this study progress. In other words, contemporary writers have to eradicate a certain mindset about how Jewishness is represented.

Contemporary Challenges and Themes

Since the immensely popular era of Saul Bellow's first real successes, and the massive critical acclaim that followed, important social and intellectual developments have meant that younger Jewish-American writers are switching the focus from previously ideological and philosophical concerns to a more overt interest in changes within America's specific versions of modernity. Some of the prominent aspects of the postmodern condition, often written about in most major literatures, are perhaps seen most acutely in the USA. Such phenomena as the communication revolution, intrusions into personal life, mass-media sales economy, secular and religious pluralism and the challenge to order and authority are having an impact on these new writers, often in a way that forces writers to take up historical perspectives, looking for revaluations of their parents' experience as Americans. The demographic changes reflect this; the tendency of settlement for successful Jews is to have moved from city to suburb to isolation – often from East to West.

If postmodernism means anything, then it must indicate the culture of confusing choice. We are able to choose allegiances and denials as well as choosing minority or majority views in a pluralistic world. Jewish-American writing has an important part to play in the question of how the literature of a global village deals with minority voices.

One expression of this has been the revisiting of family history. The almost limitless possibilities of Holocaust literature, for instance (almost a whole corpus for study in itself), has led certain writers to look again at the 'new lives' of survivors and the ways in which younger generations have been influenced in their self-concepts and relationships. In Britain, Anne

Karpf's memoir, *The War After*, provides a similar enquiry into her own self-identity in a European context, and points out that Jewish concepts such as *haimish* – homeliness and family love – had never been expressed in literature. In other words, the ordinary, physical and relational elements in being Jewish were due for expression. America has done exactly the same. In Grace Paley's stories, we find delicate and ironical vignettes of ordinary Americans who have known horror and degradation, and have only adapted and survived at a very automatic, superficial level.

The vibrancy now apparent in this literature also comes from a strong need to rediscover the ethos and spirit of the first-generation immigrants, particularly those of the massive influx of Russian Jews after the pogroms in Russia following the assassination of the liberal Alexander II. Younger writers are anxious to find revisions of the representations of the Jewish people of that foundation era. For instance, in popular film, many gross simplifications have occurred, giving images of certain aspects of Jewishness as life-denying, stultifying and negative: refusing American assimilation. One only has to think about films such as *The Jazz Singer* or *Yentl*.

There is also the need to understand what has happened to the version of Jewishness that clearly exists in a social sense completely divorced from religious practice. In other words, the accretions of Jewish cultural life and discourse. Undeniably, the contribution of Jewish thinkers, writers, entertainers and artists reflects a complex diversity: the poets and fiction-writers have not overlooked this, and their work spans rich and poor, German and Russian Jews, latecomers (since the 1930s) and first-comers (there were approximately 353,000 Jews in the Lower East Side of New York City in 1916).

For these reasons, contemporary Jewish-American writing has found renewal and impetus, paradoxically, in the historical experience that has shaped their forebears' perceptions and identities. The period of rejection and the writing from assimilated positions has proved to be only a germination stage. The second part of this book looks at the varieties of writing that have emerged, together with parallel versions of the theme of

living with duality: being American essentially but inescapably
Jewish in origins and culture.

Creativity and Intellectual Culture

The Jews are 'The People of the Book' and it is not difficult to
enumerate the number of Jewish writers in all cultures who
have achieved success in their trade. But in America, the
traditions of writing and storytelling were regenerated with a
special addition: there were oppositions to enrich the existing
methods. But the basic value placed on the intellect, on debate
and discussion, is apparent in the texts included here. It has
been argued that the United States is basically not a culture
sympathetic to such values. Saul Bellow, for instance, in a
speech delivered at the Art Institute in Chicago in 1975, says:

> Intellectuals have not become a new class of art patrons. This
> means that the universities have failed painfully. They have
> not educated viewers, readers and audiences as they should
> have done, and educated philistinism emerges.[17]

There is a lament under all this for the undervaluation of the
community of writers so noticeable in Jewish settlements such
as Isaac Singer's memories of his writers' club back in Europe, or
the description of the intellectuals in the New York ghetto in
1902 by Hutchins Hapgood. The latter has this to say on the
literary bohemia in the East Side coffee houses:

> Most of them were places where the immigrant Jews drank
> tea and talked – and they talked as no other group has talked.
> They talked about Karl Marx and Bakunin, Henry George and
> Eugene Debs . . . They talked about the performance of the
> prima donna at the Metropolitan Opera the night before.[18]

It is remarkable that the dynamic intellectual discourse
permeating the Jewish-American novel contributes much of
the overall fictional interest; ongoing existential problems may
be maintained, interspersed with more mundane or comic
registers. But at the heart of all this, there is a profound interest

by these writers in the place and purpose of thought and creativity in the modern world, in the American suburb – often depicted as bland and stultifying, and most of all, in a post-modern milieu in which any concept of artistic 'value' is increasingly challenged from popular cultural standpoints.

What cannot be denied is what Norman Lebrecht has said about Mahler and the Jewish painter Kitaj in this context: 'For Kitaj, Mahler is personal: part of this explosive brilliance that made the modern world and attracted so much hatred.'[19]

The philistinism mentioned above, then, is often something Jews abjure. This appears as a given in these texts, thus alienating even further the Jews who inhabit the fringes of acceptability, such as Philip Roth's media- and pulp-culture-oriented beings, living on the edge of civilisation; or Bellow's thugs, at once cultured and brutal in one of his motivational paradoxes in characterisation.

The Scope of this Study and Selection of Texts

It soon becomes apparent when enquiring into the subject of recent Jewish-American literature, that there has been a perspective here which has fixed the Bellow–Malamud–Roth trio as central to the themes and issues percolating through the whole corpus of work. But since the emergence of the journal *Studies in American Jewish Literature (SAJL)* as a forum for discussion, the unofficial canon has been redefined. We have had comparatively little in print in England on the contributions of Jewish-American women writers such as Ozick, Paley and Jong. The drama has also been somewhat marginalised in this respect.

For these reasons, this book will begin with a detailed survey of the *Ur-texts* – the foundations as established in the work of Cahan, Yezierska and Henry Roth, then follow developments in three main areas:

1. The fiction-writers, from Bellow's early work (*Dangling Man* and so on.) to the most recent publications of younger writers, alongside the later writing of Philip Roth and Erica Jong.

2. An examination of the playwrights and poets who have taken particular interest in the European past, whether as part of a larger Holocaust literature or as statements of identity. (For instance a comparison of Sylvia Plath's references to concentration camps with Jong's metaphorical excursions into Europe is profitable.)

3. Discussion of how social and literary commentators have explained and mediated varieties of American Jews and Jewish life – from stances assumed in popular cultural texts to serious criticism.

The basic aims of the chapters are to introduce the writers and their concerns; to place the work in historical context and to demonstrate that there is now, just as much as at earlier stages in the development of this literature, a great deal of vibrancy and intellectual rigour in the work, together with fresh constructions of identity inside another America – a society caught up in postmodern debates and self-examination. The influence of the Old World is perhaps returning, with a renewed sustenance, as the debates on the purpose and meaning of Jewish communities in both suburbia and in old urban settings continue.

Above all else, the essays are meant to initiate further and deeper explorations into Jewish–American writing, to enrich an overall understanding of American literature, and to help to place individual writers in traditions and conventions. Often, in the very particular and localised, major insights emerge, as D. J. Taylor notes in his review of Roth's *American Pastoral*:

> The 'message' of *American Pastoral* . . . is not much more than an exposé of the chief fallacy of Western Liberalism. Tolerate that which is in itself intolerant, runs the invisible sub-text beneath Seymour's dialogue with his sullen activist daughter, and it will be that tolerance as a way to destroy you.[20]

For the student approaching this impressive and rich body of writing for the first time in any depth, the central texts of this study will establish the nature of the contribution to American literature and culture which has been made by Jewish-American writers. Perhaps most significantly, that contribution has been in the expression of what realignments in identity are possible in all varieties of an immigrant people. The student of American literature will find the texts here reflect, in common with the literatures of other minority groups, to what extent all Americans have always had to reinvent themselves.

Perhaps more than any other aspect of modern writing in the USA, the Jewish strand also contains the most prominent debate about nomenclature and definition, and I am aware that there are problems in the use of the adjectives here, just as the term 'Anglo-Irish' is fraught with difficulties when applied. But the preoccupation with what exactly is implied by varying terms seems to obfuscate an already complex literary critical practice. The point to remember is that discussing 'Jewish-American' against 'American-Jewish' only serves to recall the degrees of assimilation within the artistic community, and distances the literature still further from its origins. It is to be hoped that the stress on the word Jewish in the present work will be associated with the heart of the identity itself, and with everything it evokes in the metaphors, applications and concerns of its spirit. After all, this literature is very special; indeed, it is unique in its combination of energy, revolutionary dissent and self-reflexive poetic discourse.

Notes

1. Arthur Miller, *Broken Glass* (Methuen: London, 1994), p. 71.
2. S. Lillian Kramer, 'Post-Alienation: Recent Directions in Jewish American Literature', in *Contemporary Literature XXXIV*, 3 (University of Wisconsin: Madison, 1993), pp. 571–89, p. 571.
3. Dale Peck, 'Dangerous Girls', in *London Review of Books*, 3 July 1997, p. 22.
4. George Plimpton, 'Isaac Bashevis Singer', *Interviews from Paris Review*, vol. 3 (Penguin: London, 1975), pp. 77–95 p. 89.
5. Jonathan Ramsay, interview with Woody Allen, *Sight and Sound* ,February 1994, p. 7.
6. Joseph L. Bau, *Judaism in America* (University of Chicago: Chicago, 1975), p. 5.
7. Plimpton, 'Isaac Basheris Singer', *Interview from Paris Review*, p. 83.
8. Abraham Cahan, *The Rise of David Levinsky* (Penguin: London, 1993), p. 97.
9. See Open University television programme *The Jewish Enigma* (1989), which

focuses on the Dallas, Texas, community and interviews academics and religious leaders.

10. Gore Vidal, *Pink Triangle and Yellow Star:* Essays, 1976–82 (London: Granada, 1982), p. 213.
11. *The Jewish Enigma,* Open University television programme.
12. Mathew Kalman, *Daily Telegraph,* 30 May 1997, p. 17.
13. Bau, *Judaism in America,* p. 10.
14. Ibid., p. 11.
15. Ibid., p. 15.
16. John Berryman, *The Freedom of the Poet* (Farrar, Strauss and Giroux: New York, 1976), p. 366.
17. Saul Bellow, 'A Matter of the Soul', in *It All Adds Up* (London, Penguin, 1990), pp. 73-79, p. 75.
18. Hutchins Hapgood, *The Spirit of the Ghetto* (New York, Schocken, 1965), p. 51.
19. Norman Lebrecht, 'Mahler Goes Home', *Daily Telegraph* 17 March 1997, p. A1.
20. D. J.Taylor, review of *American Pastoral, Observer* 8 June 1997.

1
The Historical and Literary Foundations: Pre-1945

Before approaching the study of the main writers in the post-war years, there are several essential factors to consider. Many are concerned with Jewish identity in the New World and with new forms of self-awareness and social aspirations, and many are specifically aesthetic and literary. What will emerge in this chapter is the extremely complex nature of the American *Diaspora*: the dispersal of Jewish people from Eastern Europe at the end of the nineteenth and the beginning of the twentieth centuies. In 1881 almost three million Jews left Russia. Between 1881 and 1914 almost two million Jews arrived in America.

There had always been exodus in Jewish history, of course, from the first flight into Egypt, led by Moses. But the emigration to America of the Russian Jews in the Pale of Settlement (an area of Russia from the Baltic to the Black Sea) was globally significant in the chronicle of the demography of Jewish experience. Irving Howe expresses it in this way:

> The year 1881 marks a turning point in the history of the Jews as decisive as that of 70 AD, when Titus's legions burned the Temple at Jerusalem, or 1492, when Ferdinand and Isabella decreed the expulsion from Spain.[1]

The notion of shifting settlement, impermanence and separateness is basic to an understanding of the literature of Jewish America. The immigrant duality is fundamental here. This sense of being reborn into a new world, with possibilities of taking on a radically different selfhood, is something which

underlies most of the writing under scrutiny here. The immigrants came from Russian towns and villages in the Pale –
Shtetls – and life there had meant victimisation, repression
and brutality. The Russian pogroms after the assassination of
Alexander II had been the immediate cause of emigration. The
new Csar, Alexander III, reintroduced the tyranny of earlier
times. Laws prevented Jews from owning land or from making
any social or career progress in Russia. In 1891 Jewish expulsions from the major cities began, and 1903 the massacre of
Kishinev took place, in which 49 people were killed and over
500 injured and maimed. In 1904 of 30,000 Jewish workers,
one-sixth were imprisoned or sent to Siberia.

All these social and economic pressures meant that emigration was the best option – particularly for the young. Many who
went to America were skilled, literate and ambitious. In the
period from 1899 to 1909, 69.8 per cent were in the age-band
14–44. Of the skilled workers, 60 per cent were in the clothing
trade.[2] They came to New York in their hundreds of thousands,
being processed in Ellis Island, and then left to flood the Lower
East Side, struggling for existence in any way they could. Some
had relatives, of course; many spent time in Settlement Houses
run by Jewish charitable organisations. Huge numbers started
street-trading after the acquisition of a cart for the peddling
trade.

The total experience of immigration and propulsion into a
new life naturally provokes some enquiries into the traumas
and challenges involved, as these are clearly integral to the
writing from the first Jewish-American writers. It needs to be
said that the leaving of their Russian, Hungarian or Romanian
homelands was itself a deeply emotional experience. It could be
seen as failure, an admittance of defeat at the hands of the
invidious state and anti-Semitism; it was often approved of by
mothers but not by fathers, as the father in the family would
expect the son to carry on the tradition of Talmud study and
tradition in which the man was central. But it was also a thrill, a
genuine opportunity to take on a new identity.

There had been a trickle of Jews going to America ever since
the known five Jews who sailed with Columbus in 1492. German Jews had settled there before this East European influx,

and there had already been a schism: a Reform version of Judaism had been established, and there was a defined, circumscribed Judaic culture and sense of community in particular areas. There were clearly discernible differences between the two groups. The Germans had moved from pushcarts to established urban capitalism and suburban living; they placed no value on Yiddish, whereas the East Europeans cultivated that language and had a folk-literature which played a part in their self-awareness and cultural sense. It was a case of the contented capitalists living alongside the urban proletariat and the former taking on the role of philanthropists and charity-organisers.

The Varieties of Jewishness in the New World

In a sense, the Hebraic world-view, as in the Old Testament, had been a fundamental element in the American social and ideological fabric since the Puritan settlers, but this was little more than a distant order of theoretical principles when it came to considering the revolutionary social changes brought about by this wave of immigrants who were to be new Americans. There were clearly going to be gradations of Jewishness in American society which were to be increasingly complex as the long but inevitable process of assimilation went on. If the settlement was going to be in some ways 'the essentially American conflict between history and desire'[3] then exactly what versions of 'history' were to be relevant and, in fact, influential on the new Americans' progress into their new identities?

To answer this question, it is necessary to reflect on the possible varieties of Jewishness in such a society. First, as Nathan Glaser has pointed out, there is the aspect of Judaism which makes it a discrete element, a nation–religion in a context in which the idea of a religion linking with a national ideology has disappeared. It is an ethnic phenomenon, but transferable to any culture, with degrees of assimilation of various intensities:

As against the Christian churches – and even the non-Christian religions like Islam and Buddhism, which have some

adherents in the United States – Judaism is tied up organically
with a specific people, indeed a nation.The tie is so intimate
that the word 'Jew' in common usage refers ambiguously
both to an adherent of the religion of Judaism and to a
member of the Jewish people.[4]

In other words, we must begin by considering the idea of
Jewishness as either a religious or as a racial feature. Glaser
points out that the secular Jewishness which functions on the
idea of a social good divorced from a creed and from ritualised
religious practice has been expressed in America partly through
the Jewish Centre – a social institution owing its origins largely
to the Settlement Houses for immigrants. These centres culti-
vate a version of Jewishness which is secular but promulgating a
moral purpose and an agenda of social cohesion.

But the central versions of 'being Jewish' are increasingly
defined by an existence within rupture, divorce from the past,
compromise with a new society and above all, by cultural and
aesthetic action rather than by religious practice. As commentators have often pointed out, a Lutheran can be Norwegian or
Polish, but a Jew is always Jewish and a member of a certain
specific nationhood. A clear example would be in Turkey,
where Jews have settled since the expulsion from Spain, and
lived as Turks in the social and civic sense, but as Jews in the
religious sense.

Of course, the Jewish-American writers also reflect other
kinds of diversity. There are Jews who follow particular varieties
of the faith, such as the Hassidim of Crown Heights, who follow
the dress-code and ethics of their eighteenth-century founder
(they have their author in Chaim Potok); the Yiddish–English
bilingual culture with literary and artistic definitions of Jewish
life, and the degrees of assimilation noticeable in the newer
generations of writers. But in the first decades of the twentieth
century, what were the most powerful influences on the writing that emerged from this new proletarian class?

As there were so many potential versions of 'being Jewish',
and also an option to lose all Jewishness and reject the past and
its concomitant belief-systems, the literary expressions of a
whole diversity of subject-matter becomes quite complex.

But there are some dominant concerns which persist and return in the decades since 1945. The heart of this is in the question of assimilation as opposed to Jewishness as an aesthetic principle – a part-bohemian way of life with residual moral structures and artistic impulses which notably appropriate the American nature and thematic material.

The people who wanted to be American while retaining elements of Judaism had the Reform movement. 'We must accept, at least in some degree, the characterisation of nineteenth century reform as a religion of economically-comfortable Jews who wanted to be accepted by the non-Jewish world.'[5] This statement hints at a remarkable split which is crucial in defining differences: first, the more established and largely capitalist Jews had a literary taste and tradition which is in contra-distinction to the new arrivals from Eastern Europe. The new urban Jews existing by peddling or sweatshop work in and around the tenements had a different basis for their narratives and artistic discourses about themselves.

First, they had a Yiddish literature, either in the established writings of Sholom Aleichem and Mendele Sforim, or in the bellettrist journalism and documentary fiction of Abraham Cahan and the *Jewish Daily Forward*. The setting the new Americans found themselves in was not a *Shtetl* but a city – they were adopting an urban consciousness and living by means of self-determination wherever possible. In terms of their writing, intellectual debate and bohemian life, there were several factors in Jewish tradition that formed these established priorities. The idea of Jewish men being scholars and thinkers, annotating and debating Talmud was long established, and study was given a high priority in their culture. The idea of a *Luftmensch* (someone who lived apparently on air) was related to the 'poor scholar' and poet stereotype. In other words, it was considered admirable to have book-learning. The mix of journalism, philosophy and religious teaching clearly gave rise to a new Yiddish literature of the sweatshops and tenements:

Morris Winchevsky (1856–1932) sometimes called the grandfather of Yiddish literature in America . . . Joseph Boshover (1973–1915), David Edelstadt (1866–1892), Morris Rosenfeld

(1862–1923) and dozens of less talented poets, mostly shop-
workers themselves, created a working class literature that
voiced the indignation and the pathos of their fellow 'slaves
of the machine'.[6]

This clearly shows what a schism existed between the sophisticated tastes of the assimilated Jews of a previous generation
and the working class in the cities. The poor Jews had a
literature initially based on parables, Talmud stories and Biblical traditions, but the secular literature had arrived.

There is a work of particular merit and insight into the new
community which gives a detailed picture of the New York
community of the Lower East Side in the early years after the
immigration from Eastern Europe. This is Hutchins Hapgood's
The Spirit of the Ghetto (1902), in which we have articles and
sketches (done by Jacob Epstein) of the inhabitants of this area,
ranging from scholars to traders. In a chapter called 'Four Poets'
we have some valuable information on the proletarian literature which made the bedrock of such writers as Yezierska and
Cahan (studied in Chapter 2).The poets are Eliakim Zunser, a
wedding bard; Menahem Dolitski, a backward-looking, ethnic
poet; Morris Rosenfeld 'The Sweatshop Poet'; and Abraham
Wald, a socialist ideologue.

It is clear that the spectrum of interests and subjects provided
by these four writers enlightens the nature of the period and
the writing very well: the range covers conservative sentimentalism, modern commentary and bardic, social-function poetry.
What they illustrate is the nature of a literature embedded in
the simplicity of a defined, ethnic colony, a sub-culture in the
process of re-formation. Of the four, it is Wald who shows the
dilemma of the writer who meets the challenge of modernity
from a position in which antipathetic cultural values have been
long established, yet the desire to write in a contemporary way
about urgent issues is given to him by America:

'Before I came to America,' he said, 'I thought it would not be
as interesting as Russia, and when I got here I saw that I was
right. America seemed all worked out to me, as if mighty
things had already been done.'[7]

On the other hand, a wealthy young Jewish girl called Rose Pastor was writing a column for the *Tageblatt* newspaper and dabbling in verses. This gives us two other vitally important issues for future developments in Jewish-American writing: the place of women writers and the class differences:

> She read constantly . . . Bookishness was considered danger-
> ous for Jewish girls . . . who were supposed to study the
> womanly arts of housekeeping . . . She had also begun to
> write poetry. Her verse was light and airy and simple, much
> influenced by Emily Dickinson. In one poem, called "My
> Prayer" she wrote:
>
> > Some pray to marry the man they love,
> > My prayer will somewhat vary:
> > I humbly pray to Heaven above
> > That I love the man I marry.[8]

This contrast is not only a vivid insight into the polarities of Jewish-American consciousness; it also suggests the degree to which assimilation of established cultural values created the new 'American' from raw material. The conflict between desire and history is notably more complicated the deeper one en-quires into varieties of Jewishness.

It is therefore impossible to talk of Jewish-American literature in terms of defining characteristics. A superficial view, distant and lodged in meaningless stereotypes perhaps provided by popular narratives in fiction and in film, presents 'typical' features of a Jewish-American. But these prove to be chimeras; there is no such creature. As the forces of historical changes intensified in the decades after the first millions arrived from the Pale, it became clear that the Americanisation of the Jews was one in which each individual could decide on particular alignments and identities. Economic factors naturally domi-nated until a settled pattern of life emerged and it became possible to make choices concerning the extent of a Jewish presence in one's life, and whether or not Judaic religious observance was to be a part of that lifestyle.

Assimilation and Adaptation

An understanding of the writing that emerged from this social upheaval and from these questions of identity requires an exploration of how awareness of being Jewish either remained within American ideology or was swamped. In some cases, of course, it was consciously erased, seen as an embarrassment or an anachronism. But predominantly, Jewishness was still defined by the past, by historical change and impact. The underlying feature of assimilation is, however, always a vulnerable, disquieting force which has persisted as an insecurity. David Mamet has addressed this in an essay on Jewish identity:

> What did it mean, then, to be 'racially' Jewish? It meant that, among ourselves, we shared the wonderful, the warm, and the comforting codes, languages, jokes, attitudes which make up the consolations of strangers in a strange land.[9]

Mamet makes it clear that, with hindsight, he sees his forebears' experience of assimilation to have been one that was always one mixing acceptance with exclusion. But the blame is largely put on the immigrants themselves. Their tolerance, their understanding, their adoption of a broad view made them in a sense quintessentially American – in the sense that American ideology takes acceptance to the point of self-denigration.

In the formative decades of Jewish-American experience, then, the process of assimilation was often only in external, communal and vocational arenas, with the domestic culture being a preserve of fundamental Jewish values. Thus religious impulses were often transferred into idealistic urges towards moralism and voluntaryism, as discussed in the introduction. It meant that being American could be, for some, a veneer, and for some a strategy for survival. Beneath these complexities of self-identity lies the abiding Jewish experience of transience and dream of a homeland. The notion of a new homeland, one of enlightened ideas and set in a frame of modernity previously unknown, was easily absorbed by intellectual effort, reconciling emigration to a 'golden land' as America was spoken of in

Europe, to a long-standing dream of a place where to be a Jew
was not to be a scapegoat. David Martin Fine links this also with
the European Enlightenment, in the case of Jewry, an awakening that came a century after the standard dates in the history
books: 'Under the flags of Enlightenment and Emancipation,
western thought had been circulating in the *shtetlach* of the
Pale since the eighteenth century.'[10]

One way of appreciating the profound impact of the broader
European ideas on Jewish life and thought is to note the difference between the microcosmic, circumscribed lives of familial
morality and the revolutionary acculturation process which,
over two generations, transformed static, almost medieval notions of gender roles in the family into lifestyles in which
independent Jewish women could enter the realms of public
life, higher education and business. The paradox also emerges
here that women in the Shtetl were usually the workers, running
the stores and the home while the men studied Talmud.

But there is another way of 'being Jewish' which has persisted
since the early years of this century. Erica Jong puts it like this:
'The older we get, the more Jewish we become in my family. My
mother's father declared himself an atheist in his communist
youth, so we never belonged to a synagogue or had bat mitz-
vahs. But we wind up in Hebrew homes for the aged and in
cemeteries with Hebrew letters over the gates.'[11]

That is to say, there is another quality or condition of
Jewishness, beyond strictly religious definition, and different
from a purely cultural one linked to American values. This
version is concerned with looking at Jewishness *from within*.
Curiously, this often claims communication with and influence from the wider, cosmopolitan sense of Jewish thought. In
recent years, Philip Roth has most notably explored these
trends, but pre-1945 it was a case of writing about social and
family life in terms of discontinuity. In an interview in 1993
Cynthia Ozick was asked about this idea of rupture and discontinuity in Jewish tradition, and she sensibly raised an
important question:

Isn't the idea of culture precisely the idea of continuity, of
heritage? So how can a culture be defined by discontinuity?

Moments of discontinuity do occur. . . . Everything new, the riotous temptations of freedom, when you had to work in a sweatshop for three dollars a week in order to survive – all of that was rupture.[12]

This is very constructive in the present context. The appeal of this Jewish-American literature, and the success of much of the classical statements of the identity questions, comes from the realisation that there was a new culture in its incipient stage. Ozick's point is surely right to a point, but then the excitement of realising that the voices who tell their stories in Henry Roth, Yezierska and Cahan are in fact a succession of selves in transit, en route towards assimilation but also moving into the duality which lies at the heart of the post-war literary expositions.

The source of the assimilation cannot be pinpointed to one event, naturally. But Irving Howe notes a feature of the contrast of old- and new- world religious impulse which is relevant here:

In Eastern Europe the ordeal of poverty had been eased by a spiritual discipline centred on the synagogue and enclosing every department of life; in American religion authority could never be monolithic.[13]

In conclusion, it is useful here to draw together the various elements in the social history that have a bearing on the literature that was to emerge with Abraham Cahan's novel, *The Rise of David Levinsky* (1917). This foundation covers mainly three areas of the immigrant experience: dual identity, the emergence of an 'American' rather than a European, and the concepts of Jewishness which remain as the second generation arrives.

There is also the presence of other forms of Judaism, the established and the minority; the intellectual and the cultural, and the politicised and even atheistic. The notion of Jewish-American writing can, therefore, embrace on the one hand literature which confronts the central issues of belief and tradition, and on the other, that body of work which monitored the new freedoms.

These freedoms were a matter of reality, not dream, even as

early as 1890, according to Joseph C. Landis, in his account of Yiddish dreams in America:

Amazingly, within a decade – by the 1890's – the contours of the American-Jewish world began to emerge. The dream of the *goldene medine* [golden land], a shattered illusion to the newcomer, began to acquire a large measure of reality as his condition improved.[14]

In the period between the expulsions and pogroms of 1881 to the first real curtailment of Jewish immigration by the Great War in 1914, communal identity and consolidation had reached a level of significant achievement, as Hapgood's social enquiry shows. The Yiddish education programmes and the charitable educational work of Julia Richman,[15] together with the social medicine and public health achievements of Lillian Wald, made possible a basis from which talented individuals could rise. 'America', in short, becomes a symbol of the aspirations of the immigrant people. The word itself acquires a resonance, connoting a whole gamut of qualities related to individualism, escape and rebirth. Learning and study were to be the avenues to success, in writing as in everything else, and with Cahan and Yezierska we have the arrival of a Jewish American rather than a Yiddish literature in the United States. The aspirations of the first writers were clearly towards more universal themes and subjects, while at the same time taking the notion of a rebirth of identity as the foundation of what they did.

Notes

1. Irving Howe, *The Immigrant Jews of New York* (Routledge: London, 1976), p. 5; this is the most comprehensive account available of the Jewish immigration experience in this context.
2. Ibid., in particular pp. 58–60.
3. David Martin Fine, 'In the Beginning: American-Jewish Fiction, 1880–1930', in Lewis Fried (ed.), *Handbook of American Jewish Literature* (Greenwood Press: New York, 1988), pp. 15–33, p. 15.
4. Nathan Glaser, American Judaism (University of Chicago: London, 1957), p. 3.

5. Ibid., p. 46.
6. Joseph C. Landis, 'Yiddish Dreams in America', in Fried (ed.), *Handbook of American Jewish* Lierature, p. 146.
7. Hutchins Hapgood, The Spirit of the Ghetto (Schocken Books: New York, 1965), p. 115.
8. Stephen Birmingham, *The Rest of Us* : *The Rise of America's Eastern European Jews* (Futura: London, 1984), p. 52. Birmingham is unusual in that he traces the rise of the wealthy in commerce, entertainment and the arts.
9. David Mamet, *Some Freaks* (Faber: London, 1989), p. 8.
10. Fine, 'In the Beginning, in Fried, *Handbook of American Jewish Literature*, p. 16.
11. Erica Jong, *Fear of Fifty* (Vintage: London, 1995), p. 85. Jong, along with Adrienne Rich and David Mamet, appears to be addressing a revisionary view of the early, formative years of the first generation. This revision is discussed in Chapter 4.
12. Elaine M. Kauvar, 'An Interview with Cynthia Ozick', *Contemporary Literature*, vol.34, no. 3. (Fall, 1993), pp. 359-394, p. 385.
13. Howe, *The Immigrant Jews of New York*, p. 94.
14. Landis, 'Yiddish Dreams in America', in Fried, *Handbook of American Jewish Literature*, p. 149.
15. See Birmingham, *The Rest of Us*, particularly the first chapter. It is significant that, despite the presence of the rich and successful Jewish immigrants in much social history, they have not been important in fictional constructions. In fact, biography of Jewish 'rags to riches' narratives is yet to be explored in depth. A book such as Frederic Morton's *The Rothschilds* (Atheneum, USA: 1962) would be representative.

2

Seminal Influences: Abraham Cahan, Anzia Yezierska and Henry Roth

The immigrants from Russia and Eastern Europe generally inherited several elements of what was, in effect, a revolution in the beliefs, lifestyles and art of a people who had always been fundamentally guests rather than permanent citizens of the lands in which they found themselves. This revolution has its beginnings in the consequences of the Jewish Enlightenment or *Haskallah*, which is discernible in the late eighteenth century, but which has no really popular dissemination and presence until the first decades of the nineteenth century. In that period the first Reform Temples were founded in Europe and in the USA. The writings of Moses Mendelssohn perhaps proved to be the most influential on general attitudes. The important result for the purposes of understanding the rise of Jewish-American writing is that there was a spread of modern European culture among Jewish communities.

At this point, note should be made of the notions of what exactly 'literature' was conceived to be in the Jewish communities that came to America. First, the cornerstone of learning was the Talmud, a massive body of commentary and scripture, which also had a wealth of stories, parables and poetry interwoven. But the Yiddish literature which developed in the nineteenth century established a few 'modern classics' which most people would have known. These were notably Sholom Aleichem (who died in the USA in 1916), Mendele Sforim and I. Peretz. The nature of their language, Yiddish, features strongly in the three foundation texts discussed in this chapter, and it is useful to reflect on Yiddish, as opposed to Hebrew, at this point. The critic Alfred Kazin, explains:

> They do not despise Yiddish because it is the tongue of everyday life . . . But by identifying it with their reduced situation . . . they embody it in an historical moment, the present and its desolation, rather than the world of eternity which is mirrored in Hebrew.[1]

The Yiddish literature which had been established as part of the *Haskallah* thus separated culture from religious text and institutionalised belief. The fact is that modernity had impacted on a religious practice which made too many untenable demands on many Jews. The Reform movement had already found a foothold in America, long before the immigration of the 1880s. A rabbinical conference in Pittsburgh in 1885 finally consolidated the new version of Judaism espoused ever since the first attempts by German Jews in the 1820s to follow a more open and flexible approach to worship.

In *The Rise of David Levinsky*, for instance, we have a great deal of information on the cultural, literary establishment in New York, and how it became actively radical, often communist and certainly bohemian. The poet and journalist character, Tevkin, spends time at the Yampolsky Cafe, frequented by 'poor working men, and that some of these were poets, writers of stories or thinkers'.[2] Tevkin's daughter reads Ibsen and their home is crammed with books and the clutter of a family more concerned with ideas and debate than order and discipline. The literary-cultural centres had been established as a part of this Yiddish literary foundation. Cahan, Yezierska and Roth all owe their achievement, in some measure, to the nature of Yiddish and to a new proletarian literature.

This American writing was indeed the first Jewish proletarian writing, and it has all the familiar features of that genre: plenty of rhetoric, a need to be didactic and to provide facts and explanation, and also a firm belief in fiction as social documentary. The first Jewish-American writing shows this didacticism. Mary Antin's autobiography, *The Promised Land* (1912), for instance, concentrates on the experience of immigration and Americanisation. The overall impulse was to compare the Pale in Russia or other homeland with the urban landscape of the New World and with the fascinating process of creating a new self.

The Yiddish literature that lies behind these first landmark novels is exemplified by Sholom Aleichem's stories, embedded in the peasant life of the *Shtetl*, in part pastoral and in part complex in its ideologies and religious strictures. The world of his stories is medieval through modern eyes: allegories about people who flout the law; the workings of the supernatural forces around the Jewish settlements; stories about remarkable feats of love, idealisation and devotion. In a sense, these stories about working men and women were ideal for use as source-texts for a new proletarian writing, politicised and confident, exciting and embodying a whole range of dualities. The Yiddish literature which the early Jewish-American writers knew was intimately bound up with the virtues and vices of the world they had left. But naturally, the attitudes to life imbued in the Jews of Eastern Europe did not simply disappear when they set foot on Ellis Island.

The early writing is always interested in the basis of emotional belonging in the 'old country'. That is why the fundamental nature of the three established Jewish-American texts are about learning, growth and change in the individual consciousness. This aspect of the *Bildungsroman*, the novel of growing and learning, is peculiarly relevant to our enquiries here: Cahan, Roth and Yezierska stand out as being representative of so many of the themes and interests that actually formed the land from which the post-1945 writers reaped their harvests. Large claims have been made in this context, and an acknowledgement of the importance of these first Jewish-American writers leads to a troublesome question:

How could such writers, whom Leslie Fiedler characterises as more alienated from the mainstream of American life than even the negro, and whose cultural ties are more intimately bound up with the American present so lately emerge as the representative novelists of America at mid-century?[3]

One answer presents itself, and that relates to the discussion so far. The assimilation of the first-and second generation-Jews from Eastern Europe was an experience which had been like no other to any other group: it presented a chance for two claims being made on self-identity. First, the dream of the golden land in which limitless opportunity was available, and second, the idea of being part of a nation, an ethnic identity in 'the land of the free'. Obviously, much of the early literature dealt openly with anti-Semitism, and the immense body of writing on that subject is complicated by the resentment of some Jews for other Jews.

But letting go of the past is the central preoccupation. Yiddish was the language of the past and also of the streets. Henry Roth allows his David to be engulfed in street Yiddish in the more modernist episodes of *Call it Sleep*. These writers were asking what is gained and what is lost in this change of identity, and language is at the heart of the explorations: after all, to be bilingual in a society in which one dominant language carries with it the entry to success is to be both specially blessed but also uniquely handicapped.

Yet there is also something else: another ingredient in this early fiction. There is a certain indefinable quality of Jewishness which arguably sustains and also gives a special quality to the prose and the syntax. 'The future Americans, thanks to the Jew in them, will have passions, enthusiasms.'[4] The immigrants were coming to a land in which people had already made decisions about social belonging and alignments. Some had reached out bravely into the American character, speaking and dressing in the 'American' way; others had maintained the social ties of their former *Shtetls* and kept their ambience narrow and local. In *The Rise of David Levinsky*, Cahan makes a special point of explaining how the workers in David's cloak factory can produce cloaks cheaper than anyone else, and avoid union complications, mainly because the workers are from Antomir, David's Russian *Shtetl*, and they are 'tied' to David the capitalist, within what is in effect, not 'America' but another version of Antomir.

But the dream of the *goldene medine* was in part actually realised. This proletarian literature emanated from a place in which these dreams were realised; success stories abounded. The hope was that 'American freedom would somehow be joined to a Jewish community life.'[5] A definable base of acquired values might have been removed from the scene, but the excitement of being transformed from an anonymous and unvalued non-person within an anti-Semitic nation was undeniably at the centre of the new consciousness beneath the fiction.

These first Jewish-American writers, then, had a familiar tradition of Yiddish writing which was about a community with only vestigial status in the New World; it was a world passing from sight and from importance in terms of being American, but nevertheless it was a world whose containment of the quality of Jewishness – by culture as well as by religion – was undeniably a source of power and creativity in the writers who now wrestled with their new identities. The later literature, particularly in the 1950s and 1960s, was to use this first-generation duality as a touchstone for many depictions of Jewish city-dwelling intellectuals within the confusions and paradoxes of modernity: characters like Mr Patimkin in Philip Roth's *Goodbye, Columbus*, for instance.

The question still needs to be asked, though, as to why these three are representative. It would be possible to discuss several writers who produced interesting work in this period. One answer to this has been suggested by Eric Homberger, in an essay mostly concerned with Michael Gold, the author of *Jews without Money* (1930). He places the notion of ambivalence at the heart of this issue, and it is certainly very helpful.[6] Consider the various causes of ambivalence in this community of the Lower East Side. Were they to aspire to total assimilation? Was that actually possible? They often wanted to play the role of the yankee businessman but, like David Levinsky, they needed instruction in table etiquette, but there was a fundamental trait of Jewishness that maintained this ambivalence towards success, assimilation and also to complete rejection of the past. Anna Tevkin, the idealistic woman who rejects David Levinsky, is given an opinion on this: 'It simply means that at the bottom of our hearts we Jews are a sad people . . . there is a broad streak of tragedy in our psychology.'[7]

Much of what interests Cahan, Roth and Yezierska is linked to these complex reasons why Jewishness remained obdurately potent and directive in terms of self-esteem and value. In Yezierska's story, *The Fat of the Land*, Hannah Breineh, from the poor East Side, rises in the wake of her playwright son, but cannot cope with the material success this brings. This story perhaps encapsulates something of this dilemma, and in its openly didactic manner, it clarifies the situation. Hannah says to her friend Mrs Pelz:

> Why should my children shame themselves from me? From where did they get the stuff to work themselves up in the world? Did they get it from the air? . . . Why don't the children of born Americans write my Benny's plays? It is I, who never had a chance to be a person, who gave him the fire in his head.[8]

One way of understanding this early, foundation literature is definitely to see it as a body of work in search of a status. It is caught between questioning and certainty; between establishment and rebellion. Hannah Breineh has, metaphorically, returned again and again throughout the decades since 1945 in Jewish-American literature. In plain terms, the experience of emigration and duality is inescapably attractive to a writer. It immediately supplies tension, drama, social conflict and, most of all, that ambivalence of saying yes but wanting to say no, of choosing but preferring not to have a choice.

Of course, guilt also goes along with this, and guilt will play a large part in the following textual discussions. But there is also a marvellous innocence. In many ways, this early writing is childlike, Romantically-charged like a Wordsworth narrative poem, or using the simplicity of Blakean poetic diction while dealing with eternal questions. Although there was, in this period up to 1945, clearly an emergence of a typical 'Jewish Problem' novel, that strand has not persisted. Lionel Trilling's review of *The Disinherited* by Milton Waldman (1929) makes it clear that there was a lot of rhetorical over-writing going on, exploiting the superficial elements of Jewishness and using such topics as religious conversion, Zionism, anti-Semitism and nostalgia for the past as staple material.

However, the discussion of the three formative novels will show that, bearing in mind that this fiction arrived on the scene when sentiment and naturalism sat easily as a so-called 'real' depiction of American issues, the achievement of even the most purposeful fiction, with a high level of didacticism, is considerable. All three writers show versatility, enterprise and an impressive facility in delineating Yiddish-New York dialogue, and in presenting the varying language registers at work in home, street and factory.

There is also a huge amount of social history in these novels. Abraham Cahan's story explains the labour movement, the working of the peddler trade, the marriage matchmaker, the life of a travelling salesman, poor poets and wealthy intelligentsia. Levinsky mixes with the rich and the poor, the dispossessed and the failures. Roth employs Woolfian and Joycean techniques to lay bare the spirit of a child striving to survive in the heart of a dozen conflicts. Yezierska is a novelist creating a world for women's voices hewn from nothing. Her heroines grasp and strain for selfhood against all odds, but never lose the dream of the displaced, unvalued and eternally secondary.

Abraham Cahan: *The Rise of David Levinsky* (1917)

Cahan was a leading light in the radical Jewish leftist intelligentsia; he edited the influential *Jewish Daily Forward* and always seems to have been embroiled in controversy. He was born in Vilna, Lithuania, in 1860. He was a journalist first, but certainly a novelist of energy and originality. There are passages in Levinsky which hint that Cahan had admiration for Dickens, and his interest in minor characters, his relentless vitality in explaining ordinary lives together with an ability to give a social commentary of real insight make him an heir to the great Russian novelists as well as to Dickens.

Cahan died in 1951, and Isaac Bashevis Singer, in his book *Love and Exile,* makes it clear that Cahan played a large part in helping Singer into print also. Hutchins Hapgood said that

Cahan 'Spoke and wrote for directness, simplicity and humanity' and as an East Side writer, wanted to 'educate the ignorant masses of people into socialism'.[9]

Hapgood's eulogy, written at the time of Cahan's writing of Levinsky, insists on Cahan's avoidance of any doctrinaire approach. In the novel, there is an abundance of information, and a great deal of self-reflection, but at the core, we have the story of a man looking for fulfilment from a position between two desires: to accomplish something in learning, scholarship, and yet also to be an American capitalist. Cahan places the emotions somewhere between these two, making the cultural and business worlds appear to be often no more than urges, mindless desires to gain, own or win.

The novel has a loose structure, following digressions where they appeal, but slackening the impetus of the central search for stability, a woman's love and contentment. Often, a succession of women come and go, without any clear idea as to David's intentions. But wherever there is a lack of focus, there is also a language of irresistible drive and passion towards explaining the psychology of a Talmud-learned Jew in the midst of Babylon.

Cahan makes his protagonist elusive; the reader is asked to accept a range of actions and thoughts of very doubtful morality as part of unavoidable necessity, but we are made to judge, objectively. Aims and designs are elaborately thought out, and obsessions soon develop into normality.

Cahan tries to develop several ideas in the novel, all interrelated and all essentially about the interplay of the personal, spiritual life as opposed to the public, secular identity. The heart of the fictional interest in David Levinsky's story is that the people and events in the first few chapters, set in Antomir, have a profound influence on everything else, so the adult David is never happy nor fully shaped and completed as the 'American businessman' shown to the world. As David Martin Fine puts it: 'To forge an American persona that denies the historical self is an act of betrayal, one that is accompanied by a sense of loss.'[10] Paradoxically, David's story is perhaps closer in spirit to European allegory than to anything else. The three people in Antomir who haunt his future are Rabbi Sender, 'A dreamer with a noble imagination, with a soul of beauty'[11] ; his mother, who is beaten to death by gentiles as she is roused to anger by violence against her son; and Mathilda, the woman who rejects him.

When David eventually meets up with Matilda in America, all the allure has gone. But it is as if the secular world has soured, whereas the religious, spiritual aspect of him is ineradicable. David always has the shaking movement of the Talmud scholar. He learns to make money and to attract women, but the aesthetic element, the hunger for learning and the worship of the Word is always in him. Cahan uses this as a motif which enriches and explains the inner failure to live. Yet, there is an irony also. Even in the *Shul* in Antomir, David is competitive. He tries to outdo the boy who knows more Talmud by heart than himself. When David finally apologises, we have something that is crucial to the understanding of the whole novel:

> A minute later I stood in front of my hated rival, thrilling with the ecstasy of penitence.'I have sinned against you. Forgive me', I said, with downcast eyes. The Pole was puzzled . . . A suggestion of a sneer flitted across his well-fed face.

This scene encapsulates a basic element in much Jewish-American fiction, and pinpoints the core of *David Levinsky*; it foregrounds the Jewish enjoyment of suffering. Penitence brings on 'ecstasy' for David. He has thrilled to the excitement of competition – and notably, against a Pole, the oppressors of the Jewish inhabitants of the *Shtetl* in many writings. The Pole has a 'sneer'. Cahan is opposing expressions of very deep and elusive components of the religious nature of Judaism in this context, and David carries this with him to America. He even exploits it in his compatriots. The ability to do without, to be denied pleasure and fulfilment is the issue here.

But in the early chapters there is also Naphtali, the free-thinker: this boy first induces David to think about secular dissent and non-sacred literature. But Naphtali also introduces David to the poetry of Tevkin, whom he meets later in America. Everything in the pre-America chapters is purposeful, didactic and often indicative of Cahan's need to place Jewishness in one context, and with the pre-eminence of the man over the woman, the sacred above the secular, and the past before the present. America then comes to represent that challenge of the present, the escape from time and convention, which has become a defining aspect of modernity.

As the novel progresses, we have a gradual recession of this Jewish *Shtetl* identity, as personified by Sender. In America, David applies Psalm 104 to the New World, and Cahan is making links between the 'America in the mind', which is timeless and symbolic, and the America which is in the process of construction. 'When the discoverers of America saw land at last they fell on their knees and a hymn of thanksgiving burst from their souls' says David on arrival.[12] Cahan uses Psalm 104 as a device for defining David's notion of America with the ambivalence that is to persist: 'So I was praying God not to hide His face from me, but to open His hand to me; to remember that my mother had been murdered by Gentiles and that I was going to a strange land.'[13] But this land is full of ambiguities. It has 'hostile glamour', and this glamour is applied to both Matilda and America. Constantly in the novel, Cahan uses women as emblems of a surface, ephemeral attraction: alluring in their sexuality in the new secular life David experiences as America itself.

This gathers more interest as David the capitalist, the central theme of the novel, is more elaborately detailed. This business world is the site of continued historical interest. Cahan the journalist steps in, and we are given insights into the acquisitive mind; David's story is to be the quintessential American one (perhaps with ironical reference to Howells' novel *The Rise of Silas Lapham*), and the rise here is only 'non-American' in the superficial sense of the manners and attitudes David has to learn when success enables him to enjoy social intercourse with WASP Americans. One of this class even teaches him table etiquette. The social history, following the rise of the Jewish entrepreneur from pushcart peddler to successful businessman, is often explained through descriptions and images of clothing. The intricacies of dress and fashion provide Cahan with a metaphor for Americanisation through superficiality. The fact that David succeeds through making cloaks is the focus of this irony. A cloak hides all, covers the body, and is associated with night-time.

Constantly, David explains change and growth – and the inevitable duality of being Jewish American – through clothes. He arrives with a poor tailor, Gitelson, and later, they meet again and David helps his friend. The 'higher things' he has yearned for, such as being a Doctor of Philosophy[14] are left behind and he even employs his former teacher, Bender, then takes to the road. Here, clothes attain even more significance: yet the lonely man within David, as he dines with business colleagues and says he loves America, comes to use fashion, make-up and hair as symbols of his delusion, the success that has kept him from 'the higher things':

> The riot of prosperity introduced the fashion of respectable women covering their faces with powder and paint in a way that had hitherto been peculiar to women of the streets, so I pictured civilisation as a harlot with cheeks.[15]

Cahan has David read Max Nordau's book *Degeneration* (1895) and this prompts him to say that civilisation was 'honeycombed with . . . conventional lies, with sham ecstasy, sham sympathy, sham smiles.'[16] Cahan increasingly makes David's ambivalence one which strides two apparently discrete worlds, parallel but eternally alien. But there is a subtlety beneath all this which makes the novel one of the most influential of the foundation texts.

This concerns the extent to which David has brought 'America' with him from Antomir. Again, the explanation of clothing helps here: 'It was the Russian Jew who had introduced the factory-made gown, constantly perfecting it and reducing the costs of its production . . . Nor it is apish copying. We make it our business to know how the American woman wants to look.'[17] But of course, the *American* woman is in the process of being re-formed, renewed, and multi-cultural influence is stealthily at work even in David Levinsky's own story. The rich irony all the way through the novel is that we have an American narrating, a voice and sensibility explaining how that urban proletariat was made into the new formation of total America, not just the self-identity of a perceived ghetto. David's business makes it to Fifth Avenue.

Yet, ultimately, the 'higher things' have eluded David Levinsky. The scene in Yampolsky's Cafe, where he finally meets the poet Tevkin, is Cahan's instrument for foregrounding the reversal of his protagonist's aspirations. Tevkin insists that Russia is better than America: 'There is too much materialism here, too much hurry and too much prose ,' but David replies in a way which deepens the ironical materials of the narrative devices:

> 'Comfort ye, comfort ye, my people, saith your God', I quoted gaily. 'It's all a matter of mood. Poets are men of moods.' Again I quoted, 'Attend unto me, oh my friend, and give ear unto me, oh comrade' I took up the cudgel for America.[18]

This reverses the Rabbi Sender–David relationship of the first chapters. Here we have the poet preaching a secular, very prosaic gospel of American selfhood, against the openly sentimental and backward-looking praise of the Jewish past. David takes up the 'cudgel' – there is a fight to be fought. Throughout the novel, this has been an internalised turmoil, with a desperate urge to retain the Jewishness of Antomir and obey the past, reward his mother's sacrificial death at the hands of the *goyim*. But the novel ends with David having absorbed this new creation which he has actually shaped, outwardly as a man in the public sphere, and inwardly, as a spiritual force losing its guilt at the loss of the 'higher things'.

The Rise of David Levinsky, then, has several sub plots defining the sites of narrative debate which are to make the rich interplay between reader and text in the novels of third-generation Jewish Americans. As with Yezierska and Henry Roth, it also helps us to understand why specific texts have been singled out as those which are representatively 'Jewish American'. For instance, Ben Hecht, a Zionist, wrote novels and stories before 1945, but no process of canonical formation of the Jewish-American texts has claimed hegemony for that work. The answer is surely in the fact that writers such as Cahan textualised Jewishness not in terms of the 'problem novel' as some novelists may have done in Britain in the 1840s, with a need to campaign for social change; he gives us social historical process as a concomitant force with the important one of individuals becoming Americans.

Anzia Yezierska: *Hungry Hearts*

Anzia Yezierska was born near Warsaw in 1881. Her career as a writer took her eventually to Hollywood, but she left the place in disgust. Disenchanted by such success, she wrote an account of what happened when the big film studios had 'bought' her work. Riva Krut comments, 'Yezierska found herself isolated from the very people who had given her creative sustenance: "I am alone because I left my world".'[19] The collection of stories published under the title *Hungry Hearts* in 1920 is remarkable for many reasons. Here was a woman writer, writing in English not Yiddish, who knew Russia as a child but experienced the Jewish *Shtetl* world of Orthodox Judaism, where women were ancillary to men. She produced fiction from her early confrontation with the American Dream which uses a dialectal discourse of rare power and expression in order to give a voice to people who were doubly dispossessed. Her women are embedded in the ideology of the *Hausfrau*, expected to maintain, in their urban poverty, the high ideals of their former lives. Their purpose is to serve, but Yezierksa explains their dreams and yearnings.

These stories express more directly and starkly, the immigrant's condition of non-being, in a limbo between poverty and hope, desire and repression. The women in the stories are generally bilingual, and their 'Yinglish' dialogue conveys a deep duality. This fiction is remarkably close to the stylistic features and genre conventions of Yiddish originals. There is a noted heightening of emotional velocity; symbols are used very directly, and there is an unrestrained use of sentimentality. All this is in the service of difference, of separateness, and the fiction is built on the privileging of the Jewish women and the cultural 'Other' of the educated American. *Hungry Hearts* re-counts the hunger of the dispossessed female, in search of the American nature within a frame of 'higher things', as in Cahan. The same aesthetic and spiritual hunger gnaws at Shenah Pessah, who loves and worships her academic American lodger, John Barnes.

Again, Shenah dresses 'American' and tells Barnes of her desire for knowledge:

> 'I'm through for always with old women's shawls. This is my first American dress-up.'
>   'Splendid! So you want to be an American! The next step will be to take up some work that will put you in touch with American people.'[20]

But the narrative thrust is dependent on Shenah's naive self-deception that he cares for her, while Barnes is simply studying the assimilation process. His thesis is on 'Educational problems of the Russian Jews' and he feels only sympathy for her. The interest for students of Jewish-American literature is specifically in Yezierska's juxtaposition of two distinct discourses: one is embedded in the world of romance, idealisation and childhood innocence, and is unworldly. It is a personality in the process of formation. The other is assured, single-minded and nothing more than an instrument of a dominant ideology. The potency of the story is in Shenah's insistence on matching dreams with reality.

Her family setting is deeply framed by poverty and manual work of Dickensian proportions, but Yezierska continues the aspirational fervour. Shenah proclaims 'with Jewish fervour': 'Can I help it what's in my heart? It always longs in me for the higher. Maybe he has forgotten me, but only one hope drives in me like madness – to make myself alike to him.'[21] The Romantic convention of introducing the normal suitor, the reliable type of her own people, in Sam Arkin, is used to test her resolve.

She, like Levinsky, accepts the expected, but her dream, her hunger, is never abated. The focal strength of the stories as a group is in the use of the Yiddish syntax and vocabulary to contain the discourse of sentimentality and, paradoxically, of realism. Most of the stories in the collection have the ongoing concern for the beauty and appeal of status, success and colour – sheer attractiveness and style, as opposed to the dowdiness of the ghetto and the tenement. Yezierska takes up a theme that has only recently been reintroduced: the lives of women within the Jewish immigrant community. Even in the post-1945 period, the women writers have not had the same level of critical attention. Tillie Olson's astonishingly innovative story 'Tell Me a Riddle' (1961) is one of the few texts to have had an acknowledged impact on the reception of this writing. So the stories in *Hungry Hearts* give genuine insights into the lives and aspirations of the women in the East Side. Again, it is the isolation, the entrapment inside the morals and sexual politics of Orthodox Jewish domesticity that surrounds the narratives. But the success of this subject-matter also brings with it a direct commentary on the social rifts reflected. In the story 'The Free Vacation House', for instance, the female narrator applies for time at a vacation house, and we are suddenly given a parable of the America which threatens, and is remarkably unfree. The house has rules and discipline. It represents order and rationality. The woman's family and children-oriented mind expresses the minimised spirit of the immigrant who still has her former self within:

> But still she went on. The children over two years dassen't stay around by the mothers. They must stay by the nurse in the playroom. By the meal-times, they can see their mothers . . . We must always listen to the bells. Bell one for getting up. Bell two for getting babies' bottles.[22]

The increase in rules creates a more prominent use of Yiddish syntax: 'I was thinking for why, with so many rules, didn't they also have already another rule, about how much air in our lungs to breathe.'[23]

The recurrent concern, though, is for a series of poetic interpretations of 'America' as a mental construct and as embodied in the Other – the binary opposition in the texts for what is complete rather than the immigrant's aspiration for completion. The stories tell of social mobility, of arranged marriages, impossible goals in society, generational conflict and status in the hierarchical order of the East Side. Perhaps the most informative thread in all these is the prominence given to education, schoolrooms and books. Book-learning and teaching become the apotheosis of Americanisation. They are the high road to personal completeness. In 'The Miracle' we have a dialectic exposition of the Americans-to-be and the Americans perceived as complete and defined. The teacher in the story says, 'Though you work in a shop, you are really freer than I. You are not repressed as I am by the fear and shame of feeling. You could teach me more than I could teach you. You could teach me how to be natural.'[24]

The immigrant Jews are called 'the creative pulse of the America to be'.[25] Even at the level of small talk among the Yiddish-speaking ladies, the future is the focus in life: 'What did I tell you? In America children are like money in the bank.'[26]

Yezierska's stories then are boldly didactic statements of a social context enfolding a desperate search for new identities and status in the immigrant women. In shifting the subject to the domestic life and to the poetics of the ordinary experience, Yezierska initiates something that Olson, Paley, Jong and Ozick were to continue: and the mediation of Jewish-American literature is still unfortunately dominated by the initial impact of Bellow–Malamud–Roth. Unfortunate in the sense that the women writers, more attuned to the wealth of material in the domestic world of cultural Jewishness as well as in the Orthodox or even Hassidic contexts, have radically innovative perspectives to offer. The difference between Cahan and Yezierska is immense, despite the fact that both wrote at length about the internal assimilation that goes on, unseen but just as profound and angst-ridden as that of the overt world of business, university and media.

Yezierska's stories also gave precepts as to how to write dialogue, and how to give the sinews of Yiddish syntax their place in textualising by impressionistic methods, the voices of a community still brimming with their Russian *Shtetl* consciousness. In the language we find the most transparent expression of a condition, an inner debate and, at the same time, a dialogue of the dispossessed with the powerful. Increasingly, as the stories include the modern issues, generational and artistic, the stylistic interplay becomes laden with the language of internal discord: 'The trouble with us is that the ghetto of the Middle Ages and the children of the twentieth century have to live under one roof.'[27] Benny, Hannah's son and one of the first intellectuals in this early fiction to foreshadow Bellow and Roth's focal characters, says to his mother. His words are entirely divorced from the grammar and syntax of Hannah herself, whose characteristic expressions are 'Oi weh!' and 'Gewalt!'

Henry Roth: *Call it Sleep*

Henry Roth, born in 1906 in the Austro-Hungarian Empire, came to New York in 1907. *Call it Sleep* has had a remarkable impact on the general conceptions of how the second-generation immigrants textualised a point of radical change in assimilation, a watershed. Roth published nothing else until he began work on a six-book work, beginning with *A Star Shines On Mt. Morris Park* in 1994. His first novel, though, has been distinguished for special critical attention in recent years, and the central reason for its importance, it could be argued, is its impressionistic and poetic evocation of Jewish childhood and 'rites of passage' narrative at a time when, as Irving Howe has said, 'a subculture finds its passion at exactly the moment that it approaches its disintegration'.[28]

There are also some wider considerations to be noted at this point. Lewis Fried summarises a basic tendency in terms of the Jewish faith in the 1930s: 'During these authors' lifetimes, the individual ceased to find Judaism at the core of his existence and came to expect that a theology would revolve around the self and its needs.'[29]

In Roth's case, what is certain is that the adult world around David Schearl is experienced through a child's eyes, distorted, cruel, often bestial, violent, self-hating and intransigently self-seeking – with the exception of Genya, David's mother. Genya is constructed carefully as a sacrificial figure; she is the eternal feminine in the composition of everything kind, emotional

and selfless in David, but his overbearing impulse is one of fear
and joy in extremes.

It is a novel of the street; a multitude of voices articulate a
raucous, aggressive urban America in the chaos of creation. Roth is
capable of conveying a dazzling range of voices, argots and slangs,
all actively enveloping the Yiddish of the street urchins; but we
have the Italian street-cleaner, the Irish policeman and Leo,
David's friend in Book IV. Overall, the novel textualises a kind
of birthing: we sense that Roth's carefully constructed poeticism,
and Romantic rhetoric, sited close by the impressionistic modernism of the world apprehended through the senses, is a delivery
of a soul into a sensual, tactile microcosm of humanity.

Stream-of-consciousness interiority are interspersed with realistic data; Roth avoids any hint of reportage, and, unlike
Cahan and Yezierska, his novel universalises well into a tradition of the *Bildungsroman*, the impingement on the world of
necessity and growth on to a static, meditative personality.
David is alive on the streets; they provide vision and poetry as
well as companionship, excitement and fear. On arrival in
America, his father, Albert, is waiting for David and his mother,
and Roth makes both Albert and then Genya's sister, Bertha,
into truly multi-dimensional characters. Albert is brutalised and
threatening. Bertha has life in abundance, crude, unmannered
and offensive, yet intensely human and humane.

The birthing of David into an America in which the ethnic
constituents have settled and cohabited into a firmly established
set of norms and tastes is a means of foregrounding the emergent
perspectives of anti-Semitism, estrangement and difference in the
Jewish community of the Lower East Side. Yet we learn all this
detail of the greater world only partially, as David's encounters
with the street-dwellers reveal this reshaped urban America. With
Leo, as David watches the kite-flying for instance, Roth distances
us from the intensely restricted inner world of David's imagination and introduces a concept of otherness and identity which
reverberates through the texts in post-1945 literature:

'My name's Leo Dugovka. I'm a Polish-American, You're a
Jew aintcha?'
'Y-yea.'[30]

and, in the same scene:

> 'A man and a lady!' Leo turned his head aside to crow. 'Oh boy, wot Jews don't know! Dat's a scapiller see? An dat's a pitcher o'de holy Mudder.'[31]

David's Jewishness is placed in the wider context of an America which has absorbed and transformed. The dominant forces of economics and crime rule the external world; in the inner domesticity of the Schearl family and in the *Cheder* with Rabbi Pankower, the Orthodox Jewish faith is manifested through fear and violence. This is a world of darkness, of cellars and glowering small bedrooms, of bullying and anger. But in the street, David at least learns the rules of survival, and that type of assimilation is Roth's contribution: showing with astounding ingenuity, and with Joycean lyricism and depth, the dissensions of the spirit and of the human condition within the Jewish-American self-regard. The past may have receded as a perceptively influential drive, as in Cahan, but the nature of 'being a Jew' has now attained a specific social problematic. Section 7 of Book III, for instance, has all this in miniature: Passover, a fight in the street with an Italian, an epiphanic experience, a confrontation with hoodlums and an abundance of natural activity in an immediate environment as vivid and full of multiple meanings for David as a Wordsworthian revelation.

The epiphany is as deftly handled as the much-discussed epiphany of Joyce's *Portrait of the Artist as a Young Man*. David simply watches a tug in the harbour, but concludes: 'It was as though he had seen it in another world, a world that once left could not be recalled. All that he knew about it was that it had been complete and dazzling.'[32]

The epiphany, and several other meditative and lyrical passages in the novel, make it clear that *Call it Sleep* is, in one sense, a novel primarily about the emergence of a social personality in all human infants; but the Jewish context forces interpretations on us which invite a spectrum of readings, all concerned with assimilation and new identity. The final section, in which David's injury is recounted, is done through an assembly of proletarian voices and in drama as fragmented but convincing as some passages in T. S. Eliot's *The Waste Land*. Henry Roth demonstrates here the essentially Jewish qualities of speech, relationships and sub-group bonding which constitute a self-conscious minority – but the third generation, like David Schearl – are forging links with the 'Polish-Americans', and although young Leo does not call his friend 'Jewish American' but simply 'a Jew', one sense that the macrocosm which is constructed through a fresh, vigorous American ideology, will claim further degrees of assimilation, and on the human, relational level. After all, ironically, David's real father may have been 'a goy'.[33]

Roth has taken up fiction again in recent years, and his later work will be discussed in Chapter 9. The point to emphasise here is that he is still searching for the narrative devices that will bring the focus clearer and place the hard, tactile reality of life on the streets to the reader in a semi-didactic way. *Call it Sleep* does this by means of distortions and documented, selective detail. Roth has always wanted to take the 'growth of a poet's soul' into his fictional domain in this sense; his narratives are concerned with the specific perceptions of childhood and the grotesqueness of the adult world in this perspective. His strengths have been in the inventiveness of his style, and, even when derivative, it is always vibrant and interesting. The streets become a version of an Arthurian romance, with turns of events and further threats to the stability of identity around every corner. Roth makes his scenes involve both realism and picaresque.

Notes

1. Alfred Kazin, *Contemporaries* (Secker and Warburg: London, 1963), p. 275.
2. Abraham Cahan, *The Rise of David Levinsky* (Penguin: London, 1993), p. 461.
3. Rod W. Horton and Herbert W. Edwards, *Backgrounds of American Literary Thought* (Prentice Hall: New Jersey, 1974), p. 571.
4. See David Martin Fine, 'In the Beginning: American-Jewish Fiction, 1880–1930', in Lewis Fried (ed.), *Handbook of Jewish-American Literature*, (Greenwood Press: New York, 1988), p. 19; the chapter discusses several important secondary writers.

5. Joseph C. Landis, 'Yiddish Dreams in America', in Fried, *Handbook of Jewish-American Literature*, pp. 143–63, p. 147.
6. See Eric Homberger, 'Some Uses for Jewish Ambivalence: Abraham Cahan and Michael Gold', in Bryan Cheyette (ed.), *Between 'Race' and 'Culture': Representations of 'the Jew' in English and American Literature* (Stanford University Press: California, 1996), pp. 165–82. Homberger gives an excellent account of the work of Michael Gold, and relates ambivalence to modern popular narrative.
7. Cahan, *Levinsky* p. 420.
8. Anzia Yezierska, *Hungry Hearts and Other Stories* (Virago: London, 1987), p. 219.
9. Hutchins Hapgood, *The Spirit of the Ghetto* (Schocken: New York, 1965), p. 225.
10. Fine 'In the Beginning', in Fried, *Handbook of Jewish American Literature*, p. 24.
11. Cahan, *Levinsky*, p. 31.
12. Ibid., p. 86.
13. Ibid., p. 87.
14. Ibid., p. 180.
15. Ibid., p. 380.
16. Ibid., p. 380. See Stephen Arata, *Fictions of Loss in Victorian Fin de Siècle* Cambridge University Press: Cambridge, 1996). Cahan must have absorbed some of Nordau's philosophy of decline and decadence, as this has simplistic applications to urban USA at this time.
17. Cahan, *Levinsky*, p. 443.
18. Ibid., p. 459.
19. Yezierska, *Hungry Hearts* ed. by Riva Krut, p. XIX. Krut provides an excellent introduction to Yezierska's work in this edition.
20. Ibid., p. 25.
21. Ibid., p. 47.
22. Ibid., p. 109.
23. Ibid., p. 110.
24. Ibid., p. 36.
25. Ibid., p. 137.
26. Ibid., p. 201.
27. Ibid., p. 209.
28. Irving Howe, *The Immigrant Jews of New York* (Routledge: London, 1976), p. 586.
29. Fried, *Handbook of Jewish American Literature*, p. 36.
30. Henry Roth, *Call it Sleep* (Penguin: London, 1997), p. 299.
31. ibid. p. 301.
32. ibid. p. 245.
33. ibid. p. 390.

3

Jewish-American Themes in Fiction I: Bellow, Malamud, Roth and Identity Crises

Readers interpreting the foregoing chapters may be forgiven for developing the view that everything that happened which was of importance to this body of writing was in New York. Of course, there was Jewish life and culture in many other areas, but New York clearly had the mass immigration and also the first notable writers. It also had a focus for communication, media and the advancement of assimilation issues. A book such as Bernard Malamud's *A New Life* (1961), which takes 'Cascadia College' in the West as a focus, is unusual. In addition, there was also the concentration of Jewish intellectuals which has had a sub-culture celebrated throughout the whole of the period in question. But by 1945 there had been such progress and change in terms of how Jewish Americans saw themselves that any study of the writing of this period needs to pinpoint the nature of that moment at which fresh perceptions were made. That particular period of transition, roughly from the late 1930s to the early 1950s, witnesses certain important phases. First, there is a reassessment of the 1930s and of ideological change; then Saul Bellow initiates a defined way of placing Jewishness within urban culture, and finally, a 'new wave' arrives with the early work of Philip Roth. Throughout this period we also have the stories of Malamud (and parallels in Yiddish with Isaac Singer), which take more interest in the persistence of European Jewishness within American life – a world of marriage-fixers, small businesses and superstition.

However, it is also necessary to describe the literary world into which Saul Bellow arrived with his first novel, *Dangling Man*, in 1944. The consciousness and sensibility of Jewish-American literature in the early 1940s was partly politicised and partly comfortably middle class in outlook, ideologically adapted to the central American tenets of 'The American Way of Life', capitalism and liberal values. But the impact of the 1930s and Roosevelt's New Deal had been deep. As Bradbury and Temperley put it:

> Also prevalent was a feeling of personal guilt and shame, usually brought about by the humiliation of unemployment. Most Americans blamed themselves rather than Wall Street or the government. Bewilderment and shock, even a sense of imminent catastrophe, were widespread responses.[1]

The central assimilated Jewishness had become, in the second-generation immigrants, a lifestyle that was in many ways defining what 'American' was coming to mean: tolerant, vibrant, involved in technological change, acquiring family values and seeing a unity in the many. The social and cultural effects of mass communications and educational provision, together with the elimination of starvation and destitution under Roosevelt, had confirmed belief in the self-help qualities of the immigrant underclass as social aspirants. They had aspired, arrived and moved into suburbia as well as further into urban identity.

But there was still, in the art and literature, a demand for the Jewish difference to be apparent and also promulgated in the right literary channels. Saul Bellow inherited this mixture: on the one hand, a secular Jewishness which expressed itself in a certain lifestyle, and on the other, a persistent intellectualism which looked back to Europe and also tried to absorb new patterns of meanings within a perplexing modernity.

Three minor and secondary fictions of the late 1930s and early 1940s illustrate this inheritance. If Bellow has come to be seen as the dominant mediator of the Jewish intellectual puzzled in the midst of a riotous amoral *danse macabre*, then what ideals lay behind the bohemian, articulate culture from which his protagonists gain their sustenance and their sense of being? In the 1930s, an influential publication had been the *Menorah Journal*. Lionel Trilling and Eliot Cohen had been involved with this, largely with the intention of providing a forum for that intellectual diversity within academia which felt the need to express issues of Jewishness, as opposed to Judaism. As Mark Krupnick remarks:

> If they had not abandoned Jewish particularism for more universalist concerns in the crisis that followed 1929, we wouldn't be talking about them today. But their early phase of Jewish self-consciousness deserves to be remembered. It imparted to their later writing, and to the writing of later waves of the New York intellectuals, something of its characteristic style and subject-matter.[2]

Lionel Trilling, for instance, castigated some of the early Jewish writers for their too clumsy didacticism and for remaining too unthinkingly in that class of writing which gives stereotypical characters and oversimplified accounts of central issues.

The three texts which illustrate this are Trilling's novel, *The Middle of the Journey* (1947), Delmore Schwartz's story *In Dreams Begin Responsibilities* (1937) and Meyer Liben's novella, *Justice Hunger* (1956). There are themes in these fictions that give a direct and enlightening approach to the basis of much of the mainline writing of the twenty years following the Second World War. Schwartz was a very talented writer who promised a great deal, in both prose and poetry. His story was in the first issue of *Partisan Review*, another influence on this intellectualism. It deals with an allegory of understanding parents, and their life and love as first-generation immigrants. The narrator imagines seeing their lives in glimpses, on a film, and then as the father on the film breaks free from the mother, 'in terrible anger', Schwartz gives this reaction:

> I in my seat am shocked more than ever can be said, for I feel as if I were walking a tight-rope, a hundred feet over a circus-audience, and suddenly the rope is showing signs of breaking.[3]

Then, the voices of his parents come at him directly and forcefully: 'Don't you know that you can do whatever you want to do?'[4] He is dragged into the light and into the 1930s. It is a story which puts the dilemma of the younger generation very boldly; it addresses the notion of success and confidence – the need for the persistence of the qualities that first made for success in the *goldene medine*. Many of Schwartz's other stories deal with circles of bright young literary people, but Trilling's only novel, *The Middle of the Journey*, adds another dimension. He too has a young intellectual as protagonist, and also an editor and a literary journal figure in the political plot, but Trilling universalises and puts a similar question phrased in more approachable terms: 'And once more he thought of the future as a characteristic concept of the well-loved young man of the middle-class, brought up on promises.'[5] His hero, Laskell, (maybe echoing the Yiddish *Maskill* – a teacher?), confronts a variety of complacent and narrow-minded political positions, focused in New England and in rurality as well as in the urban world of small-scale journalism. Like Schwartz's work, Trilling's is consciously literary and allusive (the title is derived from Dante's *Divine Comedy*) but he faces up to current social and ideological issues more didactically.

This didactic tendency is even more apparent in Meyer Liben's stories. The notable differences between Trilling and Liben in their fiction are those of degrees of narrative subtlety and artifice. Liben is meta-fictional. He frames the story around the theoretical positions associated with some ineradicable elements of Jewishness associated with art and sensibility. Each of his chapters has an almost Brechtian interference with narrative dynamic, as in 'An aspect of the artist's relation to Great Historical Movements'. What Liben has in common with Schwartz and Trilling is an unquestioning attitude to the ways in which philosophical discussion is foregrounded and inter-woven with Jewish culture and lifestyle. In Chapter 39 of *Justice Hunger*, for instance, we have a debate on metaphysics, linked to Soviet history.[6]

In all three writers, there is a recurrent interest in Soviet Russia and Marxism. There is, however, a more palpable and unavoidable rhetoric of Leftist thought in Liben. His protagonist takes up the stance of the 1930s city boulevardier-aesthete and then a particular bohemianism is confronted by the world of ideas.

All this is a way into understanding just why Saul Bellow has been the dominant voice of Jewish America throughout the first phase of the period under review. Until the emergence of other regions, forms and originated sub-cultures and the impact of the postmodern plurality of narratives in cultural mediation, Bellow was the spokesman for that inner heartland of Jewish assimilation which not only refused to lose the quintessence of its intellectual being, but actually to use that self-identity as a basis for building a critique of post-war America.

Of course, there were other reasons for this internalising drive to understand the basis of the self in this new skin: anti-Semitism was undoubtedly one, and also the need to assert difference in a situation in which other minorities seemed to be in ascendancy. The new arrivals of the post-war years (Hispanics for instance) and the gradual establishment of sites for the cultural debate on race following Martin Luther King and civil rights, all meant that any residual Jewishness had to be treated with care, or certain types of difference and uniqueness would be capable of perpetuating myth. The film representation of Hassidism is a case in point, and in popular narrative, even as late as the 1980s, films often still constructed Jewishness as backward-looking, entrenched in a mental Euro-Jewry.[7] The cultural pluralism so typical of American life is also typical of Jewish life generally and Bellow's insistence on the nihilistic clashes in American urban life repeatedly undermines the notion of the Jew as a creature able to be assimilated. Bellow's early work, from *Dangling Man* (1944) to *Mr Sammler's Planet* (1969), presents a variety of what might be termed modes of exclusion. There have been many and diverse interpretations of these novels, but in summarising the nature of Bellow's textualisation of the Jewish American who exhibits the qualities of sensibility, intelligence, philosophical enquiry, awareness of community and dependence on a literary culture, it is necessary to locate the malaise at the centre.

It is possible to see these fictions as existential interpretations of the failure to be in a modern context; the central characters of Joseph (*Dangling Man*), Asa (*The Victim*), Tommy (*Seize the day*), Herzog and Sammler (eponymous figures), fail to cope with the aggression and materialist-led impulses of the modern urban consciousness. But also, the themes reach more deeply into a fundamental examination of the state of being-in-the-world each character exhibits. *The Victim*, though dealing with anti-Semitism, also touches on something far more universal. So it would not be unjust to insist that Bellow handles parallel ideas and explorations in each of these major novels. He often universalises, but the first concern is for the failures inherent in the confrontation of a certain moral goodness in an arena of threat, banality and brutal annihilation of basic human values.

Dangling Man establishes many of the recurrent preoccupations in Bellow's work. Joseph is waiting for military service. He is in a kind of limbo of waiting, but it soon emerges that he is waiting to be, to exist, to be justified, 'He is a person greatly concerned with keeping intact, and free from encumbrance a sense of his own being, its importance.'[9] The novel examines the ideas of how the inner life and the public life co-exist. 'He keeps his roles successfully distinct and even goes out of his way to be an excellent employee, simply to prove that "visionaries" can be hard-headed.'[10]

He asks 'How should a good man live?' and spanks Etta because she 'had a spanking coming'[11] But it soon becomes apparent that Bellow is taking on the role of moralistic chronicler of this specifically Jewish-American receptivity to such crises and contradictions. The fool plays the thinker. In the cruel man lies the poet. The anti-Semitism so prominent in *The Victim* is also present here, in the visit to the German, Will, and the calling of Joseph 'Mephisto' for no other reason than his Jewishness.[12] This illustrates Bellow's ability to give an account of the essential condition of his people through a fusion of interiority and external, often satirical material. In some prominent episodes, these accretions are made prominent as commentaries and often as authorial disquisitions on the human situation in the post-war age of anxiety. The words on personal destiny and on 'Great minds, great beauty' develop this in *Dangling Man*.[13]

In *The Victim* Bellow gives what is arguably his most rhetorical and relentlessly honest account of some fundamental qualities of Jewishness at the core of the above discussion. In dealing with anti-Semitism here, Bellow uses the subject in order to explore particular habits of mind and imagination which construct the moral corpus of being Jewish in its broadly secular sense. The American moralism is here demonstrably inherent in the Jewish sensibility. The novel deals with the 'stalking' of Asa Leventhal by a man with a grudge, a man who blames his loss of a job on Asa. This Allbee is a shadow of threat and presentiment throughout the entire novel. Interweaving a storyline of sacrifice, nobility and tolerance into Asa's character, the man gives and takes to the letter of Christ's teaching. He is a Jew with the Christian virtues, but also with far more than are called for given his position of victim. Bellow complicates through circumstances, until, again, 'destiny' plays a part. Asa sees this: 'He looked hopelessly before him. Williston, like himself, like everybody else, was carried on currents, this way and that.'[14]

Bellow takes his enquiries further. As the novel gains pace, we have debates on degrees of Jewishness, and on varieties of esteem. The debate on Disraeli is used to this effect. When Goldstone points out that Disraeli 'Showed Europe that a Jew could be a national leader'[15] Asa is forced to assess the value of the assertive, worldly Jewishness that plays to win in the gentile world. It is left to the 'sensual, powerful . . . dandy' Schlossberg to give Bellow's case for 'being human' above being Jew or gentile,[16] but in the words, 'It's bad to be less than human and it's bad to be more than human' we have Bellow's customary commentary on the progress and decline of his protagonists.[17]

In the end, though, Allbee and Asa are textualised as two extremes of the Jewish condition. Allbee is concerned with 'blame' and sacrifice. The notion of a scapegoat is contrasted with the role of selflessness. But Bellow works out two versions of egoism with alacrity, building in a sharp critique of ways of escape into reductive ideology.

Early Bellow: Establishing a Planet

In his essay, 'Where Do We Go from Here?' Saul Bellow theorises on the significance of the novel as a medium for expressing varieties of personal experience, and dismisses didacticism with an assertion of something to be found in his early work: 'The imagination is looking for new ways to express virtue.'[18] It may be argued that Bellow's handling of what several critics have seen as a fiction of revolt and accommodation is in line with an ongoing debate about to what extent Jewish novelists are 'increasingly exploring the meaning of being Jewish from within rather than from the perspective of American culture.' and implying that 'a dual identity is no longer necessary for American Jews?'[19] Indeed, Bellow's novels do deal with issues around the definition of virtue. One of the most fruitful approaches to his fiction up to *Herzog* (1964) is in terms of how the virtues inherent in a life of sacrifice and courage could be contrasted with the life of the many, of mass-culture.

In *Seize the Day* (1956), Tommy Wilhelm is under the dominance of two others: Tamkin and his father. Bellow makes a child-man of his allegorical figure. Placing Jewishness in its explicit forms, as in *The Victim*, more in the condition of accommodation to the new American culture of what Marcus Klein has called an acceptance of 'the new wealth and the corporate conscience, to the fat gods',[20] Bellow gives an account of the journey towards certain virtues inherent in Jewishness.

What begins to emerge with more clarity in this novel is Bellow's dialogic expression of that Talmudic debate at the base of fundamental Jewish being. In a sense, Wilhelm senior is a figure representing both conscience and God, or God-ness. When Tommy actually faces up to his father with his complaints, the interplay reads like a prayer and a plea on behalf of the smallness and dependency of the human condition. 'What do you want to know about my problems for, Father? So you can lay the whole responsibility on me?'[21]

Tamkin's world is the arena of the destructive element that

Bellow gives as his anti-community in the early fiction. The social settings of his novels continue a critique of the materialist society gone mad; capitalism and selfishness have undermined value-systems and dependable morality. 'Everyone was like the faces on a playing card, upside down either way. Every public figure had a character-neurosis. Maddest of all were the businessmen.'[22]

It is notable that the Jewish-American viewpoint of WASP middle-class America, with its emphasis on family values, separate spheres for the sexes, xenophobia and impetus for acquisition and career success, is often depicted as alien, a decline from human communal standards and anti-intellectual. The essays collected in Irving Malin's book on Bellow of 1968 assume that Bellow is an intellectual, but accept a Jewish, urban basis of all ideologies connected with the term.[23] In fact, the novels and stories of Bellow and Malamud are full of criticisms of the decline of the intellect in this WASP centre. In Malamud's *A New Life* (1961) Sy Levin's account of the college in the West parallels the decline of the physical landscape of America with the mental decline in the education system. His students leave when asked to think rather than submit to a robotic system of learning. Bellow insists on a similar vision.[24]

In *Mr Sammler's Planet* (1969) and *Herzog* (1964) we have much more direct and enterprising accounts of accommodation or preservation in the new America of McCarthyism, Cold War neurosis and mass-cultural mediocrity. Bellow textualises two sorts of academic intellectuals for observation in this anarchic modernity. Each has a specific philosophical base, a claim staked in the consciousness of the Enlightenment. General discussion in the mediation of Jewishness often stresses the differentiation of *Haskallah* Jewishness, from Heinrich Heine through to Franz Kafka, in terms of the degrees of acceptance of a compromise between Orthodox belief and secular virtue.

Bellow displays this site of compromise, in which the cultural Jewishness is given adherence to values of the past, and strives for these earlier, archetypal Enlightenment virtues in the face of a plurality of belief and a questioning of all authority. There is a massive assumption in both central characters that 'humanity' is an amorphous mass-term, somehow with universal virtues and qualities; yet Nazism and fascism are, in this concept, a nihilistic drive to destroy, to make creation a deistic struggle. What place is there for the good man in this view of humanity? Herzog's tragi-comic personal life dramatises many of the failures inherent in this type of idealism, but his philosophy insists on being important, in the teeth of paradox and anarchy: 'The point was that there were foolish people who could destroy mankind and that they were foolish and arrogant. . . . Let the enemies of life step down . . .'[25] Herzog inhabits a 'parlor of indignation' where 'the right-thinking citizen brings his heart to a boil'.[26]

In most significant respects, Moses Herzog represents the *Yiddishkeit* of the genteel European-cosmopolitan middle class. His attitude to Valentine betrays him as an academic and as a *Luftmensch* in contra-distinction to the proletarian, Yiddish-speaking milieu of Valentine, and Valentine sees the wasted potential in Herzog.[27]

Embracing both novels is a profound and also comic narrative of contrast, taking American notions of the past and its importance as a subject directing the basic duality of Sammler/Herzog and their deconstructions of America as a principal device in foregrounding the Jewishness in the protagonists.

The ideas about time and mutability are Jewish. Herzog is explained early in the novel: 'He was the mature generation now, and life was his to do something with, if he could. But he had not forgotten the odour of his mother's saliva.'[28] Equally, the past and the dead are central to his constructions of a moral order. 'To him, perpetual thought of death was a sin. Drive your cart and your plow over the bones of the dead.'[29]

Fundamental to the novel is Bellow's dual discussion of the intellectual life as seriously important but also rather comically grotesque. Herzog's existential act, his authentication of being in this world, where he must act and show, achieve and be what his destiny says, is often farcically given, as in his reading of the literature of Enthusiasm.[30] Also, in his quests for understanding of the self, he takes time to question Rozanov on the subject of the 'Jewish ritual bath'.[31]

Herzog's letters to the great, past and present, and his development of his own mighty project from his book on Romanticism, make him an enduring figure representing the questionable yet inescapable duty of the intellectual Jewish American to attempt to come to an understanding of post-Enlightenment selfhood, with the challenge to Orthodoxy firmly established by this time. The 1950s saw the emergence of the Jewish intellectuals and writers coming into the centre of consciousness. The literary circle around *Partisan Review* and the creators of *The New York Review of Books* were largely Jewish; the achievements of Henry Roth, Ben Hecht and others had shown that there was a need for some central and focal debates about the nature of that 'Jewish centre' and how it related both to its own past and to the wider social and political climate in which Marxist–communist theory and practice was very much in question as having any part in American self-awareness and ideological constructs.

Bellow's Herzog and Sammler contribute a great deal to this cultural interplay; their narratives locate this very specific consciousness of, as Leslie Fiedler puts it, having the 'role of the American, of registering experience for his compatriots'[32] and in Bellow's case the context is a highbrow one. If the interests of that group at that time were intellectual and philosophical, then writers needed to respond. After all, the 1950s and 1960s were also a time in which Sartre's version of existentialism had an impact on many American writers and thinkers.[33] When Herzog reflects on Martin Buber's I and Not-I thinking, for instance, it is a parody of much of the highbrow cultural discourse of the period, as exemplified in the collection, *The Dialectics of Liberation* (1968), which sprang from a conference at Chalk Farm and purposely mixed new ideas in psychology with sociology, politics and literature.[34] In other words, Bellow was conscious of a trend, a vogue, in which Jewish intellectuals were prominent, and the scope in this, from a novelist's viewpoint, was a fertile mix of parody and serious philosophical ideas interfused with the fictional elements.

But in *Mr Sammler's Planet*, Bellow goes further and is more direct in his confrontation with the pains and trials of modernity for his character. It represents, in one sense, Bellow's increasing fondness for diminishing narrative interest and diversity in the cause of authorial disquisitions. Sammler's planet is perhaps largely that circumscribed area of difference, of non-American and yet non-European identity, which is a mental space, outside time and place, existing only as a point of creativity.

But in this novel, both Israel and the Holocaust are more present, and the idea of the imagination finding new ways of expressing virtue is here again. The Holocaust and its absorption, its placing within 'history' along with more trivial and banal events, is something fundamental to Sammler's assemblies of meanings. Sammler's inner thoughts are often about a more distant view of life, essentially scientific and accepting a withdrawal of emotive vocabulary. 'More elements of reality will perhaps be incorporated in the new version. But the important consideration was that life should recover its plenitude.'[35] The result is that Bellow gives us an America which provides the necessary anonymity, the absence of a cultural sustenance which might genuinely feed the Sammlers something to re-vivify; and that Israel is a sort of rest-home and charity agency for walking wounded.[36] The 'jolly frantic music' of America is a distraction, a sort of Lethe of forgetfulness, it is suggested, in which the most horrendous events may be subsumed, hidden, placed in ritual and sanitised into normality and comprehension. The novel constructs something similar to a massive monologue inside Sammler: 'Sammler, from keeping his counsel for so long, from seven decades of internal consultation, had his own views on most matters.'[37]

What develops is a view of humankind which supports his own idea that a man among men knows how to murder; Sammler is created from annihilation, from the very fact that there was a force at work which set out to cancel out all Jewishness. Bellow's novel is one of the formative works in the context of beginning narratives about the Holocaust and its effect. In America, even the United States Holocaust Museum, designed by James Inigo Freed, was designed as a visual narrative experience.[38] The need to somehow empathise insists on being given a place in the layers of meaning which have been made about such application of evil. Sammler is a version of the prophet, and the retelling of the life in the ghetto is one which reflects the statement given in the text that, 'I am not speaking only of moral demand, but also of the demand upon the imagination to produce a human figure of adequate stature.'[39]

Bernard Malamud: Stories of Celebration and Expiation

The phrase above was given by Malamud himself, as his reasons for writing about Jews. His short stories and novels celebrate and deal with expiation. But the importance of his work is that, mostly, it explains the elements that compose the traditional character of the Jew in both religious and secular terms. His short stories focus on aspects of Jewish-American life which continue the cyclic functioning of the *Shtetl*. Within Orthodox Jewish life, the aims of the stories are mostly to reveal an inner nature, a state of being that is still coping with accelerated change and with the dream of a new life. Whereas his novels usually deal with accommodation and assimilation, the stories often locate a specific essence of Jewish consciousness inside the larger culture. The Lower East Side of c. 1920 could be the setting, but many are timeless and allegorical.

The most established and successful stories indicate the nature of the celebration and expiation: 'Take Pity' concerns pity and pride, dealing with a woman's need to build a business and keep her pride in her family and herself; 'Idiots First' explores the gap between rich and poor, and includes a portrait of the impoverished but self-negating rabbi. 'The Last Mohican' with the intellectual yet feckless Jewish scholar in contrast with the con-man and 'wide-boy'. But Malamud concentrates on particular traits which are best expressed in the surreal and the bizarre mixed with realistic devices of satire and social commentary.

Two representative stories in this respect are 'The Jewbird' and 'The Magic Barrel'. The first is a strong parable about anti-Semitism dealing with the self-hatred, that exists within Jews themselves. The storyline is comic and surreal; a talking 'Jewbird' arrives in a family, running from 'Anti-semeets' and is eventually resented, abused, reviled and cast out. The bird, Mr Schwartz, is found dead by the boy and its last words are that 'Anti-semeets' killed him. The story reads like a folktale with an urban locale; the family are depicted as hard, unfeeling and nasty. Cohen's hatred is unreasoned and driven by jealousy and resentment. The course of arrival and insult, harassment and eviction, through to ultimate destruction, mirrors the actual paradigm of recorded anti-Semitism in society, with its irrational basis.

Malamud's contribution is partly this ability to simplify by making transparent what is usually complex and resistant to analysis. Yet, as in 'The Magic Barrel', he is able to use the stuff of stereotyped Jewish-American narrative with the essence of orality as in the folktale, and to inject the required universality. In this case, the nature of love is in question, and Malamud takes this familiar theme, together with the matchmaker and the *yeshiva* student-rabbi in order to contrast intellectual with proletarian, and to use ideas of romantic love to undermine the traditional discourse of the simple tale. The story is littered with the received wisdom of Jewish self-regard: 'Out of this, however, he drew the consolation that he was a Jew, and a Jew suffered.'[40] But when Leo, the student, loves Salzman's own daughter, we are led to something deeper and more enigmatic in the closure. Leo meets the girl and 'Around the corner, Salzman, leaning against a wall, chanted prayers for the dead.'[9]

Malamud has succeeded in using the basic material of popular narrative and formal short stories to reveal the residual Jewishness within the American sub-groups preserving first-generation lifestyles. To read his novels, in contrast, is to have a vision of post-war America. He uses the devices and traditions of various genres of fiction to discover and satirise layers of American lifestyles dealt with more comfortably and also more superficially in film and television. For instance, 'He pictured the USA as a structure of highways and freeways.'[42] But more important is his textualisation of the Jew of the third generation, assimilated to America in its 'heartlands' regional existence. He succeeds in revealing features of assimilation which show it to be a term with many meanings and shades of reference, much as the sociologist Lloyd Gartner does:

There are all sorts of processes that are related to assimilation. For instance, accommodation takes place when individuals in groups within a society do not assimilate, but rather only tolerate one another.[43]

The above discussion has used the term 'accommodation' in this sense, and Malamud has demonstrated that it is possible to shift from assimilation ideas to accommodation lifestyles, particularly in individuals. His character Sy Levin leaves New York for the Far War, and takes his lifestyle, ideology and sense of Jewish selfhood with him. As an outsider in a WASP community, he commentates on the insecurities inherent in the life he observes. But he is also Everyman, with a similar voice to that of Sammler, 'Discontent brings neither cold cash nor true love, therefore why not enjoy this tender marvellous day instead of greeting it with news of everything I haven't got?'[44]

Malamud is a profitable read in contrast to Henry Roth and Anzia Yezierska, in that his stories of urban Jewish life show how far this category of writing has come in subtlety and depth since the first didactic works fixed on the dilemmas of assimilation and survival. Yet his 'celebration' of innate Jewishness somehow avoids the banal. One of his notable achievements is surely that of being able to maintain and use the inexplicable spirit of Jewish uniqueness without falsifying or distorting his subjects.

Philip Roth: Suburban Angst

Philip Roth arrived on the scene in 1959 with a collection of stories and the novella, *Goodbye, Columbus*; by the late 1960s he had written a very long socio-realist novel, autobiographical fiction and the succes d'estime, *Portnoy's Complaint* (1969). From the beginning, his writing was provocative, honest, harshly satirical, entertaining with a candour similar to that of Lenny Bruce and yet with interspersed elegies to the lost world of first-generation immigrants. His standpoint was the intelligent, dissentient voice of the new suburbs. His work was set in the geography of New Jersey, and from a basic device of using a persona, in *Goodbye, Columbus*, he created a fresh way of seeing the assimilated Jewish life of wealth, comfort and material progress. But issues of Jewish suffering as well as their triumph inhabit the fiction.

The first work from Roth concerns a librarian, a sensitive narrator who sees and reflects on a range of denizens of the suburbs. He befriends a young black boy in search of art books and friendship, but most of all he is taken up by the Patimkins, a Jewish family whose daughter, Brenda, he loves and courts. Roth contrasts three versions of assimilation or accommodation: his aunt is immersed in domesticated and small-minded but very human *Yiddishkeit*; Mr Patimkin is a materialist, embodying the work-ethic innate to his people, and Brenda herself, who is markedly different and is a clear signal to future change.

Roth specialises in his early writing in searching the spiritual life of his characters and showing them wanting. Mr Patimkin is the first in a long line of Roth creations to be inarticulate in important matters: 'I only knew that the few words he did speak could hardly transmit all the satisfaction and surprise he felt about the life he had managed to build.'[45]

The Patimkins are Orthodox and accommodated, but Roth makes it clear that he wants to compare and inevitably provide a commentary on both versions of being Jewish that his own and the Patimkin family represent. The scenes with Mrs Patimkin introduce all the elements of Orthodox Jewish life, with *B'nai Brith* and *Hadassah*, but Roth's aim is to pinpoint the dilemma of the new generation, and Neil Klugman, the main character, fumbles to explain his position: on being asked to come to the synagogue with the Patimkins, he replies, 'I sort of switch. I'm just Jewish . . . Desperately I tried to think of something that would convince her I wasn't an infidel. Finally I asked, "Do you know Martin Buber's work?" '[46]

Increasingly, it becomes clear in Roth's first four works that he is locating a specific turn in the aspirations and consciousness of the newest generation. His work parodies a range of discourses and contexts in which Jewishness as a state of being is promulgated. 'Just Jewish' is maybe the best that these new Americans can offer, but in the face of the past generations and their folly, romanticism, nostalgia and nameless fears, it is a life-choice that has to be explained before it may be defended. It does need to be defended, that much the people in the stories and novels before *Portnoy* show. Roth's first stories place identity issues plainly back in focus, with versions of anti-Semitism always handled explicitly and with effective irony. In the short stories in particular, there is much investigation of Jewishness as a shield and a convenience. That Roth made enemies and caused open debate about the importance of understanding why the young generation resisted their Jewish cultural roots and rituals is understandable, given the climate of anti-Semitism, as described in John Berryman's essay for instance.[47]

In *Portnoy's Complaint*, however, Roth selects elements of established and symbolic cultural artefacts to locate Portnoy in a new rank of American-ness, assimilated through pop and proletarianism. His baseball bat is emblematic: 'to step out and express, if only through a slight poking of the ground, just the right amount of exasperation with the powers that be'.[48] But the dissent is more fundamental. There is a whole gamut of attacks on Orthodox lifestyle and institutions. The Rabbi Warshaw, for instance, typifies this.[49] He and the synagogue come to represent everything static and bound up with mindless attention to routine and convention.

The overall perspective established in the novel is one of intentionally textualising the popular and mass-cultural reception and vulgarisation of the massive and irrefutable facts of the modern Jewish experience. Even the Holocaust is mentioned in terms which reduce it from historical event to one of trivial reference within childish play. Roth purposely set out to construct a range of appropriations here. The novel borrows and echoes several registers of talk and rhetoric concerning the nature of youth and youth-speech. The slang and obscenity inherent in the dissent powerfully voices this use of anti-establishment style.

The final effect, attained cumulatively, is one of a serio-comic denigration of certain stereotypes in Jewish life. Since taken up by Woody Allen and Billy Crystal, such references in 1969 were far more resonant because they were exceptional. Even a simple discussion such as whether or not Portnoy has a genuine complaint or simply a mundane *kvetch* is undermining some kind of stereotypical voicing of Jewish humour.[50]

Philip Roth's early work, then, in contrast to Bellow and Malamud, is more basically concerned with the acceptance of assimilation, mostly because of the appeal of the new cultural mediation of positive images of freedom and equality. It has to be mentioned, of course, that the backdrop of the Vietnam War, the assassination of Kennedy and the entire and pervasive 'invention' of the 'teenager' as a concept has a bearing, too. But the Jewish targets of this inventive and original comic novel meant that a stance had been taken in Jewish-American writing that broke unwritten laws, brought out renewed attempts at defining what mattered and what was merely outward show. The essay that Roth wrote in reply to attacks from certain rabbis and so on shows exactly how far Portnoy had gone in shaking up awareness of the process of accommodation.[51]

Roth never evaded the significance of the media in everyday experience and in the shaping of ideological processes. It has to be significant that criticism has not markedly concentrated on this aspect of his work, but from the first published fiction, he clearly saw the importance of popular forms in making the allegiances of individuals to faceless corporations and edifices. It just happens that his first target was the family, and in his case, it happened to be Jewish. Similar assessments could be made, of, say Joseph Heller in *Catch 22*. If one wanted to find Jewish satirical stool-pigeons, then the task of finding a notably Judaeo-Christian dialogue between Yossarian and God strongly anti-Jewish would not be impossible.[52] Roth's honesty and directness may have won enemies, but the originality and vibrancy of his achievement cannot be denied.

In effect, Roth was writing about the tropes of Jewish writing: the governing metaphors of that self-directed humour in this category. He simply sent up a set of conventions and was misunderstood by too many readers at the time. In fact, what was developing in his work was an increasing dialogue in which he confronted the issues involving proletarian life and middle-class consciousness in modern American culture, beginning a long succession of novels which handle these themes of class and sociological relations in ways that do not always foreground specifically Jewish topics.

Notes

1. Malcolm Bradbury and Howard Temperley (eds), *Introduction to American Studies* (Longman: London and New York, 1989), p. 287.
2. Mark Krupnick, 'The Menorah Journal Group and the Origins of Modern American Radicalism', *SAJL* vol. 8 no. 2 (1989) pp. 21–30.
3. Delmore Schwartz, *In Dreams Begin Responsibilities,* (Secker and Warburg: London), 1978) p. 8.
4. Ibid.
5. Lionel Trilling, *The Middle of the Journey* (Secker and Warburg: London, 1948), p. 155.
6. See Meyer Liben, *Justice Hunger* (Barrie and Rockliff: London, 1968), pp. 84–7; Liben's stories, published between 1956 and 1962 represent the most intentionally didactic trend in this category.
7. See in particular, *Crossing Delancey* (Joan Micklin Silver: 1988) and *Stranger Among Us* (Sydney Lumet: 1992). Both give perceptive and intelligent depictions of the communities, yet privilege only selected traits and lifestyles for plot purposes.
8. See Lloyd Gartner, 'Assimilation and American Jews' in Bela Vago (ed.), *Jewish Assimilation in Modern Times* (Westview Press: Colorado, 1981), p. 177.
9. Saul Bellow, *Dangling Man* (Penguin: London, 1971) p. 27.
10. Ibid., p. 29.
11. Ibid., pp. 71–2.
12. Ibid., p. 77.
13. Ibid., pp. 88-9; Bellow includes the 'debaters in midnight cafeterias' and again fixes on a particular sub-culture.
14. Saul Bellow, *The Victim* (Penguin: London, 1988), p. 81.
15. Ibid., p. 115.
16. Ibid., p. 119. It is interesting to note Schlossberg's origins in the cafe intellectuals depicted by Hapgood, (see Chapter 1 of this book).
17. Ibid., p. 119.
18. Saul Bellow, 'Where Do We Go from Here?', in Irving Malin (ed.), *Saul Bellow and the Critics* (New York University Press: New York 1967), pp. 211–20, p. 219.
19. Elaine M. Kauvar, 'An Interview with Cynthia Ozick' in *Contemporary Literature*, vol. 34, no. 3, (Fall 1993), pp. 359-394, p. 372.
20. Marcus Klein, 'A Discipline of Nobility', in Malin (*Saul Bellow,*) pp. 92–113, p. 92. Klein relates Bellow's work to the social setting, and works on the basic contrast of alienation and accommodation.
21. Saul Bellow, *Seize the Day* (Penguin: London, 1966), p. 53.

22. Ibid., p. 50.
23. Malin, *Saul Bellow*. Malin's collection is one of the very first to assess Bellow and the assumptions are that highbrow art is unquestioned as the central mediation of the Jewish-American consciousness. The primacy of philosophical fiction is assumed (see his introduction).
24. Bernard Malamud, *A New Life* (Penguin: London, 1968), see pp. 147–8.
25. Saul Bellow, *Herzog* (Penguin: London, 1965), p. 51.
26. Ibid., p. 51.
27. Ibid., pp. 60-1. These pages show how Bellow uses Yiddish to define a lifestyle, deftly and with a certain sense of gradations of Orthodoxy and liberalness.
28. Ibid., p. 33.
29. Ibid.
30. Ibid., p. 127. He is talking to himself here; the instinct to debate is inner – a construct of the interiority at the base of all Bellow protagonists.
31. Ibid., p. 71.
32. See Leslie Fiedler, 'Saul Bellow' *Saul Bellow*, in Malin (see note 18 above) pp. 1–9, p. 3. Fiedler places Bellow directly in the tradition of Roth and Cahan, at least in the sense of a writer who has 'worked himself up in America'.
33. See Stephen Wade, *The Imagination in Transit* (Sheffield Academic Press: Sheffield, 1996), p. 18. Here, I use Sartre's biography to assess the impact of his thought on American intellectuals at the time.
34. See David Cooper (ed.), *The Dialectics of Liberation* (Penguin: London, 1968), Notably, several contributors are Jewish thinkers and commentators, including Marcuse and Goodman.
35. Saul Bellow, *Mr Sammler's Planet* (Penguin: London, 1969), p. 17.
36. Ibid., p. 125.
37. Ibid., p. 116.
38. See the illustrated account of the museum in Adrian Dannatt, *United States Holocaust Museum* (Phaidon: London, 1996), pp. 28–51 in particular.
39. Bellow, *mr Sammler's Planet*, p. 64.
40. Bernard Malamud, *Selected Stories* (Penguin: London, 1985) p. 136.
41. Ibid., p. 143.
42. Bernard Malamud, *A New Life* (Penguin: London, 1968), p. 121.
43. Lloyd Gartner, 'Assimilation and American Jew,' in Vago *Jewish Assimilation*, p. 171.
44. Malamud, *A New Life*, p. 171.
45. Philip Roth, *Goodbye, Columbus* (Penguin: London, 1986), p. 74.
46. Ibid., p. 70.
47. See John Berryman, 'The Imaginary Jew', in *The Freedom of the Poet* (Farrar, Strauss, Giroux: New York, 1976), pp. 359-366, p. 366. Berryman takes the role of 'imaginary Jew' in a situation of blatant anti-Semitism that he witnesses.
48. Philip Roth, *Portnoy's Complaint* (Cape: London, 1971), p. 79.
49. Ibid., p. 81. The main comment here is in italics in the text: 'the synagogue is how he earns his living *and that is all there is to it*'.

50. Ibid., p. 105.
51. See Roth's defence and further exposition of his views in the long essay, 'Imagining Jews', in *Reading Myself and Others* (Cape: London, 1977), pp. 193–222.
52. See in particular Joseph Heller, *Catch 22* (Cape: London, 1962), pp. 230–1 in which there is, beneath the surreal and dark comedy, a pastiche of the dialogic relationship with God (*Yahweh*) in the traditions of exegesis (e.g. 'There's nothing mysterious about it. He's not working at all. He's playing').

4

Jewish-American Themes in Fiction II: Erica Jong, Grace Paley and Tillie Olson

The assumptions about the central importance of Bellow, Malamud and Roth have been made with several layers of reference and cultural use; not least of these is clearly the fact that Jewish characters and ideas are either constantly privileged in the narratives, or dealt with indirectly through intellectual burdens on the development of the dialogic discourse. That is, questions of identity were slowly eclipsed by questions of accommodation to American ideologies, with attendant consequences on the residual Jewishness of the characters. In Malamud's case, the actual sinews of the syntax, the Yiddish vocabulary and the concentration on the impact of the past on the present in his stories all make him more aligned with the Yiddish writer Isaac Bashevis Singer than with Roth or Bellow. His novels are a different matter. But the case of Malamud, as with Stanley Elkin also, raises again the question of definition.

This chapter summarises and interprets the work of the significant women fiction-writers in the period, and, once more, qualifications have to be made about the application of the term Jewish. The problem is stated well by Frederick Karl in an essay which seeks to link black, Jewish and women writers. Karl struggles to find adequate definition of the Jewish difference, gives a superficial case for this, and concludes that, 'Jewish novelists have, also, more or less run their course. Bellow, Malamud, Roth, Heller, Mailer, Doctorow, and others continue to publish . . . but the novelty has worn off.'[1] This illustrates the blindness to far more abiding and profound elements of recent Jewish experience in America, but also highlights the ways in which certain writers have purposely textualised Jewish life and belief, while others have simply used it as convenient material. Elkin, in an interview, for instance, talks about his story, 'The Rabbi of Lud' in merely comic terms, never mentioning any Jewish 'theme' at all.[2] Karl, in his dismissal, concludes by arguing that the decline of Jewish-American writing as a dominant and important factor only insofar as there are massive, all-embracing features which explain the ongoing concerns of American literature, and that Jewish writing has been subsumed into this. He lists 'the pastoral, Jeffersonian tradition' and 'reliance on escape and liberation as resolutions of personal dilemmas' for instance. Now, this could be easily said for any body of literature, and it avoids having to stop and consider the real case for a special difference, and indeed a renewal of vigour and sense of purpose.[3]

One of the most significant reappraisals has been that of the achievements of Jewish women writers since the 1940s. The foundation texts of Yezierska and Edna Ferber gave a whole spectrum of potential meanings and expositions of the woman writer within either the main culture or from within ethnicity. Particular writers have written about these foundations and about the impact of the social revolution after the Second World War, for instance, in the significant rise in the number of women in employment, but equally, as Betty Friedan's writings in the 1960s have shown, there was still an accepted rationale of the subservience of women and a pervasive ideology of domesticity and separate spheres. Friedan talks of 'this mystique of feminine fulfillment became the cherished and self-perpetuating core of contemporary American culture' (1963).[4]

But for the writers and intellectuals within Judaism, secular or Orthodox, conservative or accommodated, there was a persistent and deep residual Jewishness which, combined with the various stages in the development of a range of feminist theories and cultural mediations since the 1960s, led to a fresh revisionist writing (and discourse around the professionalisation of writing). This new writing had to deal with Jewishness on several levels, and it is possible to distinguish these in three major agendas:

1. The fictional commentary on accommodation and change.
2. The adoption of feminism and its relation to Jewish womanhood.
3. The philosophical and reflective examination of identity across generations, class and ethnicity.

But before assessing the work of some of the main representatives in these areas, it is necessary to look at some fundamental notions of women within Judaism and how these may relate to creativity and writing. The issues relating to identity and Jewish women's writing have been put simply and clearly by June Sochen. The basis of the identity question is clear: in traditional Jewish life, with separate male and female spheres, 'it was very difficult for Jewish women to identify themselves in ways other than the traditionally prescribed one' and, in writing, they are facing an additional issue of being and becoming.[5] Sochen also distinguishes the various degrees of identity traits. These create certain attitudes to the subject of fiction, which we shall see in the work of the writers in question: some remain fixed in the domain of 'being Jewish in America', while others 'it is the successful merger of American and Jewish values that predominates'.[6] Finally, Sochen points out the importance of seeing this corpus of work in terms of a central, established American tradition, with conventions to which Jewish women writers have to acknowledge and adapt. 'She is identifying with a literary tradition in America and in so doing allying herself with a whole set of American cultural beliefs.'[7]

A productive way to see this issue and its ramifications in recent writing is to compare three expressions of these fundamental Jewish statements about a woman's place and 'virtues' within orthodoxy. First, in traditional Yiddish fiction such as Y. L. Peretz' story, 'A Passion for Clothes'. Here, a wife who desires the fashionable dressings of the body in this transient world is punished. Her Hassidic husband, who is away from home talking theology when Satan tempts her, condemns her and she dies, being replaced in his home by an abused servant. Near the opening of the story, Peretz writes: 'Stan realised, however, that he could never persuade her to commit a *gross* sin, for she was truly a pure soul.'[8] So the woman is punished with death even for a peccadillo. Second, we have Yezierska, who as discussed above, is concerned with the basic feminine virtues of thrift, fidelity and work persisting even within a capitalist economy. Indeed, these, virtues, innate to this ideology of womanhood, in which a supportive and secondary role is instinctive to a woman, are a formula for success in 'pushcart' America.

Finally, where do we place the second- and third-generation women writers in comparison? Daniel Walden has summarised the most recent position, and we shall place Jong, Olson and Paley within this:

> The truly Jewish writer, Barbara Gitenstein claims, will turn into what Ozick says is a New Yiddish language appropriate to the liturgical mode. Perhaps in a similar vein, Norma Rosen's drive . . . comes from sources beyond the rational, perhaps the 'soul'.[9]

It is interesting to note that, in the fiction of Olsen and Paley in particular, there is a quality of what may be termed the 'irrational', a new-Romantic ethos mixed with an impressionistic social realism which confronts both the complex multi-cultural present and the semi-mystical Jewish past. We will examine Cynthia Ozick's work in a later chapter, but the present interpretation needs one further preparatory discussion: that of the American canon and its inclusion or otherwise of women writers. Nina Baym has argued forcefully that the political process involved in omitting women from the canonical texts has largely meant that critics have 'arrived at a place where Americanness has vanished into the depths of what is alleged to be the universal male psyche'.[10] Baym sees the centrality of 'socializers and domesticators' in American literature, and shows the reversals of this in women writers. When Jewish Americans of the first-generation immigrants adopted this, the result was clearly a pastiche of the romantic, idealised male, and the construction of a feminity which found strengths and resources within Jewishness which contributed further interest to an established formula of stereotypes. Yezierska's men apply to this configuration, and her women are aspirational, only emerging into selfhood with Americanisation.

Clearly, then, any reading of Jewish-American writers needs to keep these caveats in mind, but also there is a requirement to acknowledge difference, and even perhaps a claim to places in a new 'canon'. The space for individual creativity and the burgeoning of women writers in this context is remarkable when one recalls the fundamental position on women's individuality within Orthodoxy, and this is something that Jong, for instance, being brought up in a secular milieu, has a deep interest in. In terms of the orthodox statements of these limitations the expression is mainly in gender-valuing (for example a bar-mitzvah and circumcision for boys but often no recognition for a girl, nor attention given to coming-of-age), but there have been significant changes. 'With the new interest in Jewish feminism, many people have reassessed their needs and values and have written their own brit [covenant] ceremonies.'[11]

Jacqueline Rose, in an essay on Dorothy Richardson, has added some extra interest to the debate on the canon and on Jewish womanhood with her distinction between 'civic-being and species-being'.[12] The argument concerns the relinquishing of the public domain 'even in the name of feminist self-determination'. In terms of the actual subjects of, say, Paley's fiction, there is a significant shift back to the 'species-being' as a way of understanding the immigrant experience in her own community and family – and its importance for the revisionist recent generations.

Erica Jong: *Fear of Flying*

When *Fear of Flying* appeared in 1973 it appeared to have the perfect mix of both contemporaneous, even trendy concerns and a vigorous feminist playfulness in tune with much of popular film and music at the time. The account of marital and sexual anarchy together with hyperbolic satire on psycho-analysis was understood in relation to Woody Allen and to Philip Roth. Indeed the text makes reference to Roth and to its own status as a send-up of several modes of writing about American Jewishness, but it also attempts to say something about how women's consciousness relates to the Holocaust within a familial context, and how creativity is a specific dilemma to be resolved along with sexual maturity. The heroine, Isadora, is consciously formed within certain cultural and literary cross-reference and the adopted tone is a fusion of the surreal and the autobiographical *Bildungsroman*.

In her preface to the 1996 edition, Jong locates Isadora in relation to Henry Miller and to Roth. But she insists that the book validated the feelings of selfhood in a great number of women readers. She stresses the heroine's *chutzpah* and honesty, yet finds weaknesses in the female fantasy depicted. What is not stressed is the deep and prolonged fictional discourse on being a woman in a Jewish family which has an ambiguous and often unvoiced relationship with its European past and to its Jewishness.[13]

In Chapter 9 we have the open reference to Portnoy and mother/Isadora and mother. The Jewishness in *Fear of Flying* is distanced and undermined from the start. In this chapter, it is an account of creativity and the failed artist, the guilt involved, and the barriers to fulfilment. 'I couldn't rebel against Judaism because I hadn't anything to rebel against' says Isadora.[14] She learns about women from men, and sexuality becomes the way towards this self-understanding. The Jewishness becomes increasingly a separate state of being – a parallel life. There is a parable by Dovid Bergelson which explains this alter-ego of the 'Night Jew': the Jew within the being of every gradation of Jew from orthodox to assimilated. His story, 'At Night', gives very much the same expression to this element of being as Jong's, but Jong makes high comedy and insightful satire out of the material.[15] In the end, though, as Isadora realises, the central function of psychoanalysis, the focus of the novel's narrative impetus, is to show 'how fettered one still was to the past'.[16]

The core of the novel is the contrast between the two stances taken on the past. For her family and its distancing from the reality of past experience, it is a case of 'We bought the future by talking about the past' but there are unwritten rules and only superficial enquiries. Whereas Isadora's search for her Jewishness is doomed to be artificial, distorted, academic – a constructed fabrication, myths mixed with dry facts. She expresses the strategies of this impulse to know:

> For the first time in my life, I became intensely interested in the history of the Jews and the history of the Third Reich. I went to the USIS or Special Services library and began poring over books which detailed the horrors of the deportations and death camps.[17]

Jong gives Isadora the capacity to fantasise as much about being a victimised Jew as about sexual fulfilment. Every version of self-discovery is parody or written into pastiche. The intense interest in Germany and German culture, even to the idea of what is '*geistig*' in them, a fundamentally sensitive and civilised way of being German, is accounted for and dealt with in individuated fantasy, ambivalent and critical, from a position of empathic suffering with the Holocaust victims. In other words, the novel attempts to construct the paradigm of distanced empathy, of the impossibility of approaching and understanding of the past of Jewish history. The mass-culture embracing the central storyline only serves to emphasise the isolation of such a search and the futility of ever coming close to the actual Jewish nature of the people from her past.

The explanation of her family is Isadora's foundation for her search, and the definition of who she is quite clearly undergoes a negative strategy from early in the novel. 'But like it or not, it was the only religion I had. We weren't really Jewish; we were pagans and pantheists.We believed in reincarnation, the souls of tomatoes . . . And yet with all this, I began to feel intensely Jewish and intensely paranoid.'[18]

The parallels with Plath's poem 'Daddy' are also purposeful: the mediation of a secondary Jewishness through culturally fabricated fragments of historical process are used in Chapter 4 to locate Jewishness as a superficially recognised and misunderstood universalism: 'I was every bit as Jewish as Anne Frank' she concludes, after listing the iconic elements of the Holocaust, from lampshades to soap, much as Plath does in the poem.[19]

In her early writings, Erica Jong expresses this standpoint from which later generations of Jewish Americans have to attempt to make sense of what has been mediated as a cultural myth, a meta-narrative of racial suffering through which a new being has evolved. The anti-Semitism from within and from outside which had been fundamental in much of Bellow and Roth's fiction had gone some way towards explaining the reasons for the reappraisal of the past and what that core of Jewishness represented by the 'Night Jew' might be. Some of this thinking has developed into statements by such writers as Edmond Jabès that the Jew represents the quintessence of the modern artist.[20]

Erica Jong has delved more deeply into this fictional commentary with the publication of her autobiographical work, *Fear of Fifty* (1996) and here, in a section headed,'How I got to be Jewish', there is more on this theme. This essay explains a great deal about the Judaism twice removed, and how this distance relates to the ways in which identity, naming and class-rating have been crucial to the Jewish experience in the Diaspora (in every second culture). Jong provides a perceptive and honest discussion of class in this respect. She uses acculturation to express her critique, basing much of the argument on naming and identity:

> I figured out pretty soon that in my school I was high class, but that in the world I was not. The kids on television shows and in reading primers did not have names like Weissman, Rabinowitz, Plotkin . . . There was another America out there in Televisionland.[21]

This essay is one of the clearest and most perceptive statements of the Jewish identity question in American writing, and Jong's insistence on constant change, anonymity, classification and worldly success as criteria for existential affirmation are full of valuable insights into the fictional domain of her own and many others' writings. The 'other . . . proper America' is a phrase that resonates throughout Jewish-American writing since Cahan.[2]

However, being an outsider in that sense was a badge of merit, says Jong, and the merit was an inner strength. What the reader derives from *Fear of Flying* and everything it represents is the dynamic and questioning nature of the intellect and the degree of sensibility in that Jewishness which is elusive in Isadora's quest. That quest into being and into the meaning of the past is taken up by others in a more confrontational way, and with a gentler reception of other classes and viewpoints, but Jong's adoption of many of the tenets of a particular 1960s feminism has meant that her fiction is never unaware of the important questions, and even when apparently superficial, there is little justice in the criticism that her Jewish characters are placed in the narrative simply for 'token' reasons.[23]

Grace Paley: Stories of New and Old Lives

Russell Reising, in his critique of Nina Baym's thoughts on the canon, asks how any revision of the theoretical paradigm would 'alter the definition of Americanness?'[24]

One answer is potentially demonstrated in the fiction of Olsen and Paley, who have arguably reinvented the ways in which fiction from Jewish-American positions can revise several definitions of their ethnic experience and the degrees of assimilation effected since the 1940s. Olsen has made original forays into interiority and made use of her proletarian experience; Paley has provided an entirely fresh construction of community, its assumed stability and the resistance to adaptation and understanding within its ranks. There are many points of departure here, into her achievement, but one is hinted at by one of her poems, 'Drowning (1)' in which she re-creates the Middle Passage in terms of universal being:

> first friend of my thinking head
> dear flesh
> farewell.[25]

The lines hint at her basis for writing, often a need to express the sense of being-in-the-world by physicality, by emotive ties,

by irrationality and by anonymously maintaining a circumscribed life. Paley was born in New York in 1922, the child of
immigrants from Russia, arriving in 1905. She started writing in
the 1950s, and in her two collections of stories, *The Little
Disturbances of Man* (1970) and *Enormous Changes at the Last
Minute* (1975) she writes of Jewish family life from the standpoint of various narrators, but perhaps most successfully in the
stories with Faith Darwin writing about her parents and about
the larger community in the urban sprawl around her sad one-
parent families, aged nostalgics and failed artists.

As Anne Hiemstra comments, 'The dialectic of Jewish and
American attitudes forms an almost paradoxical synthesis in a
number of her most fully realised characters' and she mentions
'ancestral grief bumping up against and American present-
ness'.[26]

The story in which Paley addresses the question of what it
means to be a Jew in the world today is perhaps 'Faith in the
Afternoon'. Here she applies the customary method of irony
and implication based on an array of almost detached voices,
and the frame of the story is one in which we are asked to be an
'independent thinker of the western bloc' and asked to think of
our grandchildren.[27]

The fiction gives a mix of voices from Faith's parents' experience, as she herself lies and reflects 'under a pillow . . .
seasick from ocean sounds' and the characters fire rhetorical
questions at us from the interplay of dialogue and monologue.
What accrues is a demonstration of Jong's point about how
'proper Americans' relate to the flawed self-perceptions of
immigrants: 'Her grandmother pretended she was German in
just the same way that Faith pretends she is American,' and her
mother asks Faith, 'When will you be a person?'[28]

What Paley does which breaks with more that has gone
before is interweave the larger environments of ideological
reference with the microcosmic constructs of the Jewish idea,
the Jewish assumption of suffering and sacrifice, of giving and
tolerating. A sentence such as, 'Faith really is an American and
she was raised up like everyone else to the true assumption of
happiness.'[29] Faith's husband Ricardo, 'seen running after
women', is in that assumption of happiness too, but the more

Paley follows her enterprise into Jewish suburban retreat, the more she also takes the questions into the wider community. In two stories in particular, she textualises the idea of communal intermixture and the universality of minority psychology. In 'Faith in a Tree' scenes from a playground expand into a version of American priorities and aspirations, with a sad commentary on the isolation within family breakdown; in 'The Long-Distance Runner' she takes us into that area of comparative ethnicity, her narrator venturing into a black-American community abutting her own, and exploring her own family's former dwelling-place.

The latter story exemplifies Paley's ability to dramatise great, culturally significant trends by de-scaling them into human terms. The narrator is out of her neighbourhood, and yet very close to her parents' past. The black youths surround her, and she retreats into the apartment-building in which her past reclaims some of her thoughts. What at first becomes a scene of fear, as she is surrounded, suddenly leaps into another dimension as a tall black youth talks of his African father. He is cosmopolitan, grandiloquent, articulate; he smashes any presentiment of threat or even of stereotypical outcomes at that point. Equally, the narrator's knowledge of wild flowers unites, surprises and ultimately transmits a version of humanity common to all, in childhood, in innocence and most of all in relating to one another on terms other than what is mediated the dominant American ideology.

Another dimension to Paley's fiction is her attitude to the generational distance created by those differentiated perceptions based on degrees of accommodation to American centrality, to the acquisition of the 'happiness' given by the acculturated ideology of optimism. A comparison of Paley's fictional representation of the first-generation Jews to that of, say, Yezierska's reveals a revisionary view which contains a large amount of honesty, even to the point of unreserved objectivity and analysis. In 'Faith in the Afternoon' the Dickensian Mrs Hegel-Shtein has dominated the events when we become aware of a social commentary with rather more perspicacity in it than usual, and the expression of anti-Semitism is couched in bland terms, acceptance mixed with wisdom:

'Brilliant. The husband played golf with the vice-president, a goy. The future was golden. She was active in everything. One morning they woke up . . . Someone uncovers a little this, a little that . . . In forty-eight hours, he's black-balled.'[30]

The comments on social change gather and each reference adds to the impact: 'The war made Jews Americans and Negroes Jews. Ha ha. What do you think of that for an article? "The Negro: Outside in at Last".'[31]

Where Grace Paley really finds her own approach, however, is in the paradox of the silence and withdrawal of the articulate. In the artistic, creative and intellectual Jews of her parents' generation, the inexpressible is always suggested, usually avoided. As with Jong's parents and their silence, their non-committal to causes and identities, so with Paley: her father, for instance, at the close of 'Faith in the Afternoon', walks to the subway with Faith, and leaves something unsaid. His small talk is a disguise, an avoidance:

Mr. Darwin reached for her fingers through the rail. He held them tightly and touched them to her wet cheeks. Then he said, 'Aaah . . .' an explosion of nausea, absolute digestive disgust . . . he had dropped her sweating hand out of his own and turned away from her.'[32]

In 'A Conversation with My Father' this intention takes on a meta-fictional element. What has been autobiographical, im-pressionist writing with a clear selectivity of detail becomes a commentary on storytelling in this context. The aged father, on his sick-bed, asks for a story, a simple story. He insists on the power of the ordinary, as in the classic Russian fictions, but the narrator's relentless use of American material and modernity leads to a discussion of the necessity of telling 'plain tragedy' in this specific relation to American, sophisticated reality. The closure of 'Tragedy! You too. When will you look it in the face?' invites the reader to question the necessity for the sophistica-tion of narratives, and why, as in Paley's own work, there has been a rejection of the tragic view. The stories manipulate the resistantly American material of a dream relived and always invited, even from a recognised state in which all is a process of becoming, of changing into transmuted but desirable material. For these reasons, Paley's voices from the earlier generation are understandably harsh, detached, seeing the process of life *sub specie aeternitatis*: 'One hundred and Seventy-Second street was a pile of shit, he said. Everyone was on relief except you . . . Thank God capitalism had a war it can pull out of the old feed-bag every now and then or we'd all be dead. ha ha.'[33]

Returning to the issue of what the analysis of such additional and revisionist writings do to our concepts of the Jewish-American literature written by women, it is perhaps possible to relate Paley's achievement to a demonstration of *Ecriture féminine*. In her poem, 'For My Friend who Planted a Tree for His Daughter Jane,' she writes 'It is the responsibility of the male poet to be a woman/ It is the responsibility of the female poet to be a woman'[34] and this partly explains what her fiction demonstrates. There is an equality, a democratic domain in which gender and class, ethnicity and minority-consciousness dissolve into some fundamental examinations of how being American in the contemporary world is never explained by the superficial delineation of media-effects, double-think and family values. In fact, the persistence of minority talk and the discourse of sub-cultures is more a matter in individuals preserving the mind-sets which have ensured survival in the past than of new Americans thinking inside a postmodern malaise, or even with a repositioning of what is essentially Jewish in the proposition that there is a 'Jewish-American difference' in creativity and the making of stories. In the end, Paley's writing reflects, more than anything, a culture of orality; 'A rich verbal world of conversation and storytelling' as Anne Hiemstra puts it.[35]

Finally, Paley's fiction reminds readers that there is a massive area of family experience that has not been perceived as important in the earlier phase of Jewish-American fiction (1945–80). The Jewish family has been either a site of surreal comedy (*Portnoy's Complaint*) or stereotype social humour.

In this, Paley has played a part in the development of the impressionist, poetic short story: laconic, packed with seemingly easy constructions taken from the vernacular. This is an aspect of Jewish writing that still has to be fully explored.

Here we have the prose sinews of middle-class America as it reaches utterance, not as it is fashioned in literary style, nor shaped into elements of studied characterisation. She uses dialogue as powerfully as in the best drama, and this is a counterbalance to the rather overwritten Yiddish-American of, for instance, some pre-war drama. In Paley we have the authentic voice of a new suburbia, aware of issues of survival as sharply as notions of culture and social improvement.

Tillie Olsen: Revisiting the Silences

Time has proved that Tillie Olsen's book, *Silences*, which appeared in 1979, stakes a claim to being one of the formative texts in that revaluation of some versions of feminism which underlie American fiction. What also needs to be added is that Olsen added a proletarian dimension to this, using a broad range of references and extracts in the work, providing an anthology of exclusions from the self-definition involved in writing. Writing as an existential act, and as an appraisal of the self and its directions, was further developed in her inclusion of the proletarian element, and some of her stylistic devices echo those of the much undervalued James Hanley, who did the same thing for British writing in the 1930s and 1940s.

Olsen was born in Nebraska in 1913 but lived in San Francisco for many years. Her most notable fiction is collected in the volume *Tell Me A Riddle*, and the title-story of that collection won the O. Henry Award in 1961. Cora Kaplan, in her 1980 edition, expresses the importance of that story:

> Tillie Olsen's fiction speaks on behalf of the unnumbered, voiceless working men and women, especially women, whose needs and aspirations went unfulfilled, stifled by depression, world war and a poverty which still flourished in boom years.[36]

Kaplan also mentions that the stories were written in years of frightening overreaction to political dissent in America, and it is part of Olsen's achievement that she succeeds in approaching the inner experience of women in that period, taking in such textless diurnal routine as mothering, support, sacrifice and isolation. What is remarkably relevant to the present discussion is Olsen's marginalisation of any overt Jewish consciousness or social, combative, communal self in 'Tell Me a Riddle'. In fact although the story – recounts the dying of an old lady from cancer – with a stress on interior monologue and interwoven commentaries from husband, family and their immigrant past it dynamically rejects any confrontation with Jewishness. The woman's dying and her younger life, are equally secularised, even located within a shifted focus in which Jewishness is excluded and womanliness placed in the centre.

In the hospital, for instance, a rabbi visits her simply because she is listed as being 'of his religion'. She tells him to go. She says, 'Tell them to write: Race, human; Religion, none.'[37]

In this episode, we feel her apartness, and we feel the terrifying separateness of being a woman, being defined as distant from other, more active and overt family values. In this section, she is seen again, looked at with fresh eyes, appreciated for what she really is. The buried identity surfaces in crisis. This theme is a common one in Olsen's work, and 'Tell Me A Riddle' is notable for its placing the scrutiny of selfhood on a forgotten, neglected source of identity: the one which has been stereotyped into invisibility. This is the mother-figure.

Olsen writes in a tradition that is partly related to something profound in the Jewish narration of interiority. So much of Paley and Olsen's fiction is parallel to that strong dramatic monologue found in Pinter, Kafka and indeed in much Jewish humour. Olsen actually places the early European (Russian) life of her dying woman at the periphery of any observable privileging of notable meaning-patterns. Where Bellow initiates a convention of isolation within a complex network of social relationships past and present, Olsen reduces to a minimum. The result is a variety of internal dialogic structures in the story, where past and present consciousness interact in a formative dialectic. Any overt intellectualism or purposeful symbolism is omitted. The allegories of Kafka, the appeals to the audience from Pinter to universalise, the inner dilemma of Bellovian protagonists as Everyman in a devalued human purgatory – all are absent in 'Tell Me A Riddle'.

Where there is reference to the past, from inside the confusion, the dreams, the half-waking states, it is devalued, reduced to impressions, devoid of any openly given material that might be Americana. 'She sat close to him and did not speak. Jokes, stories, people they had known, beginning of reminiscence, Russia fifty-six years ago.'[38]

In other words, what Olsen achieved in this influential and innovative story was the narration of the Jewish experience from a standpoint of the margins: her fiction works inside the consciousness of the 'silences' and discontinuities of women's lives within that ideology of exclusion. Where, in the tradition from Yezierska to Ozick, there is a concept of Yiddish as difference, *Yiddishkeit* as a location of inner dissent and a platform for the renewal of varieties of invigorated Jewishness inside assimilated communities, in Olsen the assumption is the political stance of woman on the periphery in the arenas of identity, the political and the ideological.

In fact, the woman, who is named in her gradual decline into death by her husband with the nomenclature of non-human terms such as 'Mrs Excited for Nothing' similar, or simply as 'grandma' by the children, is a fusion of typicality and individuality. In one register she is textualised as woman in general. 'You remember how she lived – eight children and now one room like a coffin.'[39] Her claim to individuality is negated from a range of stances, most notably her nullification in the domesticity and dogma of Judaism: 'Religion that stifled and said: in Paradise, woman, you will be the footstool of your husband, and in life – poor chosen Jew – ground under, despised.'[40]

The story is remarkable for many reasons, but the emphasis here is on the status of the story as representative of Olsen's innovations. In stylistic matters, her fiction places the accommodated Jews in urban America as being silent. The silence is the site of a dialogic dissent, a catechism which never arrives at a satisfactory conclusion regarding the way in which Jewish interior lives have never been, in a real sense, more than immigrants in their own minds. Paley's father-figure commenting on 'Blacks' as US citizens within the northern cities is one example of a more open statement of this gradual emergence of the American Jew into perceiving that he or she 'should' have been instated into full membership of the American Dream. By the end of the decade of imperialism abroad and mediated WASP family ideology at home, ethnic elements of Judaism in the diaspora seemed less important to many. A comparison of the three varieties of writing about Jewishness by women has to venture a conclusion linked to the marginality they occupied until recently. In fact, the prominence of women writers and intellectuals in arts and media in recent decades has quite clearly brought about some revisionist perspectives on why certain selected traits of Jewishness have tended to define the norm.

Where was it ever confirmed, for instance, that the depiction of Jews in American society should limit the humour inherent in the Jewish view of philosophy and lifestyle to male-centred ideology? Film and verbal narrative have established a paradigm in this respect in which issues of class, gender and ethnicity have been frozen in time, as if change is barred and only certain specified subjects are considered acceptable. One sure marker of this has been the decline of the use of Yiddish in the fictions by women since Yezierska. It is surely a consequence of these versions of narrow-minded or complacent attitudes to what constitutes Jewish sensibility that any reading of Paley or Olsen demands a realignment of priorities; equally, Erica Jong has shown that the intellectualisation of the Jewish and the feminine in her writing has been simply a phase, and that the primary experience of womanhood is a more fundamental source of creative sustenance.

'Tell Me a Riddle' also includes this hidden element of the woman's mind, creative sources, vibrancy and spirit. In her dying, the rise of her hidden, previously silent responses to her reading and thinking burst through the pain. As Cora Kaplan says, 'The broken-up prose of the last section of the story mimes Eva's disordered capitulation . . . giving us her words as a concrete poetic testament.'[41] The textless history of working women, suffering mothers, identities in limbo find their voice, and it cannot always live in the silence that Olsen visits. In a broader sense, the story is simply the beginning of what is potentially an energetic revival of Jewish women's writing, and, as Chapter 7 will examine, there are cogent arguments for this being the case. Returning to Frederick Karl, it is not difficult to challenge his statement that Jewish-American writing is 'played out'.[42]

Notes

1. Frederick R. Karl, 'Black Writers–Jewish Writers–Women Writers', in Boris Ford (ed.), *The New Pelican Guide to English Literature*: vol. 9 American Literature (Penguin: London, 1991) pp. 566–82, p. 581.
2. See Peter J. Bailey, "A Hat Where there Never was a Hat"– Stanley Elkin's fifteenth interview', *The Review of Contemporary Fiction*, Summer 1995, (RCF: Normal, Illinois, 1995) pp. 15–26, p. 20. Elkin has always insisted that he is not primarily a Jewish writer, but a writer who is Jewish.
3. See Karl, Black Writers – Jewish Writers – Women Writers', in Ford, *The New Pelican Guide to English Literature*, pp. 581–2.
4. Betty Friedan, 'That Has no Name', in Anders Breidlid et al., *American Culture* (Routledge: London and New York, 1996), pp. 115–19, p. 116.
5. June Sochen, 'Identities Within Identity: Thoughts on Jewish American Women Writers', *SAJL*, vol. 6 (1987), pp. 6–10, p. 6.
6. Ibid., p. 7.
7. Ibid., p. 9.
8. Y. L. Peretz, 'A Passion for Clothes', in Joachim Neugroschel (ed.), *Great Works of Jewish Fantasy* (Picador: London, 1976) pp. 374–80, p. 374.
9. See Daniel Walden, 'Jewish Women Writers and Women in Jewish Literature: An Introduction', *SAJL*, vol. 6, As note 5. pp. 1–5, p. 4.
10. See Nina Baym's discussion of the canonical issues, 'Melodramas of Beset Manhood: How Theories of American Fiction Exclude Women Authors', in Elaine Showalter (ed.), *The New Feminist Criticism* (Virago: London, 1986), pp. 63–80, p. 79.
11. Lavinia and Dan Cohn-Sherbok, *A Short Reader in Judaism* (Oneworld: Oxford, 1996), p. 180.
12. See Jacqueline Rose, 'Dorothy Richardson and the Jew', in Bryan Cheyette (ed.), *Between 'Race' and 'Culture'* (Stanford University Press: CA., 1996), pp. 114–28, p. 128.
13. See Erica Jong, preface to *Fear of Flying* (Minerva: London, 1996), pp.viii–x,
14. Ibid., p. 165.
15. See Dovid Bergelson, 'At Night', in Neugroschel, *Great Works of Jewish Fantasy*, pp. 243–5, p. 244. The resonance of Bergelson's allegory is potentially profound for anyone attempting to reconcile the mystical tradition, as in Isaac Baskevis Singer's fiction, with modern secular Jewish fiction in the USA.
16. Jong, *Fear of Flying*, p. 179.

17. Ibid., p. 67.
18. Ibid., p. 61.
19. This is a standard example of the nature of Plath's influence on this revisionist view.
20. See Paul Auster's essay on Jabès in *Ground Work* (Faber: London, 1996), in which he discusses Jabès' claims for the paradigmatic nature of the Jewish writer within modernism.
21. Erica Jong, *Fear of Fifty* (Vintage: London, 1996), p. 88.
22. Ibid., p. 91.
23. The reception of Jong's recent, (1996) fiction included comments on the artificiality of the Jewish themes and characters. A recent view is that Jewishness has become too one-dimensional In her fiction.
24. Russell Reising, *The Unusable Past* (Methuen: New York and London, 1996), p. 240.
25. Grace Paley, *Begin Again : New and Collected Poems* (Virago: London, 1992), p. 7.
26. Anne Hiemstra, 'Grace Paley', in   E. Showalter et al., *Modern American Women Writers* (Collier: New York,1991), p. 259.
27. Grace Paley, *Enormous Changes at the Last Minute* (Virago: London, 1979) p. 31.
28. Ibid., p. 33.
29. Ibid.
30. Ibid., 42.
31. Ibid., p. 47.
32. Ibid., p. 49.
33. Ibid., p. 173.
34. Paley, *Begin Again*, p. 56.
35. Hiemstra 'Grace Paley', in Showalter et al., *Modern American Women Writers*, p. 265.
36. Cora Kaplan, Introduciton, in Tillie Olson *Tell Me A Riddle* (Virago: London, 1980) p. 1.
37. Ibid., p. 91.
38. Ibid., p. 106.
39. Ibid., p. 107.
40. Ibid., p. 92.
41. See Cora Kaplan's introduction to Olsen, *Tell Me a Riddle* p. 8. Kaplan has much of interest to say about Olsen's relation to various strands of feminist thinking.
42. See Frederick R. Karl, 'Black Writers, Jewish Writers, Women Writers', in Boris Ford (ed.), *New Pelican Guide to English Literature: vol. 9 American Literature* (Penguin: London, 1991), pp. 566–82, p. 581.

5

Explorations in Drama: from Arthur Miller to Tony Kushner

It could be argued that it is in the massive body of work comprising modern American drama that a specific *Materia Judaica* may be distinguished, similar to that of medieval literature which split into Arthurian, Christian and secular love, so does the drama from Miller's early plays through to Kushner's epic *Angels in America* (first published in 1994)can be divided into distinct sections. This corpus forms into (1) preoccupations with the Holocaust – the era and the aftermath; (2) the description of duality in third-generation urban Jews in a material world; and (3) a specific mediation of a new secular Jewish attitude to identity and to modernity.

But the first point to make is about the stunning diversity of this writing. Ellen Schiff has made this clear in her wide-ranging survey, *The Greening of American-Jewish Drama.*[1] She begins with the influence of Clifford Odets, then introduces the idea of an 'expanded image of Jews' and of the authors' renown in American literary life. That is, diversity once again pinpoints the problems of definition in this literature. The dramatic works which could potentially be covered in this chapter could include writing from Neil Simon, Woody Allen, Wendy Wasserstein and even the stage adaptation of the *Diary of Anne Frank*. All these were influential on Jewish constructions of new identities in some way, but such richness again presses the critic to select certain themes and preoccupations which bring the above three categories into focus.

For these reasons, this chapter analyses those plays which have dealt with ideas and subjects within the categories listed above. But there have been important watersheds in the development of this theatre. For instance, in June 1980 the Jewish Theatre Association ran a conference entitled: 'Exploring the Dimensions of Jewish Theatre'. Ellen Schiff expands on the remit here, and on the sheer dimensions of this work. She refers to the Yiddish theatre, and to the massive undertaking of the National Foundation for Jewish Culture and the Jewish Theatre Association. Their main production was a focal reference work:

Edited by Edward M. Cohen, *Plays of Jewish Interest* (1982) is an annotated, cross-indexed listing of more than six hundred published and unpublished titles, including the finalists in the NFJC's playwriting competitions and information about Hebrew and Yiddish plays in translation.[2]

Schiff's overall categories in her survey are Judaism, family life and assimilation. While these are clearly very useful in a detailed survey, for the purposes of an introductory overview, the central concern of the discussion is with identity and the past and present interests in the documenting of Jewish experience in America. For these reasons, a critical survey has to omit a large amount of interesting writing, but what cannot be denied is that in the major dramatists who have taken Jewish identity as a central enquiry, only a limited number have made it exclusive to their work. What has happened is that themes related to the *materia* I have listed have often been parallel to other, largely philosophical concerns of the playwrights. This has been a prominent feature of this writing.

There is also the general question of certain outstanding features of American theatre since 1945 in relation to categories, sites of production and categorisation. There is a large degree of flux in the issues of definition and labelling. For instance, in her introductory survey of the same period and literature, Ruby Cohn groups Ribman, Rabe and Mamet together in terms of what she calls 'Narrower straits' in contra-distinction to 'Broadway Bound' plays. This is her explanation:

I am guided toward the latter (narrower straits) by my own impression of a playwright's compulsion. Simon alone has kept a stable footing on Broadway, whereas zigzags mark the paths of Kopit, McNally and Wilson. The dramatists in this chapter have executed comparable zigzags, and yet they seem to me further from Broadway conventions in subject and form.[3]

What lies behind this issue are two powerful cultural influences of, first the deeply held belief that American theatre should instruct, and second the notion of 'Off Broadway' and even 'Off-Off Broadway'. In other words, the struggle by serious dramatists, those who see theatre as a notable form of locating and enlightening audiences with regard to dominant ideologies and social constructs of conformity and identity, has been ongoing and has always been necessary. The lure of Hollywood is the obvious example. A dramatist such as Clifford Odets, a Jewish American who wrote directly about assimilation and cultural change, perhaps typifies this. His drift to Hollywood has been chronicled in detail by Margaret Brenman-Gibson, and filmic depictions of the influences of the studios are easy to find, along with fiction concerning this seduction.[4]

The other foundational factor here is the notion of a theatre of serious artistic enterprise, with commercial elements made secondary to aesthetic purpose. As Ruby Cohn describes it, 'Off-Off Broadway had no tradition but a rebellious spirit' and she mentions influential New York venues and people in this context.[5]

The point of departure here is to establish exactly what had been done before the 1940s in this context. Clifford Odets, Elia Kazan, Lee Strasbourg and the Group Theatre had established a platform for this social commentary and politicised theatre, but in terms of the Jewish subject-matter, perhaps Odets, for all his achievement in depicting the people and the issues around becoming American, limited and defined things too narrowly. His plays of family life and social aspiration mirror very closely the fiction discussed earlier, but his mixture of authentic and stylised dialogue, the Yiddish-American centre of the verbal power in such texts as *Awake and Sing!* (1935) can have the effect of seeming 'too Jewish' to younger Jewish Americans – that is, too embedded in past values and vestigial moral structures.

Having said this, it cannot be denied that Odets had a massive influence on how this argot had to be handled. His idiom and intonation patterns are convincing despite a tendency to infuse rhetoric. Ralph, in *Awake and Sing!*, speaks with the same flavour and tones as several characters from Yezierska, but with a settled base of American slang. The interlanguage has faded: 'I been working for years, bringing in money here – putting it in your hand like a kid. Alright. I can't get my teeth fixed. Alright, that a new suit's like trying to buy the Chrysler Building.'[6]

Arthur Miller's attitude to Odets' achievement is perhaps most enlightening on this issue of influence: 'I was troubled by a tendency in his plays to over-theatricalised excess – lines sometimes brought laughter where there should have been outrage.'[7] The interest here for the modern student of this drama is that there is now a radically new perspective on the whole question of how Jews and Jewish life are depicted, of course, and there are some basic philosophic lines of thought to be summarised before embarking on an account of the influential texts linked with the massive subjects listed at the beginning of this chapter. Arthur Miller is the link here, and also the beginning, as it is his confrontation with anti-Semitism as a theme that introduces many deeper and more complex areas of Jewish identity in the American Diaspora.

This basis of enquiry is rather speculative, but fascinating nonetheless. It demands that we consider the very nature of the Jewish writer and his or her relationship to the creations made in the texts. Theatre is per se particularly interesting as an expression of Jewish creativity. The Jews are a Mediterranean people and have the same expressive and emotive need to tell stories as is found in Greek and Italian traditions. But they also have that basis of biblical text, of parable, and a view of narrative as central to an understanding of communal definition and purpose. Therefore, the nature of the Jew as writer and of writer as Jew has attracted theorists as well as dramatists. Arthur Miller's need to find naturalistic methods such as interiority in *After the Fall* is partly a revolt from the realistic approaches of Odets and others. Miller seeks to universalise, and the theorists have done the same. The French writer, Edmond Jabès, for instance, writes of the perennial relation of the Jew to the idea of a text. Matthew del Nevo has interpreted this:

> If one is sure of one's place in the world, of one's identity, to see one's life in the book and the book as one's life, is merely a legitimation of already established structures of power and a suspension of real questioning with respect to them.[8]

This idea of the responses to the inconceivably horrific *Shoah* of the Holocaust, and of the founding of a Jewish state in 1948, with all the needed requestioning of the Jews who had dispersed across the world, is one in which redefinition of Jewish writing and subjects is called for. Arthur Miller does no less than this. In other words, the protagonists of so much Jewish-American drama have been individuals with feelings of insignificance and helplessness in an amoral world. The receding past of Jewish experience is their only way into self-revision and a clear look into their being.

For all these reasons, it seems logical to begin this survey with Arthur Miller. Since his novel, *Focus* (1945), Miller has dealt with these enormously important and complex themes with a sense of innovation and experiment, juxtaposing the pains of the interior life with the visible injustices and barbarities of the Jewish experience in modern times. That his setting is the United States is even more important, as the social and ideological atmospheres are integral to the vision. His dramatic subjects have always been close to the moral arena of decisions, dilemmas and crises of conformity and individuality. Even the plays which are ostensibly not about overtly Jewish subjects deal with the same communal issues: mass hysteria, unreason and escape from reality; the need for a stable interior life; continuity and stability across the generations, and the call of faith and doubt: these are all central to the immigrant experience in the long process of the transmutation from *Shtetl* to urban anonymity.

But there are discernible topics which repeatedly interest Miller as subjects, and particularly as theatrical narrative forms. In *After the Fall* (1964), *Incident at Vichy* (1964), *The Price* (1968), *Playing for Time* (1980), *Danger: Memory!* (1986 and *Broken Glass* (1994), he has interwoven the subjects of anti-Semitism, Holocaust experience and urban Jewish-American generational change, with a central narrative drive towards the question of what it is to be Jewish. How complex such explorations may become has been hinted at by Ronald Hayman in his study of *After the Fall*: he points out that Miller textualises betrayal as a theme linking both the Holocaust setting and the personal betrayal of Maggie.[9] That is, Miller repeatedly creates a macrocosm and a microcosm which interact creatively. This is remarkably apposite in an art that uses Jewish history as there are demands made on the artist to suggest interpretations rather than simply to describe.

For these reasons, Miller's drama is in its most directly communicative form when the philosophical dimension is lucidly present. In *Incident at Vichy* for instance, the notion that an Austrian prince, Von Berg, who has been taken as a suspect Jew, should make the ultimate sacrifice for a Jew is clearly in need of a full explanation, and Miller uses the occasion for a perceptive debate on Jewishness and its place in the amoral schema of new barbarism. Von Berg explains Nazism thus: 'They do these things not because they are German but because they are nothing. It is the hallmark of the age – the less you exist the more important it is to make a clear impression . . . What one used to conceive a human being to be will have no use on this earth.'[10]

The play begins with references to big noses and gypsies, with the assumed civilised behaviour of the captors gradually being eroded, and the notion of innate nobility being inverted across the social classes. Miller's gambits often involve establishing exactly what vibrancy, artistic elan and sheer exuberance exist among the Jews, and so makes goyish jealousy totally explicable. The articulate, often poetic lyricism of his people's imaginative impulses both explain and eradicate their brilliance: that is, the bright, dazzling intellect and they who live fully are perhaps the most obvious choice for exploitation by the narrow-minded and moderate.

The Theatre and the Holocaust

Arthur Miller's most significant achievement as a playwright handling the *materia* of the Holocaust is that of relating universalised ideas of memory and the self to that one, inescapable horror of the death-camp experience. Of course, the Holocaust has spawned a massive literature, and the number of Jewish autobiographies concerning that experience grows rapidly, building on the classic statements made by Primo Levi and Elie Wiesel.[11] The focal point of reference is the nexus of memory and present identity. As Alan Berger has said in this context:

> Writing is simultaneously an act of witnessing and penance. But refugee writing differs from that of camp inmates whose writings, as Wiesel attests, are a *matseva* [an invisible tombstone erected to the memory of the dead unburied] . . . I would add to it that these writings also serve to enlarge the reader's awareness of the manifold dimensions of the Holocaust. The issue is one of combining the writer's memory and the reader's present experience.[12]

The last sentence states what Miller has had to work for in many places, and the familiar phenomenon of anti-Semitic behaviour is often his way into the larger, less explicable subjects. At this point, a note of a key statement made outside his plays is helpful. This is his address to the Jewish Committee of Writers, Artists and Scientists, made in 1947, called, 'Concerning Jews who Write'. This piece makes it clear that autobiographical factors are crucial to the understanding of his writing on the subject, despite the fact that his voluminous autobiography, *Timebends* (1987), does not really develop the points made. George Crandell's commentary on this work makes it clear that Miller changed from a writer who insisted that his Jewishness had receded into empty gestures into someone who expanded on Jewish identity into statements on much more universal ideas. Miller, in the address, says of his generation, 'We did not yearn for some national home outside of America; we felt no ties with Europe . . . we had no personal ambitions that could distinguish us from any other American family.'[13]

Much of Miller's writing on the Holocaust and its signifi- cance is marked by the concept of what Julia Kristeva has called 'Void or Baroque speech' and of being 'strangers to ourselves'.[14] This also includes the personal satisfaction involved in turning this foreignness into art. 'Being alienated from myself, as painful as that may be, provides me with that exquisite distance within which perverse pleasure begins . . . can we be a saga for ourselves without being considered mad or fake?'[15]

After the Fall, for instance, typifies this. The events take place inside Quentin's head. The set is dominated by the wall and tower of a concentration camp. The various storylines around Quentin's life provide a commentary on individual 'sin' or responsibility. Miller includes the familiar theme of persecu- tion for political beliefs, but the plea at the emotional centre of the play is for love and sacrifice; for vision rather than immer- sion in the present, the dominance of existential complexity. 'Strength comes from a clear conscience or a dead one. Not to see one's own evil – there's power.'[16] The plea is most explicitly expressed when Quentin tries to talk about Maggie to his wife, Louise, and is misunderstood. His defence is a poetic demand for integrity: 'she was just there, like a tree or a cat. And I felt strangely abstract beside her. And I saw that we are killing one another with abstractions . . . I'm defending Lou because I love him, yet the society transforms that love into a kind of trea- son.'[17]

The problem of guilt is, naturally, central to the concept of exactly what the significance of the Holocaust was, and how the guilt inherent in any notion of sin has to be related to such atrocities. As Gerald Weales has pointed out in an essay on Miller's image of man, 'The guilt that Quentin assumes is something very like original sin: an acceptance that he – and all men – are evil.'[18] The point is that in drawing parallels between the macrocosm of world history and the individual conscience, Miller is venturing into a philosophical minefield. What starts to develop in these plays is an attempt to state intellectual empathy – the need to resituate the Jewish nature, that common ground which created separateness within a larger society in order to maintain stability, not simply the minimum needs of survival. Hence the entire intellectual and artistic enterprise of Jewish-American writing. The revisiting of this past means reinventing a particular kind of memorising, and Miller's self-appointed task has been to make all this intellectualisation theatrically interesting. The criticism of *After the Fall*, basically that the naturalistic method with the interiority of memory do not make for a unified piece, cannot be addressed to the most successful plays in this genre, *Danger: Memory!* and *Broken Glass*.

These are more recent plays and certainly since the mid-1980s Miller has refined and simplified this theme which explores memory and its presence in defining the present condition. The focus on this is given early in the play *Danger: Memory!* with Detective Fine's words: 'What you can't chase you'd better face or it'll start chasing you, know what I mean?'[19] The play concerns the murder of Clara Kroll, a woman who 'loves everybody'. Her father, Albert, is interviewed after the crime and we have her (and their) story pieced together. Once again, Miller intersperses the basic questioning session at the centre of the narrative with sub-texts and parallel mini-themes all united in the area of guilt and action, testimony and political awakening. Albert has brought his daughter up with an awareness of the moral ambivalences of intervention, and his story of how he prevented a lynching while in the forces, based at Biloxi, is given in detail, juxtaposed with Fine's avowal that his present self was born in 1945:

When they first showed the pictures of those piles of bones? Remember that? The bulldozers pushing them into those trenches, those arms and legs sticking up? That's the day I was born again.[20]

Fine has reduced his moral structures to a stage where the past is irrelevant. He says, 'I used to have a lot of questions about life, but in these last years I'm down to two – what did the guy do, and can I prove it?'[21] What we have, then, is a situation in which Kroll is hectored into questioning his potential complicity in his daughter's murder, simply because he did not act and tried to apply a flexibility and tolerance which should, according to Fine, not be part of a Jew's fabric of personality after the Holocaust. But Miller is again defending the centrality and dominance of the single, unique act. Whether that act is on a grand scale, done by thousands, or whether it is a decision by an individual conscience, it is still part of that necessary empathy of feeling and intellect which is a step towards comprehending the finally incomprehensible. Those who take Fine's stance are condemned to be released by memory at the cost of a new version of the barbarity they despise.

In *Broken Glass* these preoccupations are taken so far that they now involve the base-question underpinning these questions of identity: 'There are some days when I feel like going and sitting in the shul with the old men and the *tallis* . . .' says Hyman, Why must we be different? Why is it? What is it for?'[22]

The play concerns Sylvia Gellburg and her empathic-centred paralysis in connection with reports from Germany of atrocities against the Jews. Set in Brooklyn in 1938, the play runs three parallel plots: Sylvia's obsession with Jewish suffering, her husband's lack of affection and impotence, and Hyman, the psychiatrist's certainty under pressure. Miller confronts the issue of to what extent the Hebrew concept of *tzimtzum* – God's withdrawal from his people, to let them grow and be fully beneficent – includes the evil man does. That is, Sylvia is realising the extent of this withdrawal from the confrontation with truth. When Hyman probes the unhappiness in the marriage, Sylvia again refers to Germany: 'But how can those nice people go out and pick Jews off the street in the middle of a big city like that, and nobody stop them?'[23] The theme is further deepened by the crisis in Gellburg's business, leading to a heart-attack while under threat of losing his job, and with the implied reference to anti-Semitism on the part of Gellburg's employer. All this is Miller's way of expanding the awareness of the complex sources from which questions of Jewish identity this may grow. That the culture is deeply but imperceptibly divided is never in question. What Miller understands is that the internalisation of our sense of moral outrage is a sickness of the soul. In this sense, it is outide the therapeutic functioning of medicine, but reclaimable through love. As so often in his work, Miller gives yet another variation on the theme of dysfunctional and misplaced emotional life.

Miller has always been concerned with the fundamental issues arising from his openly stated new alignment with these positions in assimilation: his residual Jewishness is part of his vision of a society coping with increasing paranoia and moral chaos. These plays that seek to explain the revisions of Jewish-American culture's silent suffering and tolerance manage to ask some fundamental questions and, in, the process, they ask Americans to reconsider what has happened in the subtle denigration of Jewish identity, and also to think again about precisely what has been neglected.

This partly explains why so much writing by Jewish-American dramatists has been concerned with the characteristics of the Jewish temperament per se after assimilation: Wendy Wasserstein, in *The Heidi Chronicles* (1977; printed together as a trilogy in 1991) and David Mamet, particularly in *Duck Variations* (1972), *American Buffalo* (1975) and *The Disappearance of the Jews* (1983), represent some dominant approaches to the explanations of the assimilation process and what happens to the basic moral qualities instilled by tradition and family values when the postmodern pluralistic and materialistic values begin to assert themselves. Ellen Schiff points out that Wasserstein is interested in 'the question of the support available to well-educated young people looking to find their place in late twentieth-century America'.[24] The central figure of Holly Kaplan, and many of her peers with equally determined and serious intellectual-feminist proclivities acquired by discipline at Mt. Holyoke College, work for their niche in the secular kingdom. Wasserstein brilliantly depicts the ethos of success and self-development, which point to the inheritance of Yezierska's older women, who pass on the business values to their children along with cultural acquirements and liberal understanding. The basic conflict – creating both humour and social commentary on how these values are cultivated and repressed – is between innocence and experience, or the schoolroom and the urban stress of career and vocation:

Kate: I don't understand what Rita's doing. She's a smart girl.
Muffet: So what. We're all smart girls.
Holly: It's a sexist society.
Kate: I don't have any trouble.
Muffet: Kate, you don't know what trouble is. You were born in *Holiday Magazine*.[25]

David Mamet, on the other hand, in several of his major plays, delves into the ways in which certain personality-traits and basic ideological constructs in Judaism survive and express themselves inside the 'New America' of the third generation, the America in which consumerism and mechanisation have not only transformed the material world but also the interior identity concepts of what defines the essential Jewish outlook. The most silent character in the hard, offensive and dehumanised world of *Glengarry, Glen Ross*, speaks only in monosyllables and grunts. Mamet's focus is often the inarticulate male with in-built problems of expression and emotional repression. In his essays and in his novel *The Village* (1994) he is equally concerned with the dislocations of common humanity which occur within a short distance of apparent beneficence and peace. A general concern is with disenchantment and the willpower needed to continue the 'American Dream'. Mamet's theatre returns repeatedly to spaces of combat, in which the voiceless and the prolix exist side by side, but facing away. Language is something that works at relief rather than understanding. These things also establish central metaphors for existence in the bounds of the residual Jewishness. In *Duck Variations*, for instance, George and Emil work in empathy with creatures and nature, and this becomes an indirect statement of their own vacuities. Imagination, in this milieu, falls down in frustration, shown when Emil tries to express this empathy:

Emil: Whenever I think of wild things, I wonder.
George: Yes?

Emil: If, in the city, as we are . . .
George: Yes?
Emil: We maybe . . .
George: Yes?
Emil: Forget it.

In *American Buffalo* we are led to respect the trust given to young Donny when caught between the two friends, then Mamet complicates the issue by putting Donny's nature in doubt. The heart of this drama is that construction of Jewish qualities of human community and morality in a situation of testing, prejudice and pressure. John Lahr has commented on this notion of betrayal in Mamet's work.[26]

Mamet has repeatedly returned to questions of Jewish roots and what they create or instil. Ellen Schiff points out that in his *The Disappearance of the Jews*, he is directly concerned with friendship and the past. In this play Bobby and Joey are used to exemplify romanticising versions of the past and also fantasy regarding individual identity and vocation. Schiff points out that Joey, 'longs to live in a society whose best minds are devoted to the Talmud so they can be appealed to for the truth when it is required'.[27] Mamet has always been interested in the inner weaknesses of the kind of superficial thinking which creates a definition of being a Jew which relies on nostalgia, or on weak-minded acceptance of some innate inferiority filtered from the cultural mediation of the Jew as outsider. His essays collected in *Some Freaks* (1989) show that in his openly polemic attitudes, he has an agenda which can be approached and given creatively in the metaphors of the voices from 'inside' – from the vestiges of Jewish belief.

Mamet has returned to the questions again, in *The Neighbour-hood (1998)*, a set of three one-act plays, 'about being Jewish in America; about the role that a fantasy-past (or pasts) can play in the present . . . about the need to see yourself as both part of a community and a prisoner of it.'[28] John Peter has expressed the dilemma effectively here. Mamet has constantly needed to write in order to hit some nerves and see the reactions. His combative, polemic drive has given American-Jewish drama a way into postmodern doublethink which brings a clarity of vision – mainly in the sense that he writes to reveal the truth of this immigrant experience, not to continue a sentimentality or a melancholic elegy to a poeticised past peopled by portraying stereotypes and monsters.

There is a link here between Mamet's black humour about human self-delusion and avoidance of reality and the particular humour which is clearly observed in this drama, from Woody Allen's *nebbish* anti-hero, Allan Felix, in *Play it Again, Sam* (1969) to Tony Kushner's epic two-play interpretation of America and its historical imagination, *Angels in America* (1994). This humour is fantastical, parabolic, deriving from the folktale and oral tradition on the one hand, and on stand-up comedy on the other. Allen's comedy routines from his performances as a comedian gave him the way into developing a more sustained comedy of ineptness and self-delusion, but in his play, Allen's dilemmas as he looks for a partner are caught between the rabbi on one side and Bogart on the other. Allen parodies the influences of the secular world in placing his character somewhere in the no-man's land between respect for Jewish morality and imaginative contact with the media-hero. The weak and feckless character deriving from the *schlemiel* in the fiction of Peretz through to Bellow, as Sanford Pinsker has shown,[29] is a useful device for providing a commentary on the follies of the goyim. But Allen is capable of more serious parodies, as will be examined in chapter 7.

Tony Kushner's *Angels in America* is entirely different, although the multiplicity of styles does incorporate such popular forms as pastiche and Vaudeville; the two plays, *Millennium Approaches* and *Perestroika*, being 'a gay fantasia on national themes', attempt to construct an interplay of narratives fashioned around a group of gay men, and on the death by aids of one of the central characters, Also included are historical and ethnic secondary narratives, covering black experience, the Mormons going West and the urban angst of America suffering the determining metaphor of slow death. Kushner's art is further complicated by a use of the fantastic, the fabulist-centred intrusions of the angel, of inter-cutting stories, and of the dark humour of suffering. AIDS is part of a sprawling metaphor of inner decay which explores the wrongs and ill-conceived imperialism contained in the very concept of America from the beginning.

The drama begins with a funeral, and Rabbi Chemelwitz's oration is a prelude which fixes the basis of action on the notion of immigration. He talks of Sarah Ironson's life as a 'crossing' and this initiates a more widely applied metaphorical use: 'You can never make that crossing that she made, for such Great Voyages in this world do not any more exist. But every day of your lives the miles that voyage between that place and this one you cross.'[30] Prior's dying is the formative 'crossing' in one of these senses, and it provides the irony Kushner wants for the parallel stories of individuals from Jewish roots coming to cosmopolitan sensibility; and of increasing urban anonymity in the setting of America coming to the millennium. When Judaism is incorporated into the ideological agenda for a strong view of historical process, it is with self-negating humour, as in Louis' talk with the Rabbi. Louis' philosophical disquisitions lead nowhere, as the Rabbi opts out. But nevertheless, Louis' words are a central dramatic and thematic idea in the plays: he speaks of a person with a perfectionist view of human progress who 'can't incorporate sickness into his sense of how things are supposed to go.'[31]

Even the existential undercurrents in the interchanges between various versions of American crossings may be transposed to the situation Kristeva described, as summarised at the opening of this chapter. Harper, for instance, says, 'So when we think we've escaped the unbearable ordinariness and . . . untruthfulness of our lives, it's really only the same old ordinariness.'[32] It is arguably in this same technique that we find the heart of the plays' dialectic: expressed by Harper: 'Imagination can't create anything new, can it? It only recycles bits and pieces from the world and reassembles them into visions.'[33] This is the initiation of a dialogue between versions of the 'Americas in the mind', which includes some and inevitably excludes others. Thus the gay community and the black orderly, the Mormon characters and the poor, the dispossessed of the immigrant past and so on, are at different times defined in similar terms. Concurrently, Kushner places a commentary-device on American ideologies. At the centre is the implementation of a power-base, and Louis expresses this process:

> What defines us isn't race but politics. Not like any European country where there's an insurmountable fact of a kind of racial, or ethnic monopoly or monolith. I mean Dutch people are well, Dutch, and the Jews of Europe were never Europeans.[34]

Louis later expands this lecture into the idea that there is no reaching out to a 'spiritual past' and no 'racial past,' just the political.[5] The culmination of all this is a defence of the personal, the individual connections, set against the alliances with ideologies and manifestos for change or identity.

It is given to the black orderly Belize to sum up the American commentary, with the words, 'Well I hate America. I hate this country. It's just big ideas and stories, and people dying, and people like you . . . I live in America Louis, that's hard enough. I don't have to love it.'[36] Kushner's dissent is propelled from the standpoint of the disenchanted and the excluded, but in using the suffering of aids juxtaposed with the perspective of historical process, he has placed the Jewish experience in his watershed play in two ways: first, as the archetypal social other, the stranger within, and second, as the example of the version of the American who has learned to extract self esteem from himself at the expense of status and difference. Jewishness is used in the play as a motif for the displacement of the minority identity.

There is also the issue of how far the language itself in American-Jewish drama has been part of an aesthetic for such dissent. Richard Walsh, for example, in his study of Radical Theatre, places Mamet firmly with other avant-garde dramatists in his habit of making language the nexus of failure. 'Increasingly the dramatic context frames and ironies linguistic opacity: the theatrical premise remains firmly rooted in the radical loss of faith in the language.'[37] The link here with theatre of dissent is clear, and Ellen Schiff makes the point in the conclusion of her survey of the drama of the period, emphasising the American-Jewish dramatist's' place in the vanguard of the 'spokespersons for the oppressed and exploited'.[38]

This corpus of writing is certainly as healthy as ever in 1998. In a survey of American theatre in performance in February 1998, John Peter lists and discusses three new plays all dealing with being Jewish in America – and not all based in New York or in the urban elite of Wasserstein or Miller. He notes Alfred Uhry's play, *The Last Night of Ballyhoo*, for instance, which is concerned with 'being Jewish, in Atlanta, in 1939'.[39] The diversity and richness of this theatre is remarkable, and this introductory survey has had to omit several outstanding writers, for there should also be a place for discussion of Neil Simon and the inheritors of the musical tradition and of social comedy, as much of this writing is not to be labelled 'light comedy' at all.

Notes

1. See Ellen Schiff, 'The Greening of American-Jewish Drama', in Lewis Fried (ed.), *Handbook of American Jewish Literature* (Greenwood Press: New York, 1988), pp. 91–122. Schiff has ranged widely over the topic in the masterly study, identifying several dominant ideas and sub-genres.
2. Ibid. Here Schiff defines parallel traditions of social commentary.
3. See Margaret Brenman-Gibson's detailed biography of Odets, *Clifford Odets: American Playwright* (Atheneum: New York, 1981). Her account of the influence of Odets is useful here: 'Odets was substituting for the consolatory spectacles and sentimentality in the Yiddish theatre the first deeply felt and formally achieved realism in America . . . he was hoping their conflicts . . . would reach an audience not limited to Jewish-Americans:' (p. 259).
4. See particularly the film *Barton Fink*. (Joel Coen: 1991), Coen establishes a compulsive metaphor to textualise this conflict of aesthetics and commerce.
5. Ruby Cohn, *New American Dramatists* (Macmillan: London, 1982), p. 5.
6. Clifford Odets, *Six Plays* (Random House: New York, 1939) p. 66.
7. See Arthur Miller, *Plays: Five* (Methuen: London, 1995), introduction, p. XV. Here Miller compares naturalism to his own aims in giving interiority the prominence in narrative.
8. See Matthew del Nevo, 'Edmond Jabes and the Question of the Book', in *Literature and Theology,* vol. 10, no. 4, December 1966, pp. 301–17, p. 307. Del Nevo relates Jewish writing to Jabes' notion of life-experience and reading process as 'text' and how these define Jewish writing.
9. See Ronald Hayman, *Arthur Miller* (Heinemann: London, 1970), p. 63; Hayman says directly that Hannah Arendt's view is 'the Jews may have been partly accomplices to their own slaughter'.

10. Arthur Miller, Incident at Vichy, in *Plays: Two* (Methuen: London, 1988), pp. 269–70.

11. See Elie Wiesel's latest text, *All Rivers Run to the Sea* (HarperCollins: London, 1997), which appeared at a time in which several major Holocaust memoirs were published in Britain within amonth.

12. See Alan L. Berger, 'Jewish Identity and Jewish Destiny, the Holocaust in Refugee Writing', *SAJL* vol. II no. 1 (Spring1992), pp. 83–93, p. 84.

13. See George W.Crandell, 'Re-addressing the Past – Arthur Miller's Neglected Speech: "Concerning Jews who Write" ' *SAJL* vol. 16 (1997), Crandell offers a useful discussion of how Miller did a volte-face on the subject.

14. See Julia Kristeva, *Strangers to Ourselves* (Prentice Hall: Herts, 1991), p. 20. Kristeva places the Jews as strangers in the wider context of Christian historiography and cultural studies.

15. Ibid., pp 13–14.

16. Arthur Miller, *After the Fall*, in *Plays: Two* (Methuen: London, 1988), p. 186.

17. Ibid. p. 181.

18. Gerald Weales, 'Arthur Miller's Shifting Image of Man', in Robert W. Corrigan, *Arthur Miller* (Prentice Hall: New Jersey, 1969), pp. 131–42, p. 139.

19. Arthur Miller, *Danger: Memory!* (Methuen: London, 1986), p. 30.

20. Ibid., p. 52.

21. Ibid., p. 44.

22. Arthur Miller, *Broken Glass* (Methuen: London, 1994), p. 71.

23. Ibid., p. 56.

24. Schiff, 'The Greening of American-Jewish Drama', in Fried, *Handbook of American Jewish Literature*, p. 113.

25. Wendy Wasserstein, *The Heidi Chronicles* (Vintage: New York, 1991), p. 10.

26. See John Lahr, interview with Mamet in *The Times Magazine*, 24 January 1998, pp. 14–23, p. 20.

27. Schiff, 'The Greening of American-Jewish Drama', in Fried, *Handbook*, p. 115.

28. John Peter, 'Revival of the Fittest' *The Sunday Times* 8 February 1998, pp. 14–15.

29. See Sanford Pinsker's outstanding contribution to the origins and expressions of the *schlemiel* in *The Schlemiel as Metaphor: Studies in the Yiddish and American-Jewish Novel* (Southern Illinois University Press: Illinois, 1971).

30. Tony Kushner, *Angels in America: Millennium Approaches* (Nick Hern: London, 1992), p. 2.

31. Ibid., pp. 14–15.

32. Ibid., p. 21.

33. Ibid.

34. Ibid., p. 68.

35. Ibid., p. 69.

36. *Perestroika Angels in America*: (Nick Hern: London, 1992), p. 61.

37. See Richard Walsh, *Radical Theatre in the Sixties and Seventies* (BAAS: Keele, 1993), p. 37. Walsh interestingly adds Mamet to a long list of innovative dramatists, and the fact that Mametcan be added for his linguistic bravura is entirely typical of the vibrancy of American-Jewish theatre narrative.

38. See Schiff,'The Greening of American-Jewish Drama', in Fried, *Handbook of American Jewish Literature*, p. 119.
39. See Peter, 'Revival of the Fittest', in *The Sunday Times*. . . Peter suggests that the innovations and continued dynamism of this theatre would be more apparent with a directorial tradition equal to that of Britain.

6

Poetry across the Generations: Duality to Assimilation

One of the first aspects of the poetry in this period written by American-Jewish writers that strikes the reader is the marginalisation of poetry on specifically Jewish themes, even from poets who are considered to be of the first rank. In the most influential and accessible anthologies of American poetry since 1945 – those published by Penguin, Norton and Faber – there is virtually no writing directly concerned with Jewish identity. Even in the work of major poets, such as Adrienne Rich, Allen Ginsberg, M. L. Rosenthal and Howard Nemerov, there is very little. Even more striking is the absence of the Holocaust as specific subject-matter in these poets. Adrienne Rich, in the foreword to her *Collected Early Poems 1950–1970*, offers a personal explanation of this: 'Still, at twenty, I implicitly dissociated poetry from politics. At college in the late 1940s, I sat in classes with World War II vets . . . I knew women who were . . . refugees from Nazism. I had no political ideas of my own.'[1] In fact, arguably the most anthologised poem about the Holocaust is written by a gentile.[2]

Yet there is a great deal of poetry written by Jews, and of all generations. What has happened in terms of the most important poets is that so many of the fundamental statements about identity had been expressed so forcefully and imaginatively in the rich fiction of the 1960s that there was little new to say. Also, poetry in this context has always seemed to confront the Holocaust and anti-Semitism rather than deal yet again with such issues as generational conflict or Orthodox against Reform ideologies. Whereas in the theatre the huge, inexpressible concepts may be visualised, incorporated into a set or into mentalised imagery in the audience, in poetry there is a directness that perhaps evades the necessary simplicity required by definition of status and identity.

In fact, there is a certain dismissal of the well-established questions of identity in some of the poetry by many poets. Grace Paley, for instance, in 'Letter' makes fun of the whole concept of the Jewish writer as a differential status: 'They have asked for the addresses/of a couple of other Jews/Ozick and Kazin to be specific' and goes on to imagine the Jewish writers across the world, all thriving by their stated difference. Her conclusion is about a thousand Jews who fled Bombay who 'disappeared/in the terrible Yahweh-defying act/of assimilation'.[3] Only in Adrienne Rich's perspectives on historical process does the reference to changing identity take on sufficient depth and complexity, linked with her feminism and her writing on marginalisation and sexual politics. Her status as 'Split at the root, neither Gentile nor Jew'[4] is at the heart of this. It might be added in addition that a figure such as Muriel Rukeyser (1913–80), who has been highly regarded as a feminist writer and activist, has inspired more by her politicised attitudes than by her addressing of specifically Jewish issues. A recent essay on her by Marilyn Hacker stresses this, with reference to the poem 'Nine Poems for the Unborn Child': 'As far as I know, this sequence is the first to claim for this situation [the physical/mental state of pregnancy; a single woman's decision to bear and raise a child], the stature of poetic subject-matter.'[5]

For these reasons, the poets discussed in this chapter will mostly be unfamiliar to English readers, and perhaps also to many Americans. The poets in question are Irena Klepfisz, Carolyn Forché, Dan Pagis and Jerome Rothenberg. The others – Rich, Ginsberg and Shapiro – are more familiar. But the important point here is that, unlike the theatre or the novel, poetry written by Jewish-Americans who have retained the *Materia Judaica* as a focus in their work has been primarily concerned with the need to write about the Holocaust, or *Shoah*. This has entailed an understanding of the centrality of this terrible event both as metaphor and as catalyst.

The questions that will emerge from this chapter will be concerned with, in Gary Pacernick's words, poets delineating 'the Jewish past through an art of imaginative memory'.[6] Pacernick's book-length study is one of the most comprehensive introductions to this little-known body of work, and he lists the central features of the poetry as being concerned with memory and tradition, radical individualism and identification with exile and suffering. The Diaspora as a paradigm, an inner journey to selfhood, is always present, as in Gene Zeiger's collection *Leaving Egypt*, discussed later.[7]

The centre of most of this poetry, then, is the concern with suffering and exile as the destiny of the Jew. The return to the *Shoah* as focal subject is therefore of primary importance in this chapter. Before dealing with the different ways in which the poets have written about that, it is necessary to reflect on the significance of the Nazi Final Solution and the notion of the Death-camp experience as a metaphorical exploration, and indeed a confrontation with imagination itself. In Jacqueline Rose's study of Sylvia Plath, *The Haunting of Sylvia Plath*, there is a detailed analysis of how Plath exploits the suffering and the actual physical revulsion of the environment in order to create imagery of familial significance. In the course of this discussion, Rose accounts for two fundamental patterns in this writing. The first is the Freudian theory of the ego-defence mechanism of projection and the second is about language itself in the context of extreme evil and suffering. Rose's most condensed statement of this is expressed in this way:

> There is a sense, here, therefore, in which we can truly say that metaphor was arrested at Auschwitz, insofar as the figural possibilities of language . . . are one of the things the Holocaust put at risk . . . what conditions of representation can the fantasies underpinning metaphor itself be spoken?[8]

In other words, it is possible to see in Plath's poems 'Daddy' and 'Lady Lazarus' an extension of the notion of the 'non-Jew identification' with suffering. Plath, of Austrian descent, placed Nazi cruelty on her father, and even used the repulsive imagery

of the camps' bestiality and evil in the context of her psychological problems. Rose is quite right to pinpoint the importance
of what this says about memory and about metaphor. For
example, the Hassidic idea that there are three stages of mourn-
ing – weeping, silence and singing – could potentially explain
why certain periods since the end of the war have contained the
most cathartic accounts of the *Shoah*, and why at other times
that has been silence. In 1997–8 for instance, there were several
widely mediated accounts of the *Shoah* and its effects on
memory and selfhood, notably two books in the British best-
seller lists, one by the American Anne Michaels (*Fugitive Pieces*)
and the other by Ann Karpf (*The War After*). Yet, once again,
none of this was poetry.

The Yiddish proverb 'ibergekumene tsores iz gut tsu dertsey-
lin' (troubles overcome are good to tell) appears to have applied
to poetry later and less universally than in fiction. If one selects
the most familiar poems of the American-Jewish poets in this
period, they are certainly concerned with suffering, but their
concerns are more entwined with the poet's personal dilemmas, and the paradigm of Sylvia Plath becomes more appealing
as a way into the material of the Shoah as unspeakable. If, as
Michael A. Bernstein affirmed, 'The universe of the deathcamps
now functions much as the concept of the sublime did in an
earlier era: an absolute whose very existence places a demand
on us which we are categorically unable to satisfy . . . A rupture
. . . vitally connected to the theme of the unspeakable that
must always be spoken of.'[9] This explains much of the marginalisation of this writing in American poetry. The actual nature
of poetic syntax and form includes a compression of meaning,
an exactness which leaves ambiguities if done too indirectly or
vaguely. The poets who have concentrated on this subject-
matter perhaps exemplify the central problems of the American-Jewish poet more than any other writing.

In the work of Jerome Rothenberg, Carolyn Forsché and Irena
Klepfisz these attempts at offering a truth to documented
history, simultaneously comprehensive and honest, one may
see the issues of poetic statement more plainly.

Each of these poets has attempted to confront the *Shoah*
by means of narrative devices, sometimes impressionistic,

sometimes unbearably direct; the effect and method often raise the issue of the centrality of suffering in Jewish destiny, and most historical or ideological perspectives of understanding on the death camps are included within this expression. For instance, such poetry has to account for the basic function of poetry per se, in the face of such extremes of action, set against what is essentially a contemplative art, a business of withdrawal from action. Jerome Rothenberg puts this clearly in his preface to the collection *Khurbn*: 'The poems that I first began to hear at Treblinka are the clearest message I have ever gotten about why I write poetry. They are an answer to the proposition . . . that poetry cannot be written after Auschwitz.'[10]

Rothenberg's work illustrates clearly this tendency to textualise a variety of objective correlatives whilst at the same time using the barest of metaphors to express the impossibility of empathy. The difficult issue of the empathic impulse of poetry, so different from the Freudian idea of projection in Plath, is not related to a defence mechanism; rather, in this context, it is to write about the horrors in documentary mode. The process of selectivity in Rothenberg is one that foregrounds a mimetic relation of the experience itself:

> the word as prelude to the scream
> it enters
> through the asshole
> circles along the gut . . .
> it is his scream that shakes me
> weeping in oshvientsim
> & that allows the poem to come[11]

Repeatedly, Rothenberg uses the imagery of speech and words to define the notion of the unspeakable. The suffering itself is enough: style merely seems an insult. His listing of the raw data of horror needs nothing but literal language in many cases, however. The poems deal with burials, starvation, rotting corpses and smell. What develops in the collection, among other things, is the account of what was lost, or taken. It is a poetry about how one race insisted on proving what power could do, simply devoid of humanity. The paradox, which

civilised readers want to resist, that the Final Solution was a
kind of art, is given also: 'of what art can do/ what constructs of
the mind/ are thinkable/ when power assists their hands'.[12]

Similarly with other poetry focusing on the *Shoah*, there is a
grim confrontation with what metaphor cannot handle ade-
quately. Irena Klepfisz in 'Herr captain' for instance, gives the
male brutality in detailed and dynamic style, making an interesting comparison with Plath's 'Daddy'. Where Plath extends
an image into symbolic force againt the self, Klepfisz accounts
for the militaristic brutality in crudely sexual terms:

> he was hard so hard forcing bending me
> till I could not breathe slamming against me
> my mouth filled with terror.[13]

Klepfisz's collection mixes the syntax of extreme stress, of
voices from consciousness on the edge, and partly to voice
other interests in the context of oppression and sexual politics. But again, the empathic aim is expressed in a footnote to
the above poem, along with the documentary realism intended: 'In my early teens I read *House of Dolls* a novel written
by a man . . . based on the diary of an anonymous Jewish
woman who did not survive . . .'[14] The importance of Rothenberg and Klepfisz is that their work illustrates the strategies
poets have had to construct in order to establish literary
contact with a distanced and perhaps over simplified imagery
of the most formative event in Jewish history. All this is made
more difficult when it is recalled that the central current of
modern American poetry was primarily concerned with poetic
truth, an escape from established form and the discoveries of
such idioms as confessional verse or regional consciousness.
Such topics as minority poetry, and written about a distant
past, would have appeared perversely disturbing, and at a time
when the groupings across the country, along with academic
poetry and the growth of little magazines, were proving more
attractive to Jewish poets whose first aims were to succeed in
the mainstream.

After all, surveys of the poetry written since 1945, such as
Kenneth Rexroth's[15] hint that interest in history as such had

always been important as a basis for all this, are helpful but the aims were mainly autobiographical or ideological; the necessary politicisation of such poetic subjects as the *Shoah* were rather too complex for writers involved in finding sexual freedom, discovering 'America' and insisting on changes in consciousness. Such marginalisation in Jewish poets may be observed in, for instance, the work of Hyam Plutzik, whose representative selection of writings in Howard Nemerov's well-known anthology, *Five American Poets*,[16] contains only one poem about the kind of history which emerges in the younger writers such as Klepfisz; the poem is about his great grandfather, and the last lines,

> At last demanding, to close the door to the cold,
> Only *Here lies someone*
> Here lie no-one and no-one, your fathers and mothers[17]

There is surely some significance in the writing about history, in broad philosophical terms, which is a feature of this corpus of poetry, and it is a textual feature that repeatedly minimises the Jewish experience, in all but a few poets' work.

The younger writers have found narrative strategies also, to deal with this problem of empathy and suffering beyond explanation. Carolyn Forsché, for instance, in *The Angel of History*, tells a disjointed and lyrical story of a French victim of the *Shoah*, interspersed with other stories, and then relates this context with that of Japan and the atomic bomb. The narrative of displacement, peppered with French and with authenticated documentary topography, has an effect similar to *The Waste Land*, in that melancholy and large-scale commentary fuses with interior monologue and poetic motif, to piece together an account of the schism, the destruction of a culture and a consciousness that the Nazis tried to achieve. Forsché deliberately uses a rhetoric of elegy and lament to attain all this, as in section XVI, which illustrates her method:

> What has eaten these walls? wind in the mustard fields
> Death maps.
> Rat teeth.

Hurrying we find German war maps of the High Tatras where
Anna lived,
and one of Brno
as if there were a corpse in the armoire.[18]

The title comes from an essay by Walter Benjamin, in which the
Angel of History is said to have 'his face turned towards the past
. . . the angel would like to stay, awaken the dead, and make
whole what has been smashed.'[19] History as a force which
tempts us to imagine other outcomes, and other circumstances,
is in question here. Forsché, unlike Rothenberg or Klepfisz,
takes a perspective on the great watershed of Jewish experience
which juxtaposes it with other catastrophes of inhumanity,
and places together the individuated self with the mass suffering. Relentless historical process, as in Kushner's play, is here
also, placing the Jewish particularity in the same category as
other modern cultural and racial genocide.

All this is further explored in the work of those poets who
have placed themselves as less centrally American Jewish, while
still facing the *Shoah*. Even in the work of the Israeli Dan Pagis,
who wrote at times with an American stance, there is much less
directness, although he also includes the widest historical
perspective, and delineates the events of the cattle-trains across
central Europe, for instance, in terms that often avoid the
explicit:

> No no: they definitely were
> human beings: uniforms, boots.
> How to explain? They were created
> in the image'[20]

Even in the most restrained of his short lyrics on this theme,
there is a delicacy in the hard significance of meaningless
suffering: 'here in this carload/ I am Eve/with Abel my son . . .'[21]

Drawing all these poems together, it is important to see that
the significance here, for American Jewish writing as a whole, is
that at specific points in time – the early 1960s and the late
1980s for instance, there was concentrated effort to find the
adequate voice, the literal statement of the enormity of the

Shoah and also its suitability as a subject for poetry, despite the notion that there is an area of human experience which is beyond expression. Perhaps what has made the impact less notable has been the tendency of poets to commandeer such subjects as part of other, more autobiographical enterprises. An example might be Alan Ginsberg's celebrated poem 'Kaddish', written in 1959 on his mother's death. The poem is Ginsberg's only open use of Jewish experience, as he related the story of his mother's long mental illness – one in which she was suffering in part from a projection of psychological burdens absorbed at the thought of the death camps (much as discussed in Miller's play, *Broken Glass*, in the previous chapter). But, as his elegies in the Kaddish sequence search for expression of broader philosophical preoccupations, and a Blakean reach for universal statements, Naomi Ginsberg's Jewish empathy and sensitive awareness of her race's lamentable victimisation attain the status of a convenient allegory for the American disease of living without history.[22]

The Holocaust as an instrument of revisionary manoeuvres towards defining Jewishness in America is another element in the poetry which has led poets to create fresh ways of using the archetypal narratives of the Jewish historical process. Leslie Fiedler's essay on what he calls 'the two Holocausts', *In Every Generation*, contains a most explicit statement of one revisionary position:

> I feel obliged to wrestle with the question of why the threat of annihilation and the promise of redemption have continued to be the pattern of our history. Here too is the traditional text suggesting an answer [Chapter 33, Isaiah, quoted] '. . . he was chastised for our iniquities: the chastisement of our peace was upon him.'[23]

Here, Fiedler develops this notion of suffering in redemption, in maintaining a specific version of humanity defined by victimisation, as something that has to be negated in the face of the Holocaust. His conclusion is 'It is for this reason that I have found it impossible to reflect self-righteously on the Holocaust, which left me unscathed, without alluding uneasily to that other which has left me feeling like a Last Jew.'[24] The point is that poetry is the obvious means of exploring such 'silent Holocaust' metaphors, and of being revisionary about the idea of being a Last Jew in America now – the latest generation has once again re-imagined history. This is an act of purposive memory, and this takes the present enquiry into the area, once again, of the Jewish present and its reconstruction of the past. Clearly, there are methods of writing about this in poetic form which lend themselves to intellectualism and the poetry of the academy. But Fiedler has always been a mediator and rebel in challenging accepted ideas, and his essay is totally honest, despite qualifying phrases.

Memory and its nature is the key here, and the second most assertive corpus of American-Jewish poetry has been largely concerned with memory. The discovery made by Adrienne Rich, that her father had denied his Jewishness and that she had not been informed of her half-identity, and that she had to assert that element in her, was done in a prose essay – not in poetry. Yet her poetry is almost always concerned with memory and history. On the one hand, we have individual discoveries within assimilation, and on the other, the recurrent use of the story of Israel, the Exodus and the Diaspora. Somehow, the *Shoah* has come to be the catalyst which has regenerated a sense of what memory actually is in terms of a racial and cultural definition.

Paradoxically, it is in attempts to explain the *Shoah* that the seeds of these historical revisitations have been made. Ignaz Maybaum has said that there is no rational explanation: 'We are a remnant and we must seek with the Hallelujah of the redeemed at the Red Sea', Emil Fackenheim insists that it was an expression of God's will that the chosen people should survive; Eliezer Berkovits states that we must place the *oleh*, – the immigrant, as the new means of shaping a Jewish identity (rather than the universal image of the *Torah* student). Yet Richard Rubinstein says 'We stand in a cold, silent, unfeeling cosmos, unaided by any power beyond our own resources.'[25] These various statements provoke such dissent and pluralist responses that the role of the literary as opposed to the philosophical writing on such historical process is left open to multiple expressions and ideologies.

As a result, history and memory take centre stage in much recent American-Jewish poetry. In Gene Zeiger's collection, *Leaving Egypt*, the tone is set for this tradition of oppositional discourse, set against history as a meta-narrative of the Jewish people; it makes a renewed effort to use domesticity and interiority as the focus of interest. In this collection, we enter Grace Paley's microcosm again. Zeiger plainly exploits the resources of her mother's language and lifestyle in order to textualise elements into her poetry that are more readily perceived as the material of fiction, as in 'Vus is Gevain, is Gevain', in which memory in its smallest, most familiar arena is a stepping-stone to a larger question. We move from 'Her questions rain on me/the same ones over and again' to a closure which asserts and repeats that acceptance which has been the lot of the Jewish people, in the massive political context and in their marginalisation and philosophical ontology:

> Beyond her, the open window,
> the deep green of trees. She turns
> to look me in the eye and sings:
> 'Vus is gevain, is gevain. Is nisht du.'
> What is gone is gone. It is not now.[6]

Zeiger can also explain the sense of objective distance, of alienation from the immigrant mentality felt by the New York intellectual poet on the eve of the millenium.

'God and my mother have grown to resemble each other/ remote and distracted the two of them moving.' In the title poem, she takes on the larger themes and successfully relates them to this domestic, small-scale life of the assimilated, seeking for the meanings of that first-generation existential assertion.

> . . . At thirteen, book in hand, I thought I heard
> the boxcars rattling to Auschwitz, smelled the
> urine-soaked straw.

However Zeiger herself had more urgent discoveries to make, claiming womanhood: 'You see, for decades I said little, wrote my name/ the only word I had.'[27]

Gene Zeiger represents the centre of this other tradition, the poetry that looks for answers in the meta-narrative *only as perceived in the mundane, the experiential*. This explains why so much poetry by American-Jewish writers has attempted to be lyrical inside a framing narrative; it has also been experimental and escaped formal restriction. Irena Klepfisz interweaves prose and stream of consciousness. Rothenberg is attracted to the flexibility of documentary data. What cannot be denied is the total confidence on the part of these poets in their inheritance as manipulators of language; their cultural acquisitions have been an identified strength in this search for the expression of memory. Adrienne Rich says that from her father's perfectionism in learning and bookish culture she was made to feel at a very young age, 'the power of language and that I could share it'.

At the heart of this rediscovery through poetry is the need to, as Rich puts it, 'flirt with identity'.[28] That is, if only residual elements of Jewishness are left as the poet seeks to tackle such fundamental subjects, then is not the act of composing poetry itself a venture into the unknown? This explains why the metaphor of language itself returns again to be accommodated to the theme of history and memory. It is in Adrienne Rich's poetry that we see this most clearly, though it is in Zeiger, Rothenberg, Klepfisz and Pagis also. It is perhaps in this aspect that the most obvious difference is seen between the generation of Karl Shapiro and that of the contemporary writers. Shapiro's work, notably in *Poems of a Jew* (1958), represents that forthright certainty of social commentary, politicised after his military service in the Second World War, a certainty of what composes the identity of a Jewish artist. As Stephen Stepanchev says, for Shapiro, 'Being a Jew is the consciousness of being a Jew, and the Jewish identity, with or without religion, with or without history, is the significant fact . . . This identity involves an "intimacy" with God, but not necessarily with Judaism.'[29]

It may be that Shapiro's generation, in being close to the occurrence of the *Shoah*, language and metaphor were not a problem. A response had to be given, and anti-Semitism, being revised after the death camps, becomes a more meaningful part of modern American life mostly with hindsight. That is, what the Final Solution says about anti-Semitism is also something that, in a cyclical way perhaps, also reconstructs some elements of newly affirmed identity in later generations.

Certainly in Adrienne Rich we have a special case-study. Rich's mother was gentile and her father was assimilated in the sense that he put career and ideologies of WASP America first. But there is clearly an enormity in most denial. Do you deny history if you deny your Jewishness as a part of your public, communal self? Fiedler's 'silent Holocaust' becomes explicable through a scrutiny of how memory may disappear in everyday life, and yet poetry has accepted the role of being an archaeologist of memory, relocating a disjointed history for children of those who knew the immigrant experience in America.

At this point, before turning to look at Rich's work in this respect, it needs to be emphasised that, with history and memory still in mind, there is another way of defining American-Jewish poetry, and that is through the qualities of vision that may be seen in poets such as David Ignatow, Philip Levine and Howard Nemerov. For reasons of space, the present chapter is confined to the summary of those poets who deal overtly with the material so far dealt with. Gary Pacernick rightly points out that in Nemerov, for instance, we 'see, in his biblical poems . . . and other poems profound reading of God's influence in both nature and in human society'.[30] It could be argued that American-Jewish poetry has in fact been vibrant and extremely relevant to the ideologies of Judaism yet in some 'hidden' manner, in allegory and in tropes of rhetoric; but in limiting the study to the common theme of language and memory, it is possible to see the most influential writing more clearly. This is where Adrienne Rich's work can be shown to exemplify both these viewpoints; she writes only occasionally about openly Jewish subjects. But her exploration of the concepts of cultural 'Other', stranger and immigrant, voices more insistently and persuasively than the more abstract and philosophic poets the focus of interest in this body of writing: She may be placed in the same category as Muriel Rukeyser, as primarily concerned with power and empowerment, women's experience and the influence of historical process. Rukeyser's credo is stated in the lines:

> Woman, American, and Jew,
> three guardians watch over you,
> three lions of heritage
> resist the evil of your age[31]

Her inspiration is in biblical study and the work of the prophets, and she extends the idea of oppression to universal applications, like Rich. Her work is essentially that of a proletarian writer, aligned with Steinbeck more than poetry of meditation and isolated self. She is a participant, educated and motivated by change. Her prizing the work of Rabbi Akiba is, as Pacernick asserts, important because he was her 'crucial link to her ancient heritage'.[32] Adrienne Rich's work makes more sense in this perspective.

Rich's poetry, from *A Change of World* (1951) onwards, is interlaced with cyclical poetic discourse on the massive meta-narratives of America alongside the allegories of empowerment exemplified in her poem to Elvira Shatayev in 'The Dream of a Common Language' (1974–7). The poem shows how Rich's contribution is often that of the allegorist who manages to extend the particular into the universal with ease and power. Shatayev was a mountaineer and the leader of a women's climbing team. Unfortunately, she and her team died in a storm on Lenin Peak in 1974. Rich somehow makes her emblematic of Everywoman's struggle, and the vocabulary framing the narrative also makes it possible to see Shatayev as also representative of the marginalised, the disenfranchised – a Jew, a woman, the dispossessed. For instance, in the closure:

> In the diary torn from my fingers I had written:
> *What does love mean*
> *what does it mean 'to survive'*
> *a cable of blue fire ropes our bodies*
> *burning together in the snow We will not live*
> *to settle for less We have dreamed of this*
> *all of our lives*[33]

In her early poems, we see this tendency to universalise very well. The idea of history, of memory, or arrival and identity – all transmutes into existential statements. When they are openly Jewish assertions, it is easy to match them with the more universalised images. In the poem 'Readings of History' for instance, the first sections insist on the triviality of history as demonstrated in art. Then she shifts to the notion of hermeneutics – of Dilthey's ideas of interpretation and bias. The impossibility of finding truth in history is given in an image that could be any time or place: 'What, in fact, happened in these woods/ on some obliterated afternoon?' Section IV faces the impossible questions of our relations with ancestors, and finally to face up to how Jewish awareness has any impact at all:

> Morris Cohen, dear to me as a brother,
> when you sit at night
> tracing your way through your volumes
> of Josephus or any
> of the old Jewish chronicles,
> do you find yourself there, a simpler,
> more eloquent Jew?[34]

There are few poets in this period and context who can define and describe the complexity of that duality that has persisted – the suffering Jew as opposed to the invisible, residual Jew today in America – Fiedler's Last Jew. Rich's position is explained in her poem 'At the Jewish New Year', in which she handles the urge to cancel memory and history altogether; forgetting should begin with

> those age-old arguments
> in which their minds were wound
> like musty phylacteries

yet, they 'still burn like yellow flames/ But their fire is not for us'. Just as it seems there is a dismissal, the poem ends with an affirmation that there is a function of memory which is essential in Jewishness: 'The task of being ourselves'.[35] And in 'White Night', translated from the Yiddish of Kadia Molodowsky, Rich insists that the passage to one's self in a still-new life is still evocative of the journeys in steerage:

> I'm a difficult passenger, my ship
> is packed with the heavy horns, the *shofars* of grief.[36]

Rich's version of the imperative to insist on memory is that of the parable; her poems on history and redefinition of the self impinge of the archetypal literature of the arrival of the stranger. In 'The Strayed Village' it is possible to read the narrative of the lost, the ephemeral, as in so many of her poems concerning topography and the past. A man travels a thousand miles to find a village gone. No-one can explain its disappearance. The stranger comments, after attempts at verification and meetings with a local:

> We found ourselves as if by acquiescence
> using to speak of it, as if we thought
> someday to come upon it somewhere else.[37]

As Helen Vendler has commented on Rich's work, 'In *A Change of World* Rich struck all the notes of her generation's inchoate responses to Europe.'[38]

Finally, it has to be said that there is a sense in which American-Jewish poetry has still not attained that state of confidence in any direction and vision which is apparent in the theatre and in fiction. The excitement is there, however, and in the poetry of Gene Zeiger and Carolyn Forsché in particular, it may be argued, there is a shaping of new registers for applications to overfamiliar subjects. The kind of exploratory and innovative fiction and discursive prose being undertaken by Paul Auster, for instance, seems to be finding its way into the equivalent poetry. There is an argument that the poetic voice has been lodged in Miller's theatre and in Kushner's to a large extent, and that the *Shoah* has perhaps been too dominant; that anti-Semitism has been the subject of fiction, and that the areas of domesticity, neighbourhood and the call of the religious life are also firmly present in prose. Also, autobiography has become an increasingly prevalent form in which to deal with these things. In 1997–8 alone, there was heated debate on Martin Sherman's play about gays in the *Shoah*, *Bent*; several bestsellers which included biographical material on the death camps; Elie Wiesel's autobiography, *All Rivers Run to the Sea* and Binjamin Wilkomirski's memoir, *Fragments*, of the camps which was discussed in the context of a major symposium on the Holocaust and literature during Jewish Book Week in Britain. Wilkomirski's book illustrated the time-lag thesis – that he found a voice for the inexpressible, and the newspapers asked, where is the poetry to equal what we know through Anne Frank, Primo Levi and Wiesel?

There is a sense in which most of the fundamental aspects of Jewish identity and assimilation were said in the poetry during the earliest phase – with poets such as Louis Zukofsky and Muriel Rukeyser, but their work was still very close to doctrine and to the second-generation concerns with progress built upon initial survival. The inheritance of European anti-Semitism was still perceptible, and accepted as part of life. As material for poetry, it often took second place to such subjects as Jewish tradition, social change and Marxist agendas. The one certain fact about this poetry is that it has had to be flexible: it comes from no certain origin or Ur-text and has no forebears to equal that of, say, Yezierska in prose or Odets in the theatre. But then, one aspect of the American poet, one may argue, has always been his or her isolation – a refusal to be labelled. This also raises questions about the marginal, partly non-literary figures who are difficult to classify; even Bob Dylan would be under scrutiny here; but searching for Jewish themes in the Beat and Pop/folk approaches to writing is likely to lead to digressive qualitative discussion. The only significant element in Jewish writing that is perhaps comprehended in this marginality of literary culture is the fundamental quasi-religious or even secular belief-systems uncodified in 'Rock'.

Notes

1. Adrienne Rich, *Collected Early Poems 1950–1970* (Norton: New York and London, 1993), p. 20.

2. See the sequence 'Camps and Fields' but in particular the poem 'A Camp in the Prussian Forest' with its terrible and ironic lines 'In soil that does not yet refuse/Its Usual Jews' in *The Complete Poems* (Faber: London, 1971), p. 167. Randall Jarrell gives the serviceman's response, something captured in documentaries such as *Liberation* (Channel 4, 1994).

3. See Grace Paley, *Begin Again* (Virago: London, 1992), p. 44.

4. Rich, *Collected Early Poems*, p. 164.

5. See Marilyn Hacker, 'The Classic Poem: Muriel Rukeyser', *Poetry Review*, vol. 87 no. 1 (Spring 1997), pp. 39–41.

6. See Gary Pacernick, *Memory and Fire: Ten American-Jewish Poets* (Peter Lang: New York, 1989), p. 6.

7. Pacernick works by relating his selected poets to well-defined features of Orthodoxy and then introducing social commentaries and inner rhetoric of style. This restriction is effective in isolating main trends in each context.

8. See Jacqueline Rose, *The Haunting of Sylvia Plath* (Virago: London: 1991), Rose's extended examination of Plath's tendency to align with Freudian projection theory is illuminating in the entire literary context of the idea of metaphor per se in dealing with trauma. It also presents a paradigm for discussing attempts at empathy and issues of intention in art.

9. See Michael A. Bernstein, 'Homage to the Extreme', *Times Literary Supplement*, 6 March 1998, pp. 6–8. Bernstein discusses the psychic capacity to engage with how this genocide was or was not unique in the experience of European Jewry.

10. Jerome Rothenberg, *Khurbn and Other Poems* (New Directions: New York, 1983), p. 4.

11. Ibid., p. 12.

12. Ibid., p. 21.

13. Irena Klepfisz, *Different Enclosures* (Onlywomen Press: London, 1985). Klepfisz mixes forms, prose and poetry, with a clear intention to focus on topics linked by questions of power and deprivation, as quoted on the book cover. 'A Jewish lesbian/feminist activist'.

14. Ibid., p. 12.

15. See Kenneth Rexroth, *American Poetry in the Twentieth Century* (Herder: New York, 1971), Rexroth's anecdotal method has the advantage of naming names and locations for most of the influential groupings, academic placings and small magazines having any importance in the developments in the poetry scene since 1945. His privileging mechanisms also demonstrate the process of selection.

16. See Howard Nemerov, *Five American Poets* (Faber: London, 1963). Nemerov's anthology provides a typical example of those assimilated poets whose work, while having undoubted stylistic exhuberance and innovation, evades any didactic elements with reference to Jewish thought in any direct sense. His poets are primarily academic and literary.

17. Ibid., Hyam Plutzik, 'After Looking into a Book belonging to my Great-Grandfather, Eli Eliakim Plutzik' p. 59.

18. See Carolyn Forshe, *The Angel of History* (Bloodaxe: Newcastle, 1994), p. 40.

19. Ibid., see the epigraph, referring to Benjamin.
20. See Dan Pagis, *The Selected Poetry of Dan Pagis* (University of California: Berkeley, 1989), p. 33. Pagis, an Israeli, nevertheless proves a valuable read in the present context. His stance illustrates the effort at distancing the subject, even using science-fiction imagery, written from an American standpoint.
21. Ibid., p. 39.
22. See Alan Ginsberg, 'Kaddish and Related Poems', in *Selected Poems 1947–1995* (Penguin: London, 1996), Here, Ginsberg extends metaphors into Biblical and elemental areas in reference to his mother ('O Ruth who wept in America') and in one sense he celebrates and laments different layers of meaning in the idea of exile. An interesting note regarding the Jewish writers in the Beats: Micheline for instance, born in New York and Jewish, exemplifies the assimilation into more than a culture. It extends into a sub-group ideology which cancels Jewish concerns. Yet perhaps even Micheline's poetry owes something to the Jewish apocalyptic vision and mysticism (see his poem 'Poet of the Streets', in Ann Charters, *The Penguin Book of the Beats*, (Penguin: London, 1993), pp. 396–8.
23. Leslie A. Fiedler, *Fiedler on the Roof* (David Godine: Boston, 1991), p. 162.
24. Ibid., p. 181.
25. See Lavinia and Dan Cohn-Sherbok, *A Short Reader in Judaism* (Oneworld: Oxford, 1996), pp. 154–59 provide a succinct account of various philosophical positions vis-a-vis the Holocaust and belief.
26. See Gene Zeiger, *Leaving Egypt* (White Pine Press: New York, 1995).
27. Ibid., p. 56.
28. Rich, *Collected Early Poems*, p. 113.
29. See Stephen Stepanchev, *American Poetry Since 1945* (Harper and Row: New York, 1965), p. 66.
30. Pacernick *Memory and Fire*, p. 7.
31. Ibid., pp. 216–17.
32. Ibid., p. 217.
33. Rich, *Collected Early Poems*, p. 6.
34. Ibid., p. 165.
35. Ibid., p. 198.
36. Ibid., p. 276.
37. Ibid., 101.
38. See Helen Vendler, *Part of Nature, Part of Us*: Modern American Poets (Harvard: Mass., Camb. 1980), p. 241.

7

The Mediation of Jewishness in Cultural Texts: Cynthia Ozick, Leslie Fiedler, Paul Auster and Woody Allen

One feature of American Jewish writing that is perhaps the most celebrated and also most misunderstood is the bellettrist discursive tradition. This massive corpus is an uneasy mix of Higher Journalism, literary essay, autobiography, humour and polemic. A case could be argued that this writing is the most important and also the most suited to that particular temperament that has come to be known as New York Jewish intellectual. It includes groups who have been associated with certain journals and magazines, such as *The New Review of Books*, the *Partisan Review*, and, in earlier times, the seminal *Menorah Journal*. In the period under review, it begins with Lionel Trilling and ends with David Mamet, but it is commodious enough to include the writing of Woody Allen and Leslie Fiedler.

Essentially, it is writing specifically about Jewishness: about assimilation and Diaspora, of course, but more prominently about the intellect. The centrality of the intellect and the importance of intellectual education is the foundation. One tradition is that of the *Luftmensch*, the freethinker, bohemian, nomadic and artistic. The alternative is the Talmud scholar. The interest in the American context is the resulting fusion, giving a literary scholar who happens to entertain or indeed the entertainer who takes learning and intellect as the subject – sometimes the butt – of the satire.

Before concentrating on the major writers in this category, it is useful to reflect on how this subject impinges on some wider, more seriously mediated constructs of the Jewish intellectual. This is outstandingly significant, as this figure is established as a focal protagonist in the work of almost every writer under review. In stories of the *Shtetl*, or the New York ghetto; in Bellow's novels of disenchantment and in Roth's often-savage satires on a media-led proletarian society, the truly interesting constructions of modern Jewishness are intellectual. Paul Auster, for instance, has written about the work of Edmond Jabès, whose major texts concern the centrality of the book in Jewish learning and cultural life, even to the point of arguing in philosophic terms on how we should define the Jewish artist.[1]

The construction of the 'Jewish thinker' in the highbrow media is of particular interest here. There are hundreds of discursive essays and statements available to the effect that Jewish thinkers have offered especially valuable contributions to modernism and to commentaries on the condition of the intellectual and artist in modernity. Two typical examples are George Steiner's autobiography (and indeed his own life and work) and the influence of Yosef Yerushalmi's book *Zakhor: Jewish History and Jewish Memory* (1982) as discussed by Jeremy Treglown, who writes of the book in a way that defines this category of text: 'Short, hugely learned and wide-ranging, the book is about what history-writing is, why civilisations need it, and how it relates to religion and other imaginings.'[2] The point here is the sheer ambition and comprehensive reach of the book and the mind behind it. It represents how, at one end of this spectrum, the scholar is the archetypal figure: the assumed value given to scholarship and the exercise of the intellect is never in question.

For George Steiner, this is a subject relevant to his own situation, and also important in his writing about this aspect of Jewishness. In his essays and more prominently in his autobiography, *Errata*, he expands on the theme of how the role of the intellectual establishes an inescapable integument of that sense of being Jewish that bookishness and a passion for

ideas instil. His discussion of the commonalty in the achievements of Jesus, Freud and Marx and how their thinking relates
to the universal sense in which Jewishness is defined through
the need for philosophic perspectives on the *Weltanshauung* of
the artist.[3]

This intellectualism also relates to the academic world, and to
dissent. There has always been a strand of radicalism and
individualism in these texts, even when the style is purely
humour in surreal dimensions. The work of Woody Allen
and Lenny Bruce always suggests this. The stock figures of
the *nebbish*, the *schlemiel* and the bookworm-farceur are all
two-dimensional in that they are potentially comic but also
open to serious interpretation. A large part of all this is the
nature of allegory; much of the prose in these categories takes
the form of mock-tale, parodic prose imitating conventional
Jewish discourse. In many ways, there is a genre of fiction that
also finds a place in this category: didactic, overtly concerned
with issues or with historical understanding. Notable in this
context is some of the work of Cynthia Ozick, a figure whose
status becomes increasingly significant as time passes.

There is also the factor concerning the inheritance of the
modern writers in these diverse traditions of prose writing.
Many look back to the Yiddish culture of what might be called
a second *Haskallah*, the Enlightenment as it influenced late
nineteenth-century Yiddish art and writing. Emanuel Litvinoff,
introducing his anthology of Jewish fiction, summarises this:

> The most phenomenal upsurge of Jewish creativity in mod-
> ern times, however, occurred in the Russian empire scarcely
> more than one hundred years ago when Jewish writers
> changed from Hebrew to Yiddish. . . . Not only were they
> provided with poetry, stories and plays about their own lives,
> they also read translations of Tolstoy and Shakespeare, Plato
> and Marx . . . The pale students burning like tapers with the
> flame of Talmud were . . . hungry for intellectual suste-
> nance.[4]

The cafe intellectuals written about by Hapgood (see
Chapter 1) and the line of development that takes us to

Herzog and Zuckerman is clearly a manifestation of a fundamental spirit of enquiry, a need for free thought and an interest in learning and culture per se that goes deeply into the spirit of Judaism. Hence, this corpus of belles-lettres and criticism – cultural and biographical rather than textual in most cases – is far more significant than it may at first seem. There is such a huge amount of writing in these categories that it would seem sensible and useful to discuss the work of four representative writers, rather than attempt a survey of everyone who might claim to be relevant to this area. Each one of the four – Auster, Fiedler, Allen and Ozick – represent only the most visible and evident elements in all this writing. A case could be made for many tireless and widely published writers having an influence (Sam Girgus, Irving Howe, Alfred Kazin and Samuel Pinsker for instance), but their work is either more directly literary criticism, or historical. In the case of Irving Howe, he would need a book-length study to do justice to his achievement. The important points to keep in mind are that three influences merge in the work of these writers: (1) the privileging of intellectualism; (2) the tradition of radicalism and satire and (3) the essentially surreal, profoundly comic vision of the Jewish tradition of commentary, narrative and autobiography that come together in individualistic creative modes of writing – even to the extent of confronting such taboos as Nazism, anti-Semitism and the guilt of the assimilated. The allegorical narrative drive is central here. It is an approach that may be seen at work not only in the Yiddish stories of Isaac Bashevis Singer and the pastiche of Allen, but most powerfully in the writing of the Israeli, Amos Oz, who also writes of immigrants, Jewish identity and the force of memory.[5]

The following discussions of the four writers, then, are not meant to be any hierarchical order; nor are they biased towards any high cultural view at the cost of proletarian or democratic values. There is also no intention to include a surreptitious implication that there is a new canon of American Jewish writing which might exclude some of this on the grounds of either trivia or insult. In fact, there is a topic that has to be touched on before the summaries of the four writers may proceed, and that is the notion of what is a fitting subject or even a suitable style for modern American-Jewish writing, and the ways in which this relates to the foundational nexus of intellectual interchange and political agenda given by the *Menorah Journal*, particularly in the influential essay by Eliot Cohen in 1925 called 'The Age of Brass'. The issue here was one of perceived splits in the moral perspectives on how Jewish identity and behaviour from within assimilation was doing more damage than active anti-Semitism by gentiles. A version of inner anti-Semitism in the radical and satirical writings of some Jewish writers were seen to be deplorably self-negating.

Mark Krupnick has assessed the importance of this, and he also points out the importance of Lionel Trilling's rejection of the group around that influential journal in 1931:

> Most would have seconded Trilling's damning judgement that 'As the Jewish community now exists it can give no sustenance to the American artist or intellectual who is born a Jew.'[6]

The most potent and also cogent more recent account of this issue was given by Philip Roth in his essay *Writing about Jews* (1963). Clearly, Roth had had to experience the revulsion and abuse of certain Orthodox Jewish voices in the aftermath of his contentious *Portnoy's Complaint*, but at least it forced him to rethink and to state very lucidly the dissensions and identity problems inherent in writing about the dialectics of inner, emotive Jewishness as opposed to the Americanised 'Good Jew' versions given in his new suburbia, where residual Jewishness is losing out to wealth, accommodation and the glittering prizes of academia and Corporate America's post-managerial revolution.

Like Trilling, Roth had to understand and react against the moral myopia of Orthodox Jewry. As he defends his story, 'Epstein', for instance, he is driven to define literature as if addressing a junior class, reminding them that intentions and purposes in art are not always the face value or the immediate subject as constructed. The fact that Roth is compelled to explain at great length what the function of the committed imagination is enlightens the whole problem of division inside Jewish consciousness in America. It mediates that problem as one of a dualism seemingly insoluble until the secular spirit of the new American-Jewish sensibility is recognised as something dynamic, exciting and firmly in a creative phase that seeks to redefine the American-Jewish intellectual.

But the question of how to write about Jewish identity and also how to realign sensibilities and imaginative visions with the notion of Jewishness rather than Judaism remains as a basic point of contention. Mark Krupnick suggests that the ideological stance of the *Menorah Journal* was, once again, the archetypal statement. Elliot Cohen's statement that 'American Jewry must be made to see that a life of apology is a shameful apology for life'[7] may explain what was reacted against rather than what was positive, but one aspect of this is easy to pinpoint: the place of anti-Semitism as a catalyst leading to a new perception. The clearest statement of this has been made by Cynthia Ozick, and her seminal essay is examined below, but it is necessary to look at explanations of how more complex versions of anti-Semitism – even those from Jews themselves – came to be so influential. Partly, as with all negatives, there is an element of 'devil's advocate' in this, and like a gadfly, it leads to some genuine thought on the part of creative writers. One of the most satisfactory explanations of the Jew as scapegoat has been expressed by Slavoj Zizek, who places this unreasoned hatred in the category of fantasy: 'it is social antagonism which is primordial, and the figure of the Jew comes second as a fetish which materialises this hindrance . . . the Jew is a Kantian *negative magnitude*: the positivization of the force of "evil" whose activity explains why the order of Good can never fully win.'[8] The notion of a fetish is integral to the representations of the exaggerated Jewishness in comedic forms. Allen, for instance, has no problem in being reductive about Jewish fashion, speech and stereotyping in much of his comedy.

This is more convincing when applied to modern American-Jewish identity, because unlike the approaches using historical perspectives (such as Adorno) it places this irrationality firmly in the site of self-guilt and reactionary morality at the heart of

Roth's problem as a writer striving for free expression within undefined strictures.

A clear instance of how such problems of guilt and duality may be seen from outside, by a gentile writer, might be useful here also. Edmund Wilson, in an essay that seeks to pursue the paradox of the Judaism in the Founding Fathers of New England as opposed to the anti-Semitism that in some way flees from such extremes, insists that 'In the meantime for the Jew . . . it must become almost embarrassing to be taken for a Hebrew prophet on confidential terms with God as for a diabolical demiurge who is out to 'murder progress'.[9] Wilson's view, throughout his essay, is that a revolt from moralism into voluntaryism, as discussed in Chapter 1, leads to immense problems of grandeur, self-importance and the need for an agenda. Eliot Cohen certainly had an agenda, but it was one that proclaimed self-respect. With this in mind, an examination of how these aspects of Jewishness have been mediated will clarify this complex subject.

Cynthia Ozick

There has been a notable and prolonged interest in Ozick's work, as critic and as writer, in recent years. Her fiction, particularly the short stories (examined in the next chapter), have attracted a great deal of attention. But her cultural and polemic essays have perhaps been of even more importance, and it is in her essay 'Toward a New Yiddish', given as an address at the Weizman Institute in Israel in 1970, that we have a challenging new perspective on the American-Jewish writer. The essay confronts American pluralism, and the necessity of being different, relishing difference and cultural variation; even more, she welcomes a separate identity for the American-Jewish writer, while at the same time not dismissing any universality that may be aimed at (as in Bellow for instance). In a preface written to the essay, Ozick explains: 'To be inwardly inhibited from this openness is mental abasement. Intellectual and spiritual freedom means to be peacefully all of a piece always . . . Anything else is parochialism.'[10] She equates parochial with 'ethnic' and so provides the springboard of her argument: that there are achievements in American-Jewish writing that have either been prized for the wrong reasons, or have not been Jewish accomplishments per se. The essay begins by noting George Steiner's celebration of the nationless scholar, the rootless scholar who yet claims brotherhood by intellect rather than religion. This leads into the whole question of Jewishness within the Diaspora. What types of artists represent the achievement of Jews in the Diaspora, then? This leads to a dismissal of a superficiality (using Ginsberg as a case-study) and also to an update of America as the new Promised Land: 'Just as a Jew feels alien to the aesthetic paganism of a churched America, so now he feels alien to the aesthetic paganism of the streets.'[11]

Ozick's claims for the centrality of Jewish ideology are the boldest in the essay. She even cites the nineteenth-century novel as essentially 'Judaized' and takes the idea of the 'Jewish sense of things' being 'to passionately wallow in the human reality'.[12] This leads to a new kind of separateness, a claim for distinction that one reads as a thesis for the true understanding of the American-Jewish novel as an inheritor of these qualities, as if a mantle has been passed from another, pre-modernist milieu to a certain elite group. 'The Jewish writer . . . is all alone, judging culture like mad, while the rest of the culture just goes on *being* culture.'[13]

Her vision, which is written as a powerful assertion of confidence, is that there is a need to come out from the shadow of mimicry and absorption; she notes that 'of all Jews alive today, 45 per cent live in America, and perhaps 50 per cent have English as their mother tongue' and that there has been too much flattering of gentiles. This leads to her ultimate metaphor of the creation of a new Yavneh.[14] As a footnote explains, Yavneh was a small town in which an academy was established, during the Roman conquest. 'It was out of Yavneh that the definition of Jewish life as a community in exile was derived: learning as a substitute for homeland; learning as an instrument of redemption and restoration.'[15]

Consequently, Ozick's New Yiddish is more than a reclamation; it is a quiet revolution in self-perception. She speaks of this idiom as liturgical, and that this should embrace history. It will not be dogmatic in any way, but it should 'hardly be able to avoid the dark side of the earth, or the knife of irony.' and she insists that this will have Talmudic modes. Ultimately, this would lead to a new Yavneh, but whether this is an elite, or a separatist movement, is not clear. What is clear is that, in dismissing George Steiner's *Luftmensch* ideal of Jewish authorship and learning, she adopts the novel as a reinvigorating principle, and implicitly calls for the contact with humanity and with the Judaised novel to be valued rather more than criticism has perhaps allowed.

Is all this simply idealism? Certainly her writings have forced a rethink, and Ozick has found a formula for redefining what is needful if Jewishness rather than Judaism is to be foundational in a new literature. What is easily demonstrated is that in Philip Roth, Grace Paley and Tillie Olson there has been a depth of interest in new versions of being Jewish in modern America: a version that either avoids or belittles such conventional concerns as Orthodox versus assimilated or another Holocaust metaphor. In fact, it could be argued that what Ozick has in her vision is already there in a 'new wave' of writers, and her own stories would be in this new canon.

Ozick's most notable contribution to the debates about Jewishness within new frames of reference such as The 'American Jew' or the 'Diaspora Jew' has been her insistence that the time is right for a revisionist stance to be taken on the basic question of the condition of being a Jew in a postmodern context, and also within the context of complete secularisation. Yet her most prominent media image, and also her academic one within the microcosmic journal-centred intellectualism in which she moves, is as the approachable thinker, with views on everything literary.

Woody Allen

It is easy to disregard Allen in any traditional critical enquiry into the mainline literature of this body of work, but one only has to reflect on the widespread dissemination of Jewishness within American culture generally to understand how potent Allen's texts have been – filmic as well as literary and in a multiplicity of forms. He is, of course, a playwright and essayist. His collections of parodies, articles, sketches and belles-lettres, *Without Feathers*, (1972); *Getting Even*, (1978) and *Side Effects*, (1980), repeat much of his material both as director/playwright and as stand-up comedian in his night-club years. These contain commentaries on Jewish stereotypes and institutions (even to the extent of parodies of Hassidic tales) and give a special insight into particular viewpoints on the way in which the ideologies of Jewish textual formulations have effects on popular imagery.

In his films and plays, Allen has always been concerned to depict the Jewish family, together with a wider history of Jews in the American Diaspora, in a warm, positive and often surreal way; he has dealt with anti-Semitism openly and in comedic method which pokes fun at both Jew and Jew-hater. In *Annie Hall*, for instance, Annie says that 'You're what Granny Hall would call a Real Jew' and Allen makes Alvy Singer hypersensitive about his Jewish nature.[16] Generally, his films rely on the *nebbish* and *schlemiel* – Jewish 'losers' who have similarities to the intellectual 'nerd' of much contemporary fiction. Yet, surprisingly, in his writings, Allen is more concerned with philosophic and wider humanistic values.

Allen's writings centre on two prominent features of the American versions of the Jewish acculturation process: the family and the intellectual. His feeble yet abstracted thinkers and artists are stereotypes of the New York intellectual. In the film versions, there is often a cocoon of book-lined study, highbrow magazines and an ambient classical music of the Vienna school. The protagonist of the writing is similarly often a writer or a thinker. Allen gives gentle satire on the historical perspectives which define this type. In *No Kaddish for Weinstein* for instance, he gives a pastiche of the McCarthyist paranoia: 'Weinstein's so-called friends had all knuckled under to the House Un-American Activities Committee. Blotnick was turned in by his own mother.'[17] In his spoof of *Hassidic Tales* he uses the Jewish scholastic Torah traditions, the annotations of texts, as his target. The commentaries on the made-up stories provide an insight into the narrow textual concerns of this tradition, but somehow provide a philosophic commentary also. 'In this tale, a meaningless question is asked. Not only is the question meaningless but so is the man who journeys to Chelm to ask it.'[18]

Perhaps the most sustained and broadest salvo on the intellectual Jewish American is in the character of Needleman. Here, Allen presents a mock-profile of the man who was everywhere that mattered in contemporary history. The committed politicised individual is the centre of the piece. 'Everywhere in Europe Needleman went, students and intellectuals were eager to help him, awed by his reputation,' and 'It is easy to remember the public Needleman. Brilliant, committed, the author of *Styles of Modes*. But it is the private Needleman I will always fondly recall, the Sandor Needleman who was never without some favourite hat.'[19] Not only does Allen parody a certain type of literary memoir, but he also manages to show the importance of charisma, of public acclaim and media hype that must envelop the intellectual models and heroes of contemporary culture. The worship of the intellect is in question here: the entire tradition of the New York intellectual, post-Lionel Trilling, for instance, comes to mind when reading Needleman's 'life and works'.

Allen is also concerned with the family. His *Radio Days* is largely a celebration of the traditional values of the Jewish immigrant family: its crazy lovableness, and its capacity of love and affection. He places them in the context of the emergence of mass media, and shows a gentile society corrupt and brash, juxtaposed with the internalised satisfactions of the Jewish family. Similarly, in *Annie Hall*, in a split-screen flashback, we see the noisy, talkative and sensual Jewish family at table, alongside the Hall family eating – restrained, polite, anal. In Allen's drama, the family and the individuals who lose this intimacy are seen in sharp contrast to the gentile world. Even in the play/film, *Play it Again, Sam*, the intellectual at the centre, the *nebbish* enmeshed in the make-believe of films and able only to write intellectual commentary on art rather than be creative himself, is pathetic mainly in his loss of his wife and family roots.

Finally, it is tempting to see Allen's work as being concerned with a special kind of secular guilt: he can joke of the Holocaust, ridicule rabbis, perpetuate stereotype analysts and artists, but it is the loss of the human values of the perpetuated *Shtetl* domestication that ultimately concerns him. The macrocosmic world of American business and media provides a playground for the creative talent of the writers and comics, entrepreneurs and academics of his writings; yet there are basic failures which are easily ascribed to a profound loss, a displacement that has gone with the crumbling of Orthodoxy or even practice of worship in any form. The secular Jew is to be reduced to entertainer. Yet there is also a respect for philosophy beneath all this; Allen's people aspire to grandeur and originality. It is as if he is claiming that it is still possible to define the quintessential Jewishness of his people as creativity and mind from inside the enemy camp.

The feeling that Allen's fugitive pieces and narrative pastiche really form a basis for a potentially revisionist fiction in the genre is always present when reading fragments rather than sustained storylines, but naturally, the strengths are in the minimalism.

Paul Auster

In contrast, Paul Auster's essays and discursive prose, which mix autobiography with criticism, speculation with literary history, offer interpretations of Jewishness with a European perspective. He has done more than most to promote the modern revisionist notions of the cliché 'People of the Book' mediation. While his fiction deals with huge perspectives on cultural change and inner-city complexity, his essays and cultural writings have looked outwards to find Jewish elements in basic poetic impulses and in philosophic bases of creativity, taking as his keynote the dictum, from Marina Tsvetayeva, that, 'In this most Christian of worlds/ All poets are Jews.'[20] Together with George Steiner, Auster has probably investigated this profound basal factor in the Jewish consciousness with more breadth of enquiry than most. In fact, George Steiner's essay

'Our Homeland, the Text' is the clearest statement of the theme Auster adopts that is available to the general reader.

Steiner summarises the various relations of the Jewish people to the Old Testament and to textuality in general. His concern, like Auster's, is to understand:

> The tensions, the dialectical relations between an unhoused at-homeness in the text, between the dwelling-place of the script on the one hand . . . and the territorial mystery of the native ground, of the promised strip of land on the other, divide Jewish consciousness.[21]

Steiner's essay deals with the paradox that, 'The book is not that of life,' and that 'The sensibility of the Jew is, par excellence, the medium of the bitter struggle between life and thought, between spontaneous immediacy and analytic reflection.'[21] Where Auster fits in here is in his writing about how this tendency relates both to the Jewish element in literature and poetry, and also to the significance of memory for Jewish thought and imagination. On the literary level, Auster champions the work of the Egyptian-French writer Edmond Jabès; on the autobiographical level, he tells his own story and that of his antecedents by means of examining the shreds of memory and their centrality in self-definition.

In his writing about Jabès, Auster examines the nature of Jews and their relation to the 'book' in a metaphorical and symbolic sense. Memory itself is placed at the core of this. 'The question is the Jewish Holocaust, but it is also the question of literature itself', or in Jabès' own words 'For Judaism and writing are but the same waiting, the same hope, the same wearing out.'[22] Auster expands on Jabès' key text, *The Book of Questions*, and finds there the notion that the book itself had assumed the status of a 'homeland', much as Steiner has argued. It is no great leap of imagination to see how such thinking applies to the American situation. If memory, through texts and self-regarding commentary, is the dynamo behind the literary sustenance of the Jewish writer, then memory and imagination are inextricably linked when the actual Jewish experience of Diaspora and assimilation are written about. Thus, in Bellow and Roth's fictionalisation of dilemmas such as the status of the intellect in a world of mass media and soundbites takes on more resonance: these are social functions which arguably efface the 'memory of the tribe' as it were. The sub-culture is increasingly removed, denigrated and dies through lack of reference. It becomes a cool medium.

Similarly, Auster's advocacy of the poetic truth as opposed to the documentary is linked to his autobiographical book, *The Invention of Solitude* (1982). Here, what begins with an account of a Jewish family history located in Kenosha, Wisconsin, and indeed with the focus of his grandfather buried in the first Jewish cemetery there, develops into a study of that particular version of solitude which is caused by the inevitability of an existential act of killing. As the family drama of wife killing husband emerges, we learn of the roots of his father's strange aloofness with its origins in this internecine hatred and slaying. The first section of the book focuses on his father's living with a sad version of alienation, even from his own self; then the second section expands the idea of dissociation from the past and from memory in life and art, and how the poet aims to counteract this tendency.

In looking at mental derangement, Biblical narrative, and most of all, father–son relationship, Auster attempts to explain his Jewishness (compound with his dependency on the word) by means of this uneasy fusion of literary and familial. For instance, when his success is explained in relation to his father's continuing lack of communication: 'When ever I wrote an article for a magazine, I would set aside a copy and make sure I gave it to him. . . . I think he felt that if the Jews were publishing me, then perhaps there was something to it.'[23]

Towards the conclusion of the book, Auster admits, 'Playing with words in the way A. did as a schoolboy, then, was not so much a search for the truth as a search for the world as it appears in language.'[24] The book also deals with the kind of guilt that emerges from innocence, and the references to Anne Frank adopt her status as she has been mediated in recent decades, as a prototype symbol of this validation through the written word: a reclamation of the meaningful life by means of literary expression, of dependence on the book as a temporary home. From Talmud scholar in the stories of Malamud and Singer, to the more recent expositions by such writers as Auster and Steiner, the importance of the Book as metaphor appears to increase as revisionists address established representations.

Leslie Fiedler

Although Leslie Fiedler's name is associated with mainstream literary criticism by the English reader, there is another perspective on his remarkable achievement. He has produced a considerable body of work that deals with issues of Jewish identity, often polemic, sometimes autobiographical and always employing wide-ranging literary reference. These diverse writings have been collected in *Fiedler on the Roof* (1991) and the essays span decades of essays and addresses. In his Shakespeare criticism he has dealt with the notion of the outsider, and in his writing on the American novel, he has interwoven the Puritan themes which are of course, as Edmund Wilson has shown,[25] paradoxically often Hebraic ideologies assuming 'Puritan' labels. Therefore, it is not surprising that Fiedler has written on Jewish-American literature and identity with a very broad, cosmopolitan view. Indeed, many of his essays use reference to English and European authors and ideas.

The most striking feature of this writing is the attempt to explore the nuances and complexities of definition. In two contrasting essays, he looks at the 'Christian-ness of the Jewish Writer' and the 'Jewishness of the Christian Writer' in America. This gives a valuable account of the problems in dealing with Isaac Bashevis Singer and the status of the Yiddish writer in the present context. Fiedler defines him as American Jewish rather than Jewish-American: 'He is, in short, an émigré . . . one whose identity is involved with a dead past rather than an unborn future.'[26] If definition is to be arrived at by subject-matter, then this must be so. Fiedler points out the narrow 'claustrophobic enclave' that circumscribes Singer's fiction. In other words, the 'America' written here is one in which we are frozen in time, stuck in the pushcart seller/ matchmaker world of the Lower East Side in the bilingual world of Yiddish-home and English-street dichotomy. In asking what is American about Singer's fiction, Fiedler raises the issue of that confrontation between nostalgic literature and film that mediates and represents an anachronistic microcosm of Jewishness in the equivalent of an urban *Shtetl* and the residual Jewishness of the 'New Jewish-American' in modernity. Where Roth's protagonists, for instance, exist in a milieu of media, pop culture, noise and sensuality, where airports and hotels figure prominently, Singer still lodges in a world of arrival and threat. One major criticism is expressed in this way:

> There is in fact almost no male bonding in Singer's overwhelmingly heterosexual world. What we find instead is domestic strife and joy, demonic love; and especially, a desperate metaphysical joining of male and female flesh, which goes beyond the erotic mysticism of the *Zohar* into the realm of heresy.[27]

The Zohar in question here is the memory – in the widest sense – of being essentially Jewish, a chosen person with certain responsibilities. In other words, this is a narrative drive antithetical to modernist forms and subjects. Yet, as Fiedler says in his praise of Singer's one novel set in the United States and published in English, *Enemies, A Love Story*, the main character is like someone who has slept through the horrors of modern Jewish history as in a hayloft, and, Fiedler adds, 'an American version of a Polish hayloft would be nothing more nor less than America itself: the wilderness America of writers Singer has never read.'[28]

Fiedler has always advocated the necessity of the meeting of the alien with the native in American literature, as that implies a readiness to change, to be changed and to actively urge a fresh, invigorating version of, in this case, Jewishness to emerge. For instance, in Heller's *Catch 22*, the author's Jewish sensibility may be evident in the theological dimensions and in the perverse and *schnorrer* (fool or weakling) humour, but it is essentially an American novel, about group ideologies, and about the assimilation process caught up in survival – which comes before race, as does the market and the strength of the dollar. The locus, a site for narrative projection of revised issues of Jewishness, survival and change, has been Fiedler's concern. It goes deeper than literature, though, and he has also written about his own status as an intellectual in this condition.

His essay, 'In Every Generation', sets out his reflections on 'The Two Holocausts', and his conclusion is one that is apparently a widely held position. It leads him to think about the pattern of annihilation and redemption in Jewish history, and his own current status as a new version of his race is clearly given in his conclusion – that he has been complicit in bringing about a 'silent holocaust' within recent history. This relates to Ozick's notion of New Yiddish, in that there is a chance in new writing by American Jews to demonstrate that there is more vibrancy and energy in that silent body of people who have relinquished their Jewishness than Fiedler would allow. He cannot reflect 'self-righteously' on the *Shoah* because he feels the burden of guilt for not being actively Jewish. In adopting the role of travelling literary scholar, he has excelled in that guise that George Steiner speaks of as being the lot of the Jewish bookman: making his intellect and his scholarly domain his only 'land'.

In these ways, then, there have been a series of cultural mediations of the nature of Jewish identity in the American Diaspora. At the centre, Cynthia Ozick is not only celebrating achievement, but also adumbrating a revival with a particular intellectual manifesto that builds on new idioms, together with the language and style of the achievements of the great names of the 1960s. Each of the others has been discussed because of their representative nature. It is difficult to deny that the bookishness of the Jewish nature has found more than a natural proclivity in the New World; it has also established a version of rootedness in a country of the mind, and in some ways, the attainment of intellectual vibrancy and polymathic endeavour has been even more notable than the American-Jewish literature as such.

Notes

1. See Paul Auster, 'Book of the Dead' in *Ground Work* (Faber: London, 1990), pp. 183–9, p. 183. Auster establishes interesting links between Jabes and general tendencies in Jewish writing.
2. See Jeremy Treglown on Yosef Yerushalmi's *Zakhor* (*Guardian* 13 January 1998), p. 32.
3. See George Steiner's essays in *Language and Silence* (Faber: London, 1967). In 'Our Homeland, the Text', he ranges widely over theology and literature, noting patterns of statement concerning the metaphorical applications of text and book.
4. See Emanuel Litvinoff (ed.), introduction to *The Penguin Book of Jewish Short Stories* (Penguin: London, 1979).
5. See Amos Oz, *Unto Death*, (Fontana: London, 1977). Oz uses the Crusades as the setting.
6. See Mark Krupnick, 'The Menorah Journal Group and the Origins of Modern Jewish-American Radicalism', *SAJL*, vol. 8 no. 2, (Fall, 1989).
7. Ibid.
8. See Slavoj Zizek, *The Plague of Fantasies*, (Verso: London and New York, 1997), p. 76.
9. See Edmund Wilson, *A Piece of My Mind* (W.H. Allen: London, 1957), p. 80.
10. Cynthia Ozick, 'The New Yiddish', in *Art and Ardor* (Alfred Knopf: New York, 1983), p. 152.
11. Ibid., p. 163.
12. Ibid., p. 165.
13. Ibid., p. 167.
14. Ibid., 172.
15. Ibid.
16. See *Annie Hall* (1977), in which Allen purposely makes Singer almost paranoid about anti-Semitism, and then includes comic parody of the WASP attitudes beneath the stereotypes.
17. See Woody Allen, *Without Feathers* (Sphere Books: London, 1978), p. 196.
18. See Woody Allen, *Getting Even* (Vintage: New York, 1978), p. 48.
19. See Woody Allen, *Side Effects* (New English Library: New York, 1975), p. 9.
20. Paul Auster, *The Invention of Solitude* (Faber: London, 1988), p. 95.
21. See George Steiner, 'Our Homeland, the Text', in *Language and Silence* (Faber: London, 1963), p. 307. Steiner's discussion summarises succinctly the issues related to metaphors of 'the people of the Book' themes in commentary on this literature.
22. See Auster, 'Book of the Dead', in *Groundwork*.
23. Auster, *The Invention of Solitude*, p. 61.
24. Ibid., p. 161.

25. See Wilson, *A Piece of My Mind*. In his essay 'The Jews', Wilson speculates on the paradox of the early Puritans and New England ideology being Hebraic in sources and spirit, yet anti-Semitism even among intellectuals, developed from the same mentality.
26. Leslie Fiedler, *Fiedler on the Roof* (David Godine: Boston, 1981), p. 76.
27. Ibid., p. 79.
28. Ibid., p. 83.

8

Relocating Moralism in Jewish America: Past and Present in Chaim Potok and the later Saul Bellow

Jewish-American fiction since the 1960s can make large claims. The achievements have been impressive, and limited space in this survey means that only brief mention can be made to writers who have written on Jewish experience, but have not made that subject the central concern of their work. Undoubtedly, Chaim Potok, Philip Roth, Saul Bellow and Cynthia Ozick have made significant contributions in this respect, and their work will be the main focus of this chapter and the next. It will also be necessary to look at more contemporary writers, but the first task is to define the importance of two novelists who have written in completely different ways about Jewish America: Chaim Potok and Saul Bellow. Nevertheless, while they represent polarities of that immense spectrum of life and experience, they have something fundamental in common. They are preoccupied with the status of the intellect within Jewish identity, albeit with different uses in mind.

Chaim Potok is concerned with Orthodox dilemmas, and specifically with Hassidic Jewry in contrast to the intellectual confrontations with modernity in America. Saul Bellow has little interest in Orthodoxy as a subject, but contrasts belief with philosophical pluralism and eclecticism. In other words, both writers deal with the absence of faith, but Potok pinpoints open conflict; Bellow copes with postmodern conditions of culture and thought. In each case, though, it may be argued that the central importance of the intellect is never in doubt, but Potok sees the mind as a functioning, utilitarian device; it is to be applied and directed. Bellow sees intellect as partly a burden on the human condition, but paradoxically also a liberating principle. Both are interested in the imagination within liberal America and both see the threats of the 'junk culture' of urban modernity as fertile material for the exploration of that recession of Jewishness that has marked this literature, from their early work through to younger writers such as Jyl Lynn Felman (who is discussed in the next chapter).

Chaim Potok

Potok, a New Yorker and a rabbi, has been mainly interested in the novel as a didactic device. His novels present the dilemmas of Orthodox religious practice in the Diaspora in bold and starkly simple terms. His novel sequence built on the contrasting characters of Danny and Reuven, *The Chosen* (1966) and *The Promise* (1969) skilfully balances a storyline of open conflict between religious and secular and also Orthodox and Reform Judaism with a prominent documentary strain that informs and explains basic beliefs as the plot develops. The strength of the novels is that Potok assumes that the subjects will be taken as massively important, by readers of all persuasions. Even the gentile reader will feel the sense of urgency and significance when the Torah is discussed and explained.

But Potok also makes the characters real; the presence of secular America is always there, from the opening section of *The Chosen*, in which a baseball match is the main focus. We are always given a historical summary, and the people are located in specific places. But whereas in *The Chosen*, everything is attached to an explanation of Hassidism, *The Promise* admits raucous, chaotic, threatening America into a central position. There is less of the didactic element than in the first novel. However, Potok's didacticism is never too trying, and is always done with a lively narrative drive, as when Danny explains Hassidic history and self-definition, and Potok includes touches of convincing criticism:

That is what happened to Polish Jewry. By the eighteenth century, it had become a degraded people. Jewish scholarship was dead. In its place came empty discussions about matters that had no practical connection with the desperate needs of the masses of Jews empty, nonsensical arguments over minute points of Talmud.[1]

Yet the discussion of learned books and dogma is exactly what Potok manages to make fictionally interesting most of the time. Only occasionally does the didactic tone deviate into a style of too deliberate and simplified material, as in the account of the Depression: 'Those were terrible days, black days.'[2]

In *The Promise*, with its more vibrant account of a family caught up in divisions created by the past and by a too extreme adherence to standards and convention, there is far more constructive use made of the religion-against-dogma theme. The freethinking Abraham Gordon and his writing are at the centre:

Abraham Gordon had published five books. Each of these books had the same word written on the half-title page: 'This is the book of an apostate. Those who fear God are forbidden to read it.' I grew to loathe the writer of those words.[3]

The writer is Reuven, and the friendship with Danny is continued, but while their friendship still has its interest, the novel is dominated by the strong presence of the teacher, Rav Kalman, whose draconian regime and unbending adherence to Orthodox belief lead him to victimise Reuven, who has championed Gordon. Potok interweaves the story of the young men's friendship with this confrontation. However, the most successful element in the novel is the gradual revelation of Kalman's nature and his personal inner crisis.

Finally, the emotional and intellectual centre of the novel is the explanation of the 'remnants of the concentration camps' who have 'brought their spark to the broken streets of Williamsburg, and men like Rav Kalman who were not Hasidim felt swayed by their presence and believed themselves to be zealous guardians of the spark'.[4] Potok's insistence that we need to

understand both the value of isolation and the need for community and inheritance of values leads to a re-examination of
that moralism in nineteenth-century America which tended to
reach beyond sectarian practice and specific belief-systems. A
constant presence in the novel is the almost mythic scholar and
believer, the Kotsker Rebbe.

> He was a lonely, bitter, angry man. I think he really hated
> being a rebbe. He wanted rational and spiritual perfection in
> everyone, and in himself too. It all tore him to pieces finally
> and he ended up denying the existence of God and broke
> down and withdrew.[5]

Chaim Potok's work is primarily a dialectic; reading his
novels means handling a series of arguments and counter-
arguments, mostly founded in the polarities of extremism
and moderation, of compromise with assimilation and insistence on tradition. But whichever variety of Jewishness is in
question, there is never any doubt that such lives are special
and valuable, and that extremism can easily be understood.
What does emerge very clearly is the representation of a moral
corruption when assimilation is total. In the long opening
scene of *The Chosen*, in which the young people are swindled
at a country fair, Potok textualises a version of Jewishness that
shows he is capable of a more complex and ambiguous representation than is generally perceived. The young people speak
in Hebrew, and the old man who runs the stall listens, then
intrudes and exploits them. He speaks to them as a friend and
uses a Yiddish word. He takes their money by pretending that
they have a common bond in their immigrant experience and
in their European-Jewish roots. The whole episode is a fore-
boding of what is to come – that the real enemies to harmony
and assurance are in the ranks of Jews themselves.

In his books on the painter Asher Lev, Potok is just as
insistent on polarities, but this time it is a contrast of sacrifice
and freedom. Asher is a born creative artist; his father sacrifices
his life for the cause of European and Russian Jewry. Young
Asher simply draws and paints the simple truths of life, even to
the point of blasphemy, and his father lives in the shadow of

the superstition and mysticism of a European Ur-Judaism that still dominates lives in modern America. His father is totally dedicated to a cause that eradicates his own self. Asher also does this, with art as the all-consuming deity, but the common bond is never a uniting force always divisive.

The threat of the 'dark side' – the 'sitra alta' – is his father's threat, and Asher tells his own story with a stark simplicity that is totally compelling. Asher dreams of his mythic ancestor who questions the worth of the art Asher produces. The voice frightens him and constantly questions his reason for living. The dark side may be in the art. But Asher even draws Jesus, and in his father's response to this, we have a clarification of one of the main themes of the novel. The moralism of modern America will have to account for such thought as this:

My drawings had touched something fundamental to his being. He kept talking about my drawings of 'that man'. He would not pronounce the name. Did I know how much Jewish blood had been spilled because of that man? Did I know how many Jews had been killed in the name of that man during the Crusades.[6]

Potok locates the problems of modern American Jews and Jewish identity not in the multiplicity of forms, practices and self-definitions, but in the fundamentalist, entrenched perspectives – ideologies that are, however, totally comprehensible when explored in a fictional construct. Where much traditional fiction about Jews living in American cities with 'buried' lives of anonymity and solitariness depend on focal events such as the Holocaust or on some ancient pogrom, Potok reveals the dissent within the ranks of the Jewish Orthodoxy. He often sees only deterioration in the assimilated, but never flinches from his self-imposed need to treat the progress of the intellect as paramount. His moralism in the modern chaos of secular urban America is inadequate. His novels challenge such a concept, but it still has to be placed, because it is there, in the persistent American openness to pluralist faiths, individual worth and a sense of common decency. But if it is not good enough to live as a 'good Jew' within assimilation, what needs to be understood about the alternatives? Asher Lev's creativity is an excellent device for revealing this issue. In the end, it is Asher's mythic ancestor who resolves and placates. But this is done only through a terrible vision of truth that the artist, regardless of creed, must confront. In Paris, Asher does so: 'Now the man who had once been a child asked it again and wondered if the giving and the goodness might have been acts born in the memories of screams and burning flesh.'[7]

Saul Bellow

From his story 'The Old System' in *Mosby's Memoirs* (1968) to *The Actual* (1997), Saul Bellow has written a body of fiction that departs from previous writing in that his protagonists are gentiles; but he has also written about Jewish characters also, and mixed the two concerns of philosophic commentary on modernity and the nature of the assimilated Jew in most fictions. It is interesting to note that, whereas in the early fiction there was an intense interest in versions of Jewish survival in the new cities and in the changing self-perceptions of the third-generation people, in much recent work the focus has been on extensions of his own perceptions of that particular element of Jewish intellectualism which has informed a certain world-view, from *Partisan Review* in the 1940s right up to *The New York Review of Books* and the university culture of bellettrism as discussed in the previous chapter. Bellow's own sources for this fiction lie partly in his Chicago background. He makes Chicago an archetype of the criminal and junk culture that envelops the characters, from Citrine in *Humboldt's Gift* (1975) through to Corde in *The Dean's December* (1982).

There has been a critique of 'late Bellow' that sees his later work as quite densely reflective and bookish. Martin Amis, for instance, has written a study of this work which typifies this view. Amis sees much to admire, but notes the concentration on the physicality, the quotidian real in the Bellow's dislikes:

While he concedes that America is now ruled by drunkards, liars and venal illiterates, Bellow decides that the most vivid

symptoms of distemper can be found a little closer to home
City cops moonlight for the mob as hired executioners.
Meanwhile, 'we care' stickers are gummed to the walls of
supermarkets and loan corporations.[8]

Certainly, these novels and stories are often about an uncar-
ing society. Bellow appears to use his academic training as an
anthropologist and see human beings as purely functional
animals. But there is a current of Romanticism running
through the fiction, and Bellow is often at pains to depict
the vestiges of a poetic, highly subjective strain in his heroes.

In fact, the idea of a hero is the proper starting-point in
evaluating the later work. Again, Amis points out the nature of
Bellow's heroes:

> His heroes are well tricked out with faults, neuroses, spots of
> commonness: but not a lot of Bellow's intellectuality is
> withheld from their meditations. They represent the author
> at the full pitch of intellectual endeavour, with the simple
> proviso that they are themselves non-creative. They are
> thinkers, teachers, *readers*.[9]

This is a very useful insight. If one summarises the condition
of the main subjects/narrators of the works listed above, from
Dr. Braun to Trellman, what they have in common is that they
explain or are explained in terms of their cerebral being. They are
often literary, bookish, observers of life. When they participate,
it gives the occasion for a struggle to understand. In the story
'The Old System', Braun is estranged from his sister, who is now
dying. In his journey to her deathbed, he questions the two
edifices of his being: residual Jewishness and the need to experience feeling rather than intellect. Bellow is more direct about
Judaism in this story than in any other place in his later work.
From this story onwards, he shifts into the secular world, where
being a Jew is a matter of intellect, with feeling an expensive
indulgence. Yet Braun's inner turmoil is dramatically given:

> On the airport bus, he opened his father's copy of the Psalms.
> The black Hebrew letters only gaped at him like open mouths

with tongues hanging down, pointing upward, flaming but dumb. He tried – forcing. It did no Good.

Braun also recalls his godmother, Aunt Rose, as the 'dura mater' of the Jewish family. Bellow represents the immigrants as dour, serious, immersed in themselves, not in America. Braun has been reborn, and it is this rebirth into a new man that intrigues Bellow, from this story on into the latest explorations of survival and success. Increasingly, his heroes are successful. We have a university dean, a famous writer, a botanist, a businessman and so on. On the surface, it seems that Bellow is becoming increasingly interested in the hollowness of the secular victories gained by the assimilated. But what marks his fiction as significant in finding metaphors and motifs for the predicament of the Jewish-American intellectual is the presence of Europe. Bellow insists on relating the primacy of the intellect and creativity as the only way to understand the human condition, yet this is grounded in the thinkers of the past. His later novels constantly refer to philosophers, critics, scientists and others, as examples of the ongoing human effort to comprehend. Again, 'The Old System' is a turning point, because Braun's final sorrow is not the specific death of his sister but the universal problem of understanding the uniqueness of each life. 'And again, why these particular forms – these Isaacs and these Tinas? When Dr. Braun closed his eyes, he saw . . . molecular processes – the only true heraldry of being.'[11]

Bellow accelerates these questions as his work advances, introducing love as the directing concept, similar to the way love is examined in Auden's poetry: a version of the Romantic aesthetic at one point, but a more objectified idea at another. Each succeeding novel handles this in some way. His approach to writing about the Jewish experience in America, though, becomes more directly concerned with the European base than with the physical reality of the Jewish Diaspora in the USA. A clear way to see the difference between Bellow's working of this material and the norm is to note, in passing, how Joseph Heller treats the theme comically in his satire, *Good as Gold* (1976). His hero Gold is to write a book on the Jewish experience in America. He admits that he has no idea what that is, and has to ask his family, and even his students, about Jewish holidays. He is treated as a child by his hectoring father, and Heller uses the stand-up comic technique of such performers as Jackie Mason to satirise the absurdity of any direct attempt to deal with the subject.[12] All this helps to specify exactly what Bellow's achievement has been. He has examined those qualities of the Jewish sense of self and being that infiltrate the senses, the aesthetic perceptions and even the creativity of the modern American intellectual who carries a kind of *Mitteleuropa* sensibility inside him through the 'mean streets' of Chicago or New York. Philip Roth has done similar things with his persona-narrator of Zuckerman, which we will deal with in Chapter 9.

In interviews and articles, Bellow has often given insights into the nature of these people – the types who populate his streets, boulevards and office blocks. He has talked of this setting as 'The high comedy of the intellectual in the never-never land of the heart.'[13] His intention has clearly been to diagnose a malaise with its roots in the 'junk culture' of the American urban wastes: 'These intellectuals, now totally political, have gone over to junk culture . . . After a day of unremitting crisis, they want pleasant entertainment. They're not rushing home to read act three of *The Tempest*.'[4] As a result, his later fiction throws up certain representative characters. It could be argued that there are three basic types: the central protagonist, a man caught up in political and moral turmoil, with a need to discover love; the cultural mountebank, a dilettante who dazzles but is semi-criminal and the underworld prole – the gangster, the brute or the sensualist.

In *Humboldt's Gift* (1975), the hero, Charlie Citrine, is the creation of the immensely charismatic Humboldt, poet and talker, intellectual and bluffer. Humboldt has been a man who has been adopted by the politics of the system. He leaves Charlie with success in the material world, and a hankering for literary success of the higher type. Charlie is trying to launch a literary magazine, *The Ark*, and has employed Thaxter, a fraud with artistic eccentricities, to produce this. But Charlie is also caught up in a revenge plot with the gangster, Cantabile, and the novel can therefore shift from cultural satire to farcical crime-spoof very swiftly. The result is a mix of social comment and political satire. But everything about Charlie depends on the resonant presence of Humboldt. Citrine even philosophises with the gravitas of his master (and of Bellow himself): 'Under pressure of public crisis the private sphere is being surrendered.'[15] The aphorisms are gradually more and more convincing as Charlie matures through hard experience.

Humboldt was 'the son of neurotic immigrants'; and Charlie recalls his mentor's complexity. He insists that he was a 'fanatical schemer' but at heart, Bellow makes sure that we see Humboldt's central importance in the scheme of the novel's design:

> One of Humboldt's themes was the perennial human feeling that there was an original world, a home-world, which was lost. Sometimes he spoke of poetry as the merciful Ellis Island where a host of aliens began their naturalisation and of this planet as a thrilling but insufficiently humanised imitation of that home-world.[16]

Charlie refers to his Yiddish-speaking mother, to Humboldt's fear of American racism and to the violent Cantabile as similarly real threats – all elements that formed this insufficiently humanised imitation of a truly human, carting place. As Bellow develops these themes, it is gradually apparent that it is the need for friendship, the escape from solitude, which characterises his vision. Charlie's marriage is finished. The hard, sad world of the old men in the city baths where Charlie is hounded by the murderous Cantabile reflects the melancholy isolation of the ageing male, the lonely man of the harshly utilitarian suburbs. Humanisation is done through books, of course, and through the inheritance of European culture, but first, Bellow insists, we have to evade the fear of love and friendship that has somehow settled in the soul.

Increasingly, it is the fear of failure, of losing face, and of not sustaining the performance of the professional self that erodes these capacities for love and fulfilment. In *The Dean's December* (1982) Bellow makes his hero a gentile. Corde has gone to Europe with his wife. Her mother is dying. Back home in the

States, there has been a murder and a student is involved. Also, Corde has written articles for *Harper's* that are not fitting; they are too indulgent and woolly. We are made aware of the subtexts which form our social selves, our successes and failures, and how these impinge on relationships. As Corde waits and smokes in a Romania which somehow symbolises the monochrome, enervated human condition in the non-functional Old World, the New World has its machinations against human values.

Corde's articles have let the side down. 'The Dean's appointment had been a mistake, and it was the Provost's job to clear up the mess. Corde was an outsider, he hadn't come up from the academic ranks.'[17] In this novel, Bellow has a great deal to say, through his characters, about the moral dilemmas of America. For instance, in explaining his politics, Corde says: 'I said that America no more knew what to do with this black underclass than it knew what to do with its children. It was impossible to educate either, or to bind either to life.'[18] In a paradoxical way, Bellow's characters often retreat into the morality constructed in the European baselands, in order to understand or even try to change, their new adopted land. In *More Die of Heartbreak* (1987) we have this comment about Uncle Benn:

> I've already said that there was a Russian flavour to Uncle as there is to many Russian Jews. Somebody ought to do a monograph on the Jewish responses to the various lands of their exile, those in which their Hearts expanded and those which were most forbidding.[19]

It is worth noting here that, as Ray Keenoy and Saskia Brown have pointed out, 'Contemporary America, far from serving as a shelter from trauma, only confirms the triumph of "dark romanticism" over Enlightenment Humanism.'[20] The Enlightenment in Europe, encompassing the *Haskallah* (Jewish Enlightenment), promoted the tenets of tolerance and understanding, but also considered humanity in an egalitarian way which precluded much of the racism behind America's humanitarian image. Therefore, for Bellow's heroes to perceive America as a place that has 'expanded' or been 'forbidding' to their hearts is particularly interesting. In this context it is so because Bellow goes to great lengths to make his heroes civilised, receptive to ideas, sensitive, creative and reflective.

Love and friendship, then, are prominent in Bellow's crusade for an understanding of the human adaptations that have occurred in these 'junk culture' crises. 'For centuries love has made suckers of us' says Uncle Benn.[21] However, Bellow is not afraid to introduce a neo-Romantic aesthetic into his heroes' sensibilities, in order that they may lay claim to being redemptive voices, speakers for a new Enlightenment. Their enemy is disenchantment more than the world of media-led soundbite culture, with its instant gratification and escape from true thought. As his characters sustain themselves by thinking, they also continue to dream of man's perfectibility. In *More Die of Heartbreak*, Bellow contrasts his hero's father with his uncle. Uncle Benn is seen as 'a shlump, an incompetent' but he is defended in this way: 'He missed out on Benn's largeness of mind. Large-mindedness and strength of body were the big things in Greek antiquity.'[22]

In *More Die of Heartbreak*, it becomes apparent that Bellow is explaining the self-doubts of an elite. But the tone is one of relaxed uncertainty. Kenneth knows the failings of Benn, a man 'with his head up his arse' according to his father. But Kenneth, a Russophile, is also aware of classical ideals of perfection of mind and body. It emerges that Benn and Kenneth typify an enclave of 'barbarous America', as Kenneth calls it. The proposition that one must choose literature or life begins to be significant. Kenneth expresses it well:

> But I grant you the difficulty of making a case for enduring human bonds, everybody fears being suckered through the affections, although cynical people still adopt a lip-service attitude towards them. Philip Larkin, a poet much admired, writes, 'In everyone there sleeps a sense of life according to love.' But the sense *is* sleeping.[23]

Bellow's textualisation of the enclave of thinkers is observed moving towards a condition of reflective, discursive prose. The assimilated Jewish intellectual life, one Bellow himself admits to having experienced in certain influential phases, clearly presents us with a definition of how a sector of American-Jewishness wishes to express itself. Kenneth discusses his reading in depth – French and Russian classics – and in terms of understanding the world. His uncle is a don, a scientist, immersed in brainwork. At times, this heavy concentration on bookishness becomes a substitute for narrative integration. But the ploy is more subtle yet. Bellow carefully constructs this character in such a way that he is allowed freedom to reflect almost as if we have passages from a commonplace book. This lets a developing reflection on Jewishness emerge, as in such statements as, 'In Paris I've heard the clever opinion advanced that the ghetto is a replica of the Judean desert and that the Jews escape decadence because they lack vegetal elements.'[24]

In fact, it would not be untrue to suggest that this is about the wrong choice. It is a warning about joining the enclave of bookishness. In this way, Bellow elaborates on his thesis that if Jewish-American cultural definition is done by means of intellect, by placing the importance of thought and Enlightenment enquiry at the top of definitions in this respect, then where is the heart? Where is the sensibility that generates the poetry in a Humboldt or even in a minor figure such as Benn? In addition, Bellow has fun at the expense of this continuing stance of heightened intellect that his characters adopt. Barbara Gitenstein has seen an element of the Yiddish mock-heroic in Bellow, and this partly explains what is going on here. Again, part of this mock-heroic is a contrast of soul and mind: 'This realism is of a special kind. Though a highly intellectual realist, Bellow also insists that too much intellection must be resisted.' She mentions Sholem Aleichem's Tevye as an example of the mind–heart duality: 'his value is in the goodness of his heart'. Even more relevant to the present discussion is the suggestion that, as in the Yiddish tradition, 'the writer writes because it is necessary, because of his love of humanity'.[25] In other words, Bellow's unique narrative style, with its incisive mix of discursive thought and significant digression (owing much to nineteenth-century Russian fiction) can be placed in a tradition other than the American. The intensely 'overhumanising' nature of the Jewish imagination is also suggested by Gitenstein as a feature of Bellow's writing, notable from *Humboldt's Gift* onwards.[26]

Finally, Bellow's later fiction intensifies his interest in the enigma of being human. What he says in his exploration of love and relationships undoubtedly forms part of a continuing Jewish vision, complicated but enriched by the Diaspora viewpoint. As Kenneth says at the end of *More Die of Heartbreak*, 'The secret of our being still asks to be unfolded.'[27] Bellow has also moved on significantly from that obsession with the past as the only directing principle for American-Jewish fiction that seemed to dominate in the 1960s. As Ted Solotaroff has said,

> Harold Rosenberg, who saw more creative possibilities than Howe does in the 'open community' that American Jews now inhabit, still comes back to the idea that Jewish experience is grounded in the possibility of linking oneself 'with the collective and individual experience of earlier Jews'.[28]

Bellow has certainly reminded writers that looking to European Enlightenment ideals and contrasting them with the bland, perfunctory nature of modern urban life in America is a fruitful mode of fictionality. Despite his concentration on multiple interpretations of isolation and deprivation, of self-delusion and retreat, there is still a high level of fascination with the human comedy in his later work. Yet it has to be reinforced that Bellow always insists on a curiosity about his creations that extends to analysis. In his most recent work, the novella *The Actual* (1997), Harry is oriental-looking, 'not in the real world' and 'a first class noticer' as old Adletsky, the millionaire says. From the beginning he refers to his own life story as 'exile'. He mysteriously discloses that he has unfinished 'emotional business' in Chicago, and the phrase sets the ambiguous tone for the storyline that follows. Bellow invites the reader to judge – old Adletsky in particular – and then establishes his people at a safe distance, objectifying their lives, caught up in various transactions that mix 'emotional' with more normal commercial varieties of 'business'. Again, Bellow ensures than Jewish origins are explained, and done so with the usual gentle hints at strategies of survival. Amy's background for instance is: 'Her people were respectable. German-speaking Jews from Odessa, educated in the gymnasium. They had brought Amy up to *look* virtuous.'[29]

The Actual is particularly interesting in that the narrator, Harry, is deliberately presented as having an ambiguous attitude to the settled married lives with which he is concerned. The three couples who figure in the novella consist of a millionaire and his wife, a businessman and his wife who has plotted his death but been accepted back, and the beloved Amy, whose dead husband's body is being removed and taken to another plot. Wealth and the Jewish immersion in materialist society is the centre of the work. Bellow purposely refers to Jews in the comfortable world of business success, so that his narrator can form contrasts and criticisms with regard to the opposing world of the mind. Harry has been distanced from reality and from the commitment involved in relationships. There are cryptic remarks, however, which relate to earlier Bellovian themes:

Bourgeois habits have no claim to be sanctified or eternalised. All that is mainstream stuff, and I've never really been a mainstream type. I've always been a fairly hard judge of people. Especially if they thought too well of themselves.[30]

In his latest work, then Bellow has condensed a strand of thought that may be detected throughout his work: finally Harry proposes to Amy, the woman he has loved ever since they first met. But it has not been as simple as a mere contrast of withdrawal from the world and immersion in what Conrad called its 'destructive element'. Harry has been a cold analyst. Adletsky recruits him into his advisory 'Brains' Trust' because he observes life, sees it coolly and objectively. Bellow's later work has been primarily an exposition of the presence of a neo-Romanticism within the utilitarian, pragmatic world of American modernity, where a person is valued for functions and contributions to a multiplicity of systems.

Both Potok and Bellow are interested in the demands of the private and the personal life, but Potok's constraints are established and dogmatic; they imprison only willing prisoners, as is

the case with Asher Lev's father, for instance. Bellow's heroes
are, like Philip Roth's, unable to cope with freedoms when
these involve relinquishing segments of a formative past. There
is also the fear of commitment beneath so many of the stories.
Dr. Braun in 'The Old System' has allowed his own mind to
build the fears which paralyse his emotions at the crisis-point
which forms the story. Cynthia Ozick's verdict on Bellow's
essential achievement is a convincing one. She summarises his
characteristics, but adds this:

> To this thickness of community and these passions of mind
> Saul Bellow has added a distinctive ingredient, not new on
> any landscape, but shamelessly daring now in American
> imaginative prose. Let the narrator of 'Cousins' reveal it:
> 'We enter the world without prior notice, we are manifested
> before we can be aware of manifestation.' Bellow has risked
> mentioning the Eye of God.[31]

Ozick goes on to say that this urge to bring in a metaphysics
into narrative leads Bellow to make a more profound social
criticism than is normally achieved. It is the depth of reading in
Russian and European literature that has made the Bellovian
difference; but whatever this factor is, what cannot be doubted
is that he has constructed a vast range of Jewish intellectual and
philosophical vibrancy from within the material comforts of
the American Diaspora, and succeeded in establishing 'the
Jewish difference' in modern American writing. When Bellow
is explicit about the Jewishness of his creations, it is usually to
establish another perspective on the society rather than the
individual psyche. In *The Actual*, for instance, Harry (primarily
identified as having oriental features) refers to his Jewishness:
'When you are identified as a Jew, you are fair game. The rules
of behaviour change and you become, in a sense, expend-
able.'[32] This, when applied to Adletsky's vast wealth, had the
added irony that riches are the best form of assimilation. For
Bellow, however, it has always seemed wise to insist on the
emotions and the intellect as the true riches of the individual.
The sense of loss, and of egregious past mistakes or wrong
choices, always gives his fiction a quality of melancholy.

Redemption is possible in the resources within the self, and fiction for Bellow can describe the anterooms to these realisations.

Notes

1. Chaim Potok, *The Chosen* (Penguin: London, 1970), p. 107.
2. Ibid., p. 187.
3. Chaim Potok, *The Promise* (Penguin: London, 1971), p. 69.
4. Ibid., p. 179.
5. Ibid., p. 213.
6. Chaim Potok, *My Name is Asher Lev* (Penguin: London, 1973), p. 152.
7. Ibid., p. 282.
8. Martin Amis, *The Moronic Inferno* (Penguin: London, 1987), p. 20. Amis notes also Bellow's unique place in witnessing the formation of 'The American Idea' and this is part of the conclusion of the assessment.
9. Ibid., p. 17.
10. Saul Bellow, 'The Old System', in *Mosby's Memoirs and Other Stories* (Penguin: London, 1971), p. 79.
11. Ibid., p. 83.
12. Joseph Heller, *Good as Gold* (Cape: London, 1979), p. 110. Heller is perhaps a representative of the iconoclastic school, debunking the foundations of such issues. (See p. 1: 'I never even realised I was Jewish until I was practically grown-up.').
13. See Saul Bellow, *It All Adds Up* (Penguin: London, 1995), p. 323.
14. Ibid., p. 326.
15. Saul Bellow, *Humboldt's Gift* (Penguin: London, 1976), p. 250.
16. Ibid., p. 24.
17. Saul Bellow, *The Dean's December* (Secker and Warburg: London, 1982), p. 178.
18. Ibid., p. 201.
19. Saul Bellow, *More Die of Heartbreak* (Secker and Warburg: London, 1987), p. 31.
20. See Ray Keenoy and Saskia Brown, *The Babel Guide to Jewish Fiction* (Boulevard: London, 1998), p. 41. Their account summarises the common view of Bellow as mixing high seriousness with comic invention.
21. Bellow, *More Die of Heartbreak*, p. 10.
22. Ibid., p. 39.
23. Ibid., p. 44.
24. Ibid., p. 56.
25. Barbara Gitenstein, 'Saul Bellow and the Yiddish Literary Tradition' *SAJL*, vol.11 no.1 (Spring 1992) pp. 24–43. Gitenstein provides speculation on the origins of Bellow's imaginative and often unconsciously created material.

26. Ibid., p. 28.
27. Bellow, *More Die of Heartbreak*, p. 330.
28. See Ted Solotaroff and Nessa Rappoport (eds), The *Schocken Book of Contemporary Jewish Fiction* (Schocken: New York, 1992), Introduction, p. xiv.
29. Saul Bellow, *The Actual* (Viking: London, 1997), p. 23.
30. Ibid., p. 97.
31. See Cynthia Ozick, 'What Drives Saul Bellow?', in *What Henry James Knew* (Vintage: London, 1994), pp. 238–48, p. 246. Ozick adds an interesting dimension to Bellow studies: she notes his 'metaphysical radar'.
32. Bellow, *The Actual*, p. 44.

9

New Directions across the Generations: From Philip Roth to Cynthia Ozick

One notable feature of Jewish-American fiction since the 1980s has been the continuing contributions of writers whose reputations were made decades earlier. Although mainly associated with the 1960s, Philip Roth has expanded the scope of his fiction and his later work has been notably more ambitious, more densely layered and more concerned with ideology. Also, Henry Roth has made a reappearance with his trilogy (discussed in the conclusion) and Saul Bellow has equally shown that he is concerned with far more than simply the crisis of the Jewish intellectual in American modernity. This survival of earlier voices is far more than that. A reading of this work bears out the view that the glib acceptance of terms such as assimilation and accommodation are far more complex and multi-dimensional than might be thought with a cursory glance.

The other notable development that has become prominent in this fiction is the more openly assertive treatment of the modern Jewish experience in terms of a new use of the materials of the past. Cynthia Ozick's work in part exemplifies this. Although her writing in criticism and belles-lettres is perhaps the most well-known aspect of her work, there is no doubt that a few of her stories have caused extended critical debate about the newer perspectives on Jewish experience and historical or cultural positions. In fact, Ozick's fiction shows that there is an argument for a new siting of this revisionist perspective and younger writers such as Jyl Lynn Felman (also discussed in the conclusion) have deepened the examination of the generational change implicit in the creative insights of this corpus of work.

What is common to all these writers, however, is the need to explore the fate of Jewish-Americans within the vortex of Bellow's junk culture in one aspect, but also, and more importantly, in the social relationships of WASP America. That is, these are questions of assimilation in terms of the unseen, the quiet fusions that have occurred over a generation.

Philip Roth

Since his early work in the 1960s, Philip Roth has grown increasingly interested in several significant strands of Jewish experience in America. These have been mainly: the spiritual and intellectual life in the new suburbia; the persistence of a European sensibility; and the condition of the American Jew living in the new version of voluntaryism in a liberal culture open to postmodern uncertainties. His work in the years between 1972, when *The Breast* appeared, and 1997 his most recent novel, *American Pastoral* (1997), has moved from a use of motifs and images based on Europe and a version of *Mitteleuropa* Jewish cultural life to a more profound preoccupation with the use of a writer-narrator (Zuckerman) in order to use autobiographical material more adventurously than in the early work.

Critical interest has partly centred on the modernism in the novels dealing with Zuckerman's growth as a writer and American. The angst of modernism has interested some writers[1] whereas others have pointed out the idea of versions of exile in these novels[2]. Certainly, in the novels dealing with Zuckerman's life and eventual visit to Prague in search of Kafka, Roth manages to write about some feelings of revisiting the past that persist in much modern Jewish-American writing. Underneath all this is a current of enquiry about what it means to inherit Jewish history and how the European past always insists on a modern presence. Much of this is in *The Professor of Desire* (1977) but Zuckerman re-emerges in the three novels published as *The Zuckerman Trilogy* in 1989: *Zuckerman Unbound* (1981),

The Anatomy Lesson (1983) and *The Counterlife* (1986). Zuckerman is an alter-ego, a flexible persona, the authorial device for
exploring the essence of fiction. But there is also the character
of Tarnopol, and Zuckerman is the creation of Tarnopol, the
creation of Roth.

The fundamental stylistic ploy is these fictions if meta-fiction. Roth's interest in the fictionality of the text fuses with his
intensifying theme of the specifically Jewish strand in his
creativity. In other words, his autobiographical base is simply
a study in the metamorphosis of the life data itself into the
material of fiction. One effect of this is to suggest that we are to
fabricate with Zuckerman an interpretation of the novel as the
comprehensive art of modern society. Meta-fiction allows Roth
to interweave self-regarding references and so to use the wry
comedy of a documentary element. The trilogy forms an ambitious and multi-layered narrative that in some ways elaborates on previous preoccupations, but in others breaks new
ground.

If there is one principal enquiry it is that ever-present desire
to write about what it means to be a writer, compounded at
most points by the Jewish context also. The demands of the
vocation of novelist are, in different ways, always total. They
are ascetic, demanding a submission of the writer's nature to
the corpus of the novel, as *The Anatomy Lesson* makes clear.
Roth's literary bearings are maintained: Kafka, Chekhov, Mann,
James and Flaubert are never far away, and in *The Ghost Writer*
we even have extensive use of a James story in order to reveal an
interpretation of Lonoff himself – textualised by Roth as an
outstandingly original storyteller, and also charismatic, idealised to the point of being an allegorical figure. Lonoff is the
writer who is used by Roth to suggest the kind of idolatry given
to the prominent artists in society, mediated as being somehow
influential. Clearly, the title is a play on the two implications of
the word 'ghost' in this context.

Zuckerman Unbound moves into areas akin to earlier themes,
but turns the focus on to success. He has written his well-
received novel and he is a public figure. The first section, largely
concerned with the encounter with Alvin Pepler, introduces
several related themes which are maintained intermittently to

the end of the trilogy: the nature of art and 'schlock'; the pervasive influence of the media and of related commentary on our current concept of knowledge; the status of the novel and its status in the renegotiated art of modernity. There is also the human comedy of Zuckerman as an Everyman figure. The topography in which Nathan moves is the opposite to that of the writer Lonoff. Nathan is adrift in urban complexities, sustained by transience, instant gratification and amorality. Roth is adddressing the notion of the writer and the fictional self in the postmodern context. One of the fundamental bases of this is the common thesis that there has been a collapse of certainty, with no authoritative voices in the social institutions or ideologies around modern urban man. The resulting situation is something that impinges on every individual's sense of purpose, being and aims: 'Ordinary everyday thoughts on the subject of one who was lavish enough without an extra hump of narcissism to carry around.'[3]

Pepler is one version of the would-be writer, the alter-ego of the success at the heart of the narrative. He is a product and a victim of Bellow's junk culture, and a warning to Zuckerman that high art has to step down in order to survive. But Roth also introduces another device of deepening his writing on the nature of the writer and creativity: this time it is specifically Jewish, and is embodied in Anne Frank. The characters of Amy and Caesara are paired with Anne Frank for this reason. The use of the 'double' motif, so interesting to Roth himself in much of his work, is here used to write about the potential creativity in everyone, and also to explore that specifically Jewish quotient. In one of Roth's essays, he discusses the heroes created by various Jewish writers, and concludes:

> As I see it, the task for the Jewish novelist has not been to go forth to forge in the smithy of his soul the uncreated conscience of his race, but to find inspiration in a conscience that has been created and undone a hundred times over in this century alone. Similarly, out of this myriad of prototypes, the solitary being to whom history and circumstance has assigned the appellation 'Jew' has had . . . to imagine what he is and is not, must and must not do.[4]

That is, Anne Frank, together with Pepler the victim of pop culture and Lonoff the intellectual writer all exhibit qualities of some vague Jewishness, all open to stereotype and exploitation in art. Is there a genuine element of Jewishness, then, he asks – and is it found in literature?

Another important element in Roth's fiction has been the examination of contemporary gentile America and the Jewish assimilation into the mores and ideologies of the WASP dominance. In *The Great American Novel* (1973) Roth produced an astonishly ambitious work, rich in parody, allusion and cultural history, taking baseball as a metaphor for this centrality of American-ness that is the bedrock of everything in mainline fiction. Partly, it would lend itself to a pastiche of the various attempts at creating that American novel so beloved by reviewers and publicists, and partly it is a work of surreal fantasy, often Joycean in language and conception. Roth commented in an interview that the comedy in the book, 'exists for no higher value than for comedy itself. The redeeming value is comic inventiveness.'[5] In fact, the novel has fun at the expense of that sheer immersion in all-American values that he had previously treated in a serious and rather dour way in *When She Was Good* (1967) but he moved from small-town sexual politics and male violence to broader concerns of pervasive American ideology in the later novel. This ideology is partly one of a mythic America refusing to vanish, and finding comedy in its durability. If an attempt were made to see the novel as an allegory, with the baseball diamond being America, and the Ruppert team as representative Americans, the reading could be partially maintained, but only intermittently, so overwhelming is Roth's desire to allow comic invention to emulate many of the meta-fictional qualities of Fielding's picaresque *Tom Jones* (1749).

In terms of assessing the point Roth had reached with this novel, before going on to write *American Pastoral* and *Operation Shylock* in the 1990s, it is worth noting that he had followed a route that had been a challenge to every major American writer who has taken the nature of that vast and incomprehensible land seriously. The practitioners of film were doing the same in the early 1970s. Scorsese and Allen in their own ways were pointing towards philosophical ways of interpreting American urban society at a time when emergence from the 1960s liberations (and repressions) meant that a fragmentation was taking place. For Roth to move into the area of political writing from such introspective positions as has been assumed in the fiction dealing with Jewish identity was a total shift of focus, but it succeeded in claiming for him a candidature as, if not the creator of the 'Great American Novel', then at least as its chronicler.

It is possible to place *The Great American Novel*, therefore, in the same niche as, for instance, Ken Kesey's *Sometimes a Great Notion* and similar efforts from Mailer, Vonnegut and others. Naturally, the original conception of 'The Great American Novel' invites speculation about why such a work should be thought necessary. But for Roth, it is certainly part of his ongoing fictional interest in the sustaining mythic process of 'Middle America', the home-town ethos and the vestiges of Puritanism even within the chaos of what is increasingly seen as 'Two Americas' rich – and poor, city and state and so on. If we accept that, as a Jewish-American, Roth sees the inherent settler-myths with a cold rationalism granted to the outsider, then how much more significance does baseball attain given that Roth wanted to write a novel about something he knew. In the end, the satire is as direct and subversive as the best – Pope, Swift and Auden included; as tough as the 'Redskin' prose it accommodates, and at the same time, parodies.[6]

Roth returns to this subject in *American Pastoral*, but it is worth noting, in passing, the more directly Jewish material of *Operation Shylock* (1993). Here, this complex work is a version of a confessional, with extended historical discourse fused with the narrative: the history of Israel, the trial of 'Ivan the Terrible' (John Demjanjuk), accounts of dialogues with other writers, the narrative of the supposed Klinghoffer diary (using reference to the 'Achille Lauro') and much more. It is a novel based on the Dostoievskian idea of the 'double': 'its insistent lack of surface realism vexes interpretation'.[7]

The naming of the double, turning Roth into 'Pipik', is the principal means of attaining the narrative effects. The source of the name, linked also to the social world of the Roth aunt, Meena Gitschka, creates a being of truly archetypal nature, a fabulous, folktale entity of racial, communal meaning, so that the double may be, in this literary device, a catalyst for the textual construction of the historical dialogues that ensue. Moishe Pipik is literally 'Moses Bellybutton'; he is also another incarnation of the father and the eternal child, the child-Jew, unborn into the burdens, stigmas and dualities of Roth's Jew-hood:

> I thought then that he was like some errant son of mine, like a child I'd never had who bears the family name and the facial features of a larger-than life dad and doesn't much like feeling suffocated by him.[8]

Almost every conceivable debate about the emergence of Israel and about the Jews of the latest Diaspora is included some-where in this work. Confrontations succeed confrontations, sometimes surreal and sometimes realistic, sometimes written in tones of relaxed urbanity, in civilised address to the literate reader. But not until the arrival of Supposnik does the Shylock theme emerge and face up to the core of gentile cultural creations and denigrations of the Jew. Roth links the 'trial' metaphor in Shakespeare to the 'double' notion of Ivan's trial, and to the universal 'trial' of Jews. The gentiles' persistent, unreasoned scapegoat – the final intolerable 'double' of the book's subject – a hateful, recurrent alter-ego:

> In the modern world, the Jew has been perpetually on trial: still today the Jew is on trial, in the person of the Israeli – and this modern trial of the Jew, this trial that never ends, begins with the trial of Shylock.[9]

The novel inevitably moves towards yet another stance on the enduring paradox of why Jews are reviled. In Roth's work there has always been this agenda: his own compulsion to search out these origins, or at least to use popular cultural texts to keep asking the questions about the origins of anti-Semitism. After all, each generation has had its own apologist and edu-cator in this area, as in the 1920s with 'Benammi', who wrote a popular text explaining such hatred by means of anecdote and learning easily mixed. In some ways, Roth does the same, at least in one strand throughout his writing.[10]

In his latest novel, *American Pastoral* (1997), Roth returns to the ethos of small-town, wholehearted America in the creation of the Jew 'Swede' Levov, high-school sports hero and local celebrity who marries into an established WASP family. Swede has his wealth, from his father's Newark glove-making company, and the couple should exemplify the notion of America's finest. But Roth has brought Zuckerman back, and the writer-surrogate is to write the story of Lou, Swede's father, the Jewish businessman and moralist who finds nothing good in the morals and lifestyles of modernity. As Paul Quinn has noted, the novel engages with layers of myths:

> *American Pastoral* is crucially concerned with attempts to step outside History and into myth; and its bitter lesson is that history explodes all attempts to elude it.[11]

The novel is also a chronicle of post-war America, recording the changes in climate, moral and economic, that underlie power, and which ultimately destroy the self-help paternalism of the Levovs. The Swede emerges in the period when 'The Depression had disappeared. Everything was in motion. The lid was off. Americans were to start all over again, en masse, everyone in it together.'[12]

But the worm in the apple Roth focuses on the Levovs' daughter, Merry, who rebels and eventually becomes a political militant, being responsible for a bomb that kills a local doctor, and also she kills others. Her drift away from family WASP values parallels the decline of New Jersey and America itself; the novel's dynamism is in the depiction of the insecurities of the Levovs' safe world contrasted with the underworld and under-class of drugs and poverty which claims their daughter. The backdrop of American history is always loaded with irony, as a result of this. Even the assimilation process allowing Swede to achieve what he has is written in this mode:

> I lifted onto my stage the boy we were all going to follow into America, our point man in the next immersion, at home here

the way. The WASPS were at home here, an American not by sheer striving, not by being a Jew who invents a famous vaccine or a Jew on the Supreme Court. Instead, by virtue of his isomorphism to the WASP world.[13]

But in Seymour Swede Levov there is a disquiet. Merry develops stuttering; she goes 'wrong' and the microcosm of order begins to cave in. The novel glances at the immigrant generation, and the glove-making firm is used well here, but it is in the character of the Swede's father that we have the really important perceptions of the Jewish element in the novel. Roth makes it clear that the Swede 'loved being an American'[14] and he has even been a marine as well as marrying Miss New Jersey. But in contrast to his father, he has always kept the 'Jewboy shit' at a distance.[15] His father Lou speaks for a Jewish angle on American achievement, and thus becomes a pivotal figure in a world where people desperately need alignment with some communal sense. The daughter, Merry, eventually becomes a Jain in her revolt – probably the only one outside the East, her father thinks, in his incomprehension. Lou provides a standard commentary on social change, and everything else in the modernity of the setting is measured against this simplicity:

> The changes are beyond conception. I sometimes think that more has changed since 1945 than in all the years of history there have ever been. I don't know what to make of the end of so many things. The lack of feeling for individuals that a person sees . . . You don't have to revere your family, you don't have to revere your country . . . but you have to know you *have* them.[16]

Lou is made to speak for the cultured values of a generation long past, but the civilities he admires are made to appear desirable in the context of Seymour's loss, and of the sense of seedy and aimless urban wasteland that surrounds the estranged daughter.

If Roth is trying to point a moral lesson, it is perhaps with the Swede's gradual recognition of his weakness. This gives the novel tragic status. When Seymour sees the hollowness within, it is terrifying. He notes of himself: 'and that is why to this day, nobody knows who you are. You are unrevealed . . . That is the story, Seymour unrevealed.'[17]

There is also Zuckerman, the narrator to consider. Through a combination of his voice and that of the Swede's there is a wasteland both topographical and moral: the Jewish participation in this decline is irrationally expressed: 'Three generations. All of them growing. Three generations in raptures over America . . . and now with the fourth it had come to nothing. The total vandalization of their world.'[18] Of the many ironies in this novel, this is surely the most heartfelt and most profound: it reminds one of Leslie Fiedler's awareness of himself as one inside a 'silent holocaust' in which he senses himself as one of the 'last Jew'.

Roth has provided fiction that stimulates thought about American ideologies – and these are ones in which the Jewish dreams of fulfilment and rebirth within the Diaspora were born. It is possible to see the formative element in most of his work as essentially a commentary on political innocence and neglect, but the strongly human element in 'being a Jew' in America continues to give him sustenance as an imaginative force, and *American Pastoral* is arguably his most densely layered account of assimilation and loss of normative Jewish identity.

Cynthia Ozick

As discussed in Chapter 7, it is easy to place Cynthia Ozick's contribution to Jewish-American writing in the category of criticism, but there is much more to her work than this. In a special issue of *Contemporary Literature* devoted to her work, Elaine M. Kauvar defines the special quality of Ozick's work:

> Yet more than they have with Roth or Elkin, critics have unquestioningly regarded Cynthia Ozick as a Jewish writer whose muses not only are Jews but whose ideas are limited to Judaism. Ozick, in fact, has always treated her tradition as a threshold rather than a terminus.[19]

Interestingly, Ozick's work has attracted critics more for the intellectual debates and philosophical commentaries than from a standpoint of any notion of status. Her fiction is hard to find in Britain. Her work is not available as Roth's or Bellow's is. Yet she has been a focus of interest for some years now in academic journals. Assessments have varied immensely. Deborah Heiligman Weiner notes that, 'She still writes and still searches for meaningful modes of expression, in the hope that she can be a Jew and a writer . . . She is an idolater, she knows it, and yet she continues to write.'[20] Bonnie Lyons delves more into basic definition, and sees Ozick's Jewish qualities:

> Ozick's focus on potential for growth, which she often embodies in the figure of a child, reflects her moral stance and is part of her artistic credo. For her, great literature has a corona of moral purpose.[21]

Whatever stance one takes, what is undeniable is that her stories have generated both interest and renewed discussion as to what a 'Jewish writer' is and what he or she should be writing. Her first novel, *Trust*, appeared in 1966, and is largely about a woman's quest for a sense of identity. The theme of the awareness of historical process, and the inclusion of a concentration-camp setting give a taste of what was to come in the stories and novellas which have made her work influential. To define her difference, her special quality of language and style, is difficult. Ozick mixes realism and fantasy; she tends to give high status to internal suffering and yet external topography is important. Even more distinctive is her need to locate her fictions in a Jewish consciousness that approaches the quintessential nature of that racial suffering. She does this often through writing down, through humour and detail, as much as by overstating and being rhetorical.

The essence of her achievement is perhaps seen most clearly in the two stories 'The Pagan Rabbi' (1966) and 'The Shawl' (1980), together with the novella *Rosa* (1980 in book form). These demonstrate that Ozick is concerned with the qualities that define the outstanding elements of Jewishness: the scholarship, the experience of suffering and the involvement in community and exile. She is never afraid to use a range of textual reference that might require some effort on the reader's part, but she is also capable of writing a sparse, physical, restrained style that flourishes more potently in the aftermath of reading than in the reading itself. The short story 'The Shawl' illustrates this, and also shows how Ozick is able to deal with the subject of the Holocaust in a way that defamiliarises the reader.

'The Shawl' is the intense and internalised story of the murder of an infant in a concentration camp, and the narrator's witnessing of murder of the mother, who stuffs a shawl into her mouth as her child is thrown against the barbed wire, so that she will not speak and thus perhaps be killed also. The focal image of the shawl starts as a symbol of the only link to physical survival open to the women and child involved. The juice of the linen in the shawl is the starving child Magda's only sustenance. The fiction succeeds in its effects by the power of the objective correlatives which compose a net of brutal images around the sufferers. Such images are minimalised and graphic, sparse as the unilateral vision of tenuous survival the characters feel: 'Her knees were tumours on sticks, her elbows chicken bones' for instance.[22] This strain of the intolerable sub-life at the end of the tether is relentless up to the final voiceless suffering, and we have a final effect of the story being a symbolic interpretation of history.

It is not difficult to see how far Ozick extends the consequences of the story into both symbolism and historical setting. The cannibalism implicit in this expressed fear: 'They were in a place without pity, all pity was annihilated in Rosa, she looked at Stella's bones without pity. She was sure that Stella was waiting for Magda to die.'[23] The idea of the Jewish experience as one of being devoured by a larger society is plain; the noxious myths of medieval Europe about Jews eating Christian children is neatly reversed in this bleak vision of finality for a race and for the individual being. History is about the inevitable moments in which huge ideologies literally eat up the insignificant entities. Ozick also depersonalises the enemy. The destroyers are seen in litotes. 'A helmet' and 'a pair of black boots' are as close as we come to a definition of any delineaments of the killers. So it is the anonymity, the lack of any meaning given to the victims that generates the real power of the story.

The same could be said of the long story 'The Pagan Rabbi'. Ozick is interested in the restless dissent of the disciplined life. The dogmatic life without vision, without the towering impulses of the imagination lie beneath this story of the learned, ultra-bookish rabbi who discovers the pantheistic world of pagan Greece in a sewage-percolated field. Ozick loves to set up opposites, as Deborah Heiligman Weiner notes:

> Whether she terms it Nature versus History, Paganism versus Judaism, Pan versus Moses, or Magic versus Religion, she is talking about the same thing: the pull on the one hand of the easy life, and the pull on the other of order, sense and clarification.[24]

This order and clarification, though, is only a small part of the Rabbi Isaac Kornfeld's nocturnal communings with what he sees as a dryad. Ozick's story has a forebear in E. M. Forster's story 'The Story of a Panic' (1954), in which a very plain and provincial Englishman has a vision of Pan. The difference is that the rabbi places the vision in a new sense of cosmic order and personal philosophy – one akin to the Romantic ideology of animistic surrender to the dynamism of nature. Ozick's narrative ploy is to deepen the issues by having Kornfeld kill himself in this ecstasy, and for his learned widow to add to the recounting of the decline into paganism.

Some of the most interesting sections in the story deal with Kornfeld's changes as he develops this philosophy and has his epiphanic vision. His wife adds the comment, 'I think he was never a Jew' and tells that he began to tell surreal bedtime stories to the children: 'Rebecca cried because of a tree that turned into a girl.'[25] Clearly, the *Metamorphoses* and their enchantments were encroaching on good moral tales. In the end, this is the opposition that Ozick enjoys most. It is the deadness of a life of dry learning contrasted with the moment of epiphany and of vision. When Kornfeld sees himself as a poor scholar weighed down by a tractate, he summarises a massive negating definition of perhaps the most evergreen image of the 'good Jew':

> Its leaves are so worn they break as he turns them, but he does not turn them often because there is so much matter on a single page. He is so sad! Such antique weariness broods in his face![26]

Kornfeld also makes connections between the gods of the pagan Greek world and the creatures of Jewish literature and scripture, such as the succubus Lilith. He then sees the need to copulate with the dryad: 'As the sons and daughters of God came to copulate with women, so now let a daughter of Shekhina the Emanation reveal herself to me. Nymph, come now.' (Note that the *Shekhina* is the female presence of God in Judaism; the blasphemy is intolerable, of course.[27]

'The Pagan Rabbi' achieves many effects, but one element is certainly present as a commentary on that aspect of Jewishness that is constantly textualised as positive and admirable: the scholarly nature. The enduring image of the poor but learned rabbi and the seminarian teacher, such as attain mythic status in the tradition of Yiddish writing from Aleichem to Potok is here an object of comedy as well as a revered figure, simply because the idea of the true liberation of learning is a modern question for an essentially medieval idea. The story is also about the need for imagination, despite the risks we run in allowing its domination. It is destructive in its creative urges sometimes.

Ozick is also interested in the America of exile, and her attention is often on the community of fear in the Diaspora. We are shown America through Jewish eyes in a way far more stark and simplistic than Bellow or Malamud, for instance. Ozick, in 'Rosa', attempts to people her own American *Waste Land* with the walking wounded of a faded dream. At the centre is the meeting of Rosa, 58 years old, a refugee from New York, where she has smashed her own store after constant crime, and Persky, who is devised as the epitome of American-Jewish business success and social success. Loneliness is only the beginning of Rosa's plight. What Ozick places at the core of the story is the mental, inner life of the sufferer:

'If you're alone too much,' Persky said, 'you think too much.'
'Without a life.' Rosa answered, 'a person lives where they can. If all they got is thoughts, that's where they live.'
'You ain't got a life?'
'Thieves took it.'[28]

Rosa worships the shawl of her Magda (from 'The Shawl' and it is clear that she is paranoid and also unable to function in the present. When the psychologist Dr. Tree asks her to take part in a 'survivor study' she ascribes it to Stella.

Rosa's articulation, diverted from a social meaning, is directed only at her lost daughter and to the past. Her alienation is ultimately from herself, and Persky's attempts to communicate lead to an impasse:

'You ain't in a camp. It's finished long ago . . . Look around, you'll see human beings.'
'What I see is blood suckers.'[29]

In making Rosa into the Magda in her mind, in mixing the unhinged mind with the turmoil of past in the present, Ozick builds to a conclusion at once satisfying and also deeply ironical. The idolatry of the boxed shawl has led to an unhealthy survival ploy of one at the edge of sanity, just surviving by ultimate defence mechanisms of retreat into the static self of the past. But, ultimately, as with the Rabbi Kornfeld, Ozick has added something significant to the Jewish-American fiction written in recent decades: a confrontation with that profound symbolic power of the artefact that exemplifies the core of Jewish faith. The need to ritualise the self in some way, to embody belief and certainty in objects, has a double edge. Where 'The Shawl' established the object as a negating tool, a mix of comfort and suppression, 'Rosa' manages to objectify both the shawl as a means of survival, as a shamanistic value, in opposition to the disintegrating social world of barren, soulless Florida and crime-destroyed New York. It is a bleak vision, arguably advancing the view that in the American Diaspora, the conditions of a concentration camp are metaphorically possible, as the moral centre goes. The ambiguity of Persky in the story is perhaps the most potent of all symbolic values in the narrative scheme. His apparent, social nature hides a deeply confused perspective on the place of suffering in the Jewish experience, and at a more mundane level, he is also a victim of America comparable – with Bellow's victim in the novel, *The Victim*.

Notes

1. See Georg Lukacs, 'The Ideology of Modernism', in David Lodge (ed.), *Twentieth Century Literary Criticism* (Longman: London, 1972), p. 487.
2. See M. Tucker, 'The Shape of Exile in Philip Roth', in A. L. Milbauer and D. G. Watson (eds) *Reading Philip Roth* (London: Macmillan, 1988) pp. 33–49.
3. Philip Roth, *Zuckerman Unbound* (Penguin: London, 1989), p. 136.
4. Philip Roth, *Reading Myself and Others* (Farrar, Strauss and Giroux: New York, 1975), p. 221.
5. ibid. p. 76.
6. See Philip Rahv's seminal essay 'Paleface and Redskin' (1957), in which he says, 'Thus while the redskin glories in his Americanism, so the paleface is a source of endless ambiguities.' In *American Critical Essays* (Oxford University Press: Oxford, 1966), pp. 158–66.
7. See Peter Conradi, *Fyodor Dostioevsky* (Macmillan: London, 1988), p. 123.
8. Philip Roth, *Operation Shylock* (Cape: London, 1993) p. 185.
9. Ibid., p. 274.
10. See the very popular book of the 1920s., *Aspects of Jewish Life and Thought* by Benammi in 'Mainly About Books', vol. XV no. 2 (Spring 1922).
11. See Paul Quinn, 'Dearth of a hero', *Times Literary Supplement* 6 June 1997, p. 24.
12. Philip Roth, *American Pastoral* (Random House: London, 1997), p. 40.
13. Ibid., p. 89.
14. Ibid., p. 206.
15. Ibid., p. 211.
16. Ibid., p. 365.
17. Ibid., p. 276.
18. Ibid., p. 237.
19. See Elaine M. Kauvar, 'An Interview with Cynthia Ozick' *Contemporary Literature*, vol. 34 no. 3 (Fall 1993) pp. 359–94, p. 359.
20. See Deborah Heiligman Weiner, 'Cynthia Ozick, Pagan v. Jew, (1966–1976), *SAJL*, vol.8. no 2, pp. 179–91, p. 190.
21. See Bonnie Lyons, 'Cynthia Ozick as a Jewish Writer' *SAJL*, vol. 6 (1987) pp. 13–23, p. 17.
22. Cynthia Ozick, *The Shawl* (Vintage: New York, 1990), p. 3.
23. Ibid., p. 5.

24. See Weiner, 'Cynthia Ozick', *SAJL* p. 179.
25. Cynthia Ozick, 'The Pagan Rabbi', in E. Litvinoff (ed.), *The Penguin Book of Jewish Short Stories* (Penguin: London, 1979), pp. 247–81, p. 256.
26. Ibid., p. 271.
27. Ibid., p. 277.
28. Cynthia Ozick, 'Rosa', in *The Shawl* (Vintage: New York, 1990), pp. 27–8.
29. Ibid., p. 58.

Conclusion:

A Renaissance or Revisionism?

In his introduction to *The Schocken Book of Contemporary Jewish Fiction* (1992), Ted Solotaroff discusses the contrasts between the conventional, well-established corpus of writing in Jewish-American literature that focuses on *Yiddishkeit*, and the new writing embedded in current complexities of Jewish identity. He notes a creative plurality and a need to appreciate the demographic shifts in Jewish settlements in recent decades, and also makes an important distinction between two varieties of writing in this area, referring to the situation in the 1960s:

> There was a clear distinction between the writer who was a Jew and the Jew who was a writer, the former insisting on the right to explore the Jewish subject, as one did any other, by one's experience and imagination; the latter insisting that her or his experience and imagination were largely formed by and served the history and mission of the Jewish people.[1]

This distinction seemed like a clear one at that time, but has been increasingly difficult to maintain in the light of significant and influential events both globally and on the American domestic scene. Solotaroff and Rappoport, in this anthology, point out exactly what the acculturation changes have been in the last twenty years, with the emergence of the fourth generation of the first mass Jewish immigration, and more importantly perhaps, with the newer arrivals, from destinations other than Eastern Europe. Solotaroff adds: 'It makes more sense to us to speak of a post-immigrant culture that is coming to an end and a post-acculturated one that has been coming into being'.[2]

The influences listed in that same introduction underpin most of the significant developments in Jewish-American writing in recent years. The 1980s and 1990s have brought with them the aftermath of these events, which are: the 1967 Six-Day War, the idea of the 'open community' in the USA, newly negotiated relationships between Jews and urban black people (the issue of local school control in 1967 in New York is a focus here) and also the multiplicity of Jewish experience in the distancing of the Holocaust generation. Nessa Rappoport summarises this very well:

> So, too, will other kinds of Jews we are only beginning to hear from [write on Jewishness]: children and grandchildren of Holocaust survivors, converts to Judaism, Sephardim, descendants of *conversos* in the American South West, lesbians and gay men. Each of these groups has an idiosyncratic experience out of which imaginative writing may prosper.[3]

This anthology is a definite statement; it has a sub-text of aiming to demonstrate this richness, and to place the comforting and well-trodden writing of Yiddishkeit almost as a thing of the past. But there is the question of what will succeed, and whether or not that new writing will be as vibrant as what went before. Rappoport asserts the central Jewish creative vision, and has no doubt that it will thrive in America; she cites 'stunning formal inventiveness, imagery made resonant by millennia of use, a dazzling range of style from the sacred to the satiric and a relentless resistance to nostalgia'.[4] Certainly, when one tries to assess the worth and the direction of fresh writing, written from a position of prescient vision and from minority standpoints, one finds what Toni Morrison has hinted at with reference to colonial America: 'And it is difficult to read the literature of young America without being struck by how antithetical it is to our modern rendition of the American Dream.'[5] Morrison is discussing the first wave of writing here, but it could apply to any new wave from minorities.

Part of any effort to explain the nature of this latest type of

Jewish-American writing has to be an awareness of a whole range of quiet dissent and certain revisionist intentions. Reading the fiction of recent years in this context, it is obvious that there is still a multiplicity of forms, but that both older established writers and new voices are equally questioning and finely aware of the slackening hold of the Orthodox family, the *Yiddishkeit* values, and the extended power of the literature of suffering. Time and again in this writing, there is a mix of respect for and derision of these values. The question of what the revisionism consists of is found here. Often this is to be found in the new writers' delight in exploring what has been long neglected. Such topics as the power and influence of grandparents, sexuality and the importance of Israel occur repeatedly.

But it is difficult to make general statements. It is more meaningful to point to particular writers who may be representative. For instance, the stories of Jyl Lynn Felman are clearly significant. She writes about generational conflict, but also about the nature of the shifting exhibitions of love between people, as in her story 'A Handsome Man', from her collection, *Hot Chicken Wings* (1992), in which the male power of the first-generation immigrants is examined; Felman gives the whole range of potential arguments for that power surviving and reaching the youngest in the family. Grandfather even despises the modern rabbi, has tempers, exercises power by withholding gifts, and uses blandishments and rhetoric to get what he wants. Jessie, the granddaughter, is repeatedly told how special her grandfather is and she is told not to fight him. The story traces her growing away from him, and a final revelation hits Jessie like an epiphany, giving her a self-understanding deeper than she imagined:

> My grandfather and I were of the same world then. It made sense; I'd never understood before. We had no world; both of us were lost somewhere in between. We shared the same anger . . . I was young without a real beginning.[6]

In these stories, the failures of the older Jews are enumerated, but always with understanding. Felman can range from social

comedy with a story about an analyst, inept but loveable, to an
account of a Jewish father who puts prayer and duty above his
daughter's needs. But the real strength is found in the title-
story, in which we have an incisive and always human account
of two marginal standpoints on the Orthodox Jewishness of the
older generation. On a Jamaican holiday with her parents, the
narrator, Esther (a lesbian), meets the Jamaican Charlotte, who
is bisexual. Esther eats non-kosher food with her friend, and
hears of Charlotte's rich and sensuous life. Jamaica is contrasted
with the cloying and life-denying milieu of Florida, where the
family would normally go. But we are told that Esther has
Sephardic roots (with settlement in tolerant Jamaica) and thus
the voice of dissent is twofold.

In the eating of the *treyf* (unclean) chicken wings, Esther
learns a lesson and Felman extends it to a metaphor:

> So Charlotte was alone too, alone in green Jamaica. She had
> been eating unclean food, separate from her people, for years.
> Only she was doing just fine. It was Esther who had never
> learned that eating a little *treyf* was necessary to survive.[7]

So we have a variant in Felman's overall theme of liberations –
as in her sexuality. When making love to her partner, Esther
has to 'fight off the pious old Jew in her head'.[8]

In Lynne Sharon Schwartz's story, 'The Melting Pot' (1987),
we have an example of the critical stance taken on Jewishness
from within a multi-cultural context. Rita (half Jewish and half
Mexican) is in a relationship with the Indian Sanjay. Schwartz
creates a range of positions from which to judge the presence of
the older family values still persisting for Rita. The central
criticism is one of thoughtless obedience to convention:

> The lust to submit is his ruling passion. It is part of the
> covenant with God: obey all the rules and you will be safe. Sol
> takes this literally. He seeks out arcane rules to obey and
> seizes on then.[9]

Schwartz embodies the construction of the traditional Jewishness of the grandfather in the symbol of a room, 'like a room to

which new pieces are added but from which nothing is ever thrown away'.[10]

Reading of such younger writers leads to the view that Jewish-American literature has never been so inventive and vibrant, as Nessa Rappoport claims. But what is perhaps even more significant than the exploration of Jewishness with sexuality, pluralism and 'melting-pot' society is the confrontation of the older writers with the revisionist demands of the modern view. As discussed in the previous chapter, Philip Roth has examined layer after layer of Jewish self-awareness in postmodern America. But there has also been a major project by Henry Roth, who published almost nothing after *Call It Sleep* (1934) until his present project, an epic enterprise was initiated with the publication of *A Star Shines Over Mt. Morris Park* (1994). This is the first volume of *Mercy of a Rude Stream*, a massive fiction following the career and family of Ira Stigman from the pre-Great War years to the 1940s. The second volume, *A Diving Rock on the Hudson,* appeared in 1995 and the third, *Requiem for Harlem,* in 1998. The volumes cover far more than the years devoted to Ira, however, as the primary narrative is interspersed by a catechistic metafictional device in which the present-day Roth develops themes about writing, imagination, his personal life and identity. The novels came after a period away from writing, in which he was a woodsman, mental hospital worker and schoolteacher. The aim is to develop a six-volume work.

The central interest in this epic, in the present context, is in the devices used by Roth to place his Jewish identity, and that of his character Ira Stigman, within much more comprehensive narratives – chiefly that of America itself, much as Philip Roth has done since the 1960s. Henry Roth repeatedly undermines any attempt to heighten or mythologise the Jewish nature of his surrogate: 'Ira and his parents were not the first Jews living on 119th street. He was not, in short, without alternative of Jewish kids to hobnob with, enticing to the writer as that sort of extreme predicament might be.'[11] Even the conventional account of Jews in classic texts, so common in writing about childhood in that period, is glossed over; 'All he asked of a book was not to remind him too much that he was a Jew.'[12]

The narrative is in fact predominantly an account of the immersion in 'American' normative identity exemplified by the Italian and Irish immigrants around Ira. His affiliations are with maleness, crime, survival, urban life, education and sexuality. Far more important for the fiction is the coming to sexual awareness and the incest theme than the Jewishness, although the Roth commentary develops a thesis on James Joyce and Leopold Bloom. The account of Ira's *Bar Mitzvah*, for instance, provokes this reaction: 'he hated being a Jew; he didn't want to be one, and realised he was caught, imprisoned in an identity from which there was no chance of him ever freeing himself.'[13] As for Joyce – the point is that Roth uses his meta-fictional asides to examine universal questions such as the textualising of Bloom. For instance, Roth sees great importance in Joyce writing about Ireland from exile, and introduces Jewishness as the modernist focus for generating creative change: 'Whereas to accept his hermetic ego, exploit it, projecting his Freudian bonds on Bloom, the nominal Jew, promised him the foremost place in twentieth century English letters.'[14] There is a sub-text in *A Star Shines Over Mt. Morris Park* that is about how writing Jewishness is an easy way to avoid a writer's real identity questions.

The contention of the volumes so far in the project is that of taking America itself, with all its constituents, as the essential subject of fiction, rather than some disjointed Jewishness that sets apart, denigrates the social history behind people, and omits the central ideologies of the modern age that have formed a new American identity, with Jewishness as simply one strand in the full picture. Roth includes this just as Philip Roth did in *American Pastoral*, but with a direct statement, devoid of irony: 'Oh America, America! There was no going on beyond the outcry of remembered affection, because history would not bear out its promise . . . Still, he had a glimpse . . . of that dynamic form that was America.'[15]

The added complexity of the metafiction that Roth includes is ambiguous in the sections where the writer addresses us, and when the boldest statement about the survival of the Jews in America is put, there is an astonishing starkness in the statement:

What was left of Orthodoxy outside Israel, except for the fossilised kinkies, flaunting their earlocks and fur *shtramls* [hats]? Only the diluted remnant of rabbinical Jewry here in America. By assimilation the remnant would painlessly disappear . . . Only in Israel could Judaism thrive, only in its own land survive and evolve.[15]

In fact, reading this recent fiction, we are drawn increasingly to a self-referential, meta-fictional form. As modern theory has reminded us that stories are always aware of their form as stories, and when reflecting on this specific period of Jewish-American writing, it is apparent that the growth of this mode of fiction in the 1970s had an impact on such writers as Roth and Bellow. The discussion in Chapter 8 about the moral dimension of this fiction also reminds us that this literature has always been both philosophic and socially aware.

The contrast between Henry Roth's ambitious project and the work of writers such as Felman, Segal and Schwartz could not be more marked. Roth insists on telling a conventional story in order to dispel the bias and normality of conventional Jewish narrative in the American context. The younger writers are wanting to take the essence of the conventions and use them as a new sustenance. But the very fact that everyone avoids complacency about the familiar stereotypes and shuns nostalgia can only be a good sign. Undoubtedly there is a revisionism at work, but there appears to be no alignment with particular factions, in spite of Cynthia Ozick's requests for a rethink of the part played by Jewish intellectuals.[17] In that same interview, Ozick compliments Philip Roth for showing the way forward into both new achievements and in consolidating expectancies into established text:

At this moment I happen to think that Philp Roth's new work, *Operation Shylock*, is the Great American Jewish Novel. And, as I remarked earlier, it's set in Israel! Which doesn't prevent it from being what it stupendously is, an American novel of intricate braininess and brio.[18]

In surveying the past fifty years of achievement in Jewish-American writing, there is an abundance of 'braininess and brio' apparent in the impressive diversity of this body of literature. It would not be a statement of overconfidence to assert that each wave of new writers has brought with them a mix of the intellectual vigour and sheer vivacious need to give life to the Jewish experience in their greatest Diaspora that was first given to us by Anzia Yezierska and Abraham Cahan in the early years of this century. The Dickensian richness those writers inherited from their reading was fused with a need to depict the earthy, direct physicality of Jewish life and thought, which still persists in the latest writers on the scene. If there has to be a hallmark, a defining quality that may be relied on, it is perhaps the Jewish-American writer's wish to insist on both arrogance and tolerance, and on self-belief and tragic doubt in the core of his or her work.

The revisionism is tantamount to a review of what simplicities were given about being Jewish, about the danger of a culture of complaint at the base of the writing, and about how writing openly as a Jewish writer defines an exclusion – a celebration but also a limiting perception by readers, and the implication of certain expected narrative concerns.

What are the issues related to this important corpus of work? To most commentators, it has seemed that the writing of the unofficial canon of Jewish-American novelists in particular has been a confrontation with a counter-culture. This has, it may be argued, been a more profoundly rich and diverse *hidden* culture than has previously been realised. What strikes the reader in the central line of writing about differentiating the Jewishness of the protagonists of Bellow, Malamud, Roth and others is that it is a process of searching for reasons to be separate. The growth of a secular consciousness, the impact of European existentialism and most of all the need to redefine the nature of the 'Good Jew' as part of the American mainstream have all complicated the subject. Yet finally, the younger writers, notably Mamet and Felman, have maintained the habit of using the older generation's morality as yardsticks.

But this is to tell only half the story. There has also been a feeling that the Jewish writing within modern American literature has been the true iconoclasm. In Philip Roth's *American Pastoral*, it is the submerged dissent that maintains the fictional interest – there the drama lies, and the emotional velocity generated by the Swede's lost empires of his affections. Equally, in the writers who are indeed marginal to this study, one finds a Jewish strain: something given by their religious texts, their disposition of being counter to established formation of identity. This is evident in *Catch 22* and in *Sophie's Choice* for instance. But if one adheres to the traditions of inner dissent established in Bellow's *Dangling Man* as early as 1948, then inevitably, the focal question on this differentiated identity becomes one of adopted language. That is to say, the immense gulf between Anzia Yezierska and Bellow's Jewish consciousness is evident largely through the language of adoption, and the depiction of difference through dialectal discourse. Our textual interplay with Yezierska is often concerned with the witnessing of a child groping for an adult language, yet the power and innocence of the dialect, the New World confusion of registers, is the magnetic pull of the narrative.

With a more openly theoretical perspective, we should ask, how does the recent writing in this corpus compare with, for instance, the popular cultural texts of the post-war years? For instance, the type of discourse we find in Bob Dylan's lyrics or in the urban poetry of Ginsberg: this could be called both Jewish and mainstream. The reason is that there has been a resistance to the overtly oppositional reading that the deliberately 'Jewish' texts appeal to. What this raises in terms of the literary theory behind the work is partly one of the intended readers of this literature. Cynthia Ozick's notion of the New Yiddish is relevant here. There is often a sense of the intellectual fiction of the writers discussed in my last two chapters being written for an ideal reader who is fully informed about Judaism but also academic, pluralistic in culture and generally well read and liberal. But the texts reflect the social questioning of the version of Judaism offered by the immigrant literature.

There have been apologias for the former narrowness of the Jewish writing that looked inward. But it cannot be denied, for instance, that Isaac Bashevis Singer's work, certainly in his early and middle periods, is retrospective and is in fact historical fiction in a similar sense to that of (say) Steinbeck. However, as the stereotypes of East European Jewry have persisted in popular culture, there has been a version of 'timewarp' change-lessness in the nature of anti-Semitism. That is, if one insists on looking and acting 'Jewish' in the sense of the film *The Jazz Singer*, then readership is limited to documentary interest or meaningless sentimentalism. Chaim Potok is outstanding in the boldness with which he has presented Hassidism and secularism in polar opposition. This has been done without giving in to stereotypes, and by always taking the issues at the centre of a sub-culture as vitally important, and with no easy answers to the perceived crisis of secular, urban America.

The discussion of the Jewish-American poetry in Chapter 6 pinpoints the confusions of poetics and its relation to identity. The American scene largely precludes a serious and influential poetry of the individual without the risk of huge distortions of language and identity. Whitman would seem to be a model of potential achievement here, but what is interesting about the most prominent poetry about Jewishness which has had a wider impact is that it has been emotive, passionate and free-form. Ginsberg's *Kaddish* is surely the example here. The success of this is tied in with *Howl* and with the beat poets, of course, and this success only serves to highlight more potently the failure of other Jewish-American voices to have a wider impact.

Theoretically, poetry should be the one form in which the profoundly complex and elusive nature of the Jewish self as textualised in more sociological writings or in autobiography. In fact, autobiography may emerge as the dominant literary form in the context under discussion. For reasons of space, this has had to be excluded here, but as George Steiner's book *Errata* (1997) has shown, there is a massive potential for the place of discursive, essayist writing in this body of literature. Steiner's autobiography illustrates the natural Jewish affection for mix-ing memoirs with cultural assessment, and he gives a wide historical interpretation alongside his own life data. The crop of Holocaust testaments, as discussed in the chapter on poetry and on prose, is also evidence of the vitality and importance of this genre. In fact, the Jewish contribution to the long and respected tradition of the *Bildungsroman* could be the centre of a full study, and may yet be done with the major writers under scrutiny. In the hands of the prose writers discussed in Chapter 7, it is easy to see the link between ideology and the process of history as a sub-text beneath the self-deprecating humour, and in autobiography, this expands even further. Obviously, one conclusion we have to reiterate is that Holocaust literature is so vast that it deserves separate treatment, but it has formed a central element in the present discussion.

The broadest conclusions have to be that the major writers studied here have illustrated the various strategies that Jewish Americans have found to describe the dilemmas of their duality, and that their efforts as employing discourse specific to their traditions have brought forth 'strange fruit' but also, indisputably, a harvest of such insightful writing that it has to be noted as significant in any survey of the period. It has been, chiefly, a shift from minority insistence on factual documentation of deprivation and exclusion, to an account of multiple voices of quiet desperation among a multifarious, divided culture where other minorities rise and fall in literary movements almost every year as the focus of cultural interest relocates.

There has undoubtedly been a renaissance in Jewish-American writing, and no apologies are needed for the fact that much of this writing has been inward-looking and at times profoundly concerned with the past. The rebirth has its spokespeople and a few passionate advocates who sometimes make claims that exceed the evidence, but the younger writers, in all genres and conventions, are just as vibrant and innovative as the writers who occupy the status of an unofficial 'canon' of literature in this category.

Notes

1. See Ted Solotarff's introduction, in Ted Solotaroff and Nessa Rappoport (eds), *The Schocken Book of Contemporary Jewish Fiction* (Schocken: New York, 1992), p. xx.
2. Ibid., p. xv.
3. Ibid., p.xxviii.
4. Ibid., pp. xxviii-xxix.
5. See Toni Morrison, *Playing in the Dark* (Picador: London, 1992), p. 35. What

Morrison says about white romance is relevant to concerns of, for instance, Cahan's immigrant males searching for masculine belonging.

6. Jyl Lynn Felman, *Hot Chicken Wings*, (Virago: London, 1996), p. 66.
7. Ibid., p. 105.
8. Ibid., p. 103.
9. Lynne Sharon Schwartz, 'The Melting Pot', in Solotaroff and Nessa Rapport, *The Schocken Book of Contemporary Jewish Fiction*, p. 289.
10. ibid., p. 301.
11. Henry Roth, *A Star Shines Over Mt. Morris Park* (Weidenfeld and Nicholson: London, 1994), p. 36.
12. Ibid., p. 150.
13. Ibid., p. 161.
14. Henry Roth, *A Diving Rock on the Hudson* (Weidenfeld and Nicholson: London, 1995), p. 178.
15. Ibid., p. 161.
16. Ibid., p. 164.
17. See Elaine M. Kauvar, 'An Interview with Cynthia Ozick', in *Contemporary Literature*, vol. 34 no. 3 (Fall, 1993), pp. 259–394, p. 375.
18. Ibid., p. 394.

Glossary of Yiddish Terms

Aggadah:	Traditional Jewish literature, commentaries, aphorisms and so on.
Bar Mitzvah:	A ceremony at which the thirteen-year old Jewish boy attains the status of adulthood, of being 'a man'.
Bat Mitzvah:	A ceremony for girls when they reach the age of twelve or thirteen.
Goldene Medine:	The Golden Land (America).
Goyim:	Non-Jews, gentiles.
Haskalah:	The Jewish Enlightenment.
Hasid:	Literally, 'pious man'. A member of the movement founded by Baal Shem Tov and influenced by the Kabala.
Heimlichkeit:	Homeliness.
Kabala:	The study of Jewish mysticism.
Kaddish:	The prayer for the dead.
Luftmensch:	Intellectual, dreamer.
Midrash:	Commentary on the scriptures.
Minyan:	The ten men required in attendance before a religious ceremony may Start.
Oy gewald:	Disaster, misery.
Pogrom:	An organised attack on a Jewish community
Shabbat:	Day of holiness as a reminder of God's work of creation.
Shekhinah:	The indwelling presence of God.
Shiksa:	A non-Jewish woman.
Shul:	Synagogue.
Shtetl:	Jewish settlement in Eastern Europe.
Talmud:	The principal work of Rabbinic Judaism.
Torah:	The spiritual teaching revealed from God to Moses.
Treyf:	Food that is not kosher.

Tsadik:	A scholarly and wise man.
Yeshiva:	A Jewish day school.
Yiddishkeit:	The world of the Jews.

Select Bibliography

1. Works by and about Writers Discussed
2. Secondary Criticism and Literary Biography
3. General Background Texts

Note: The journal *Studies in American Jewish Literature* has been abbreviated to *SAJL*.

1 Works by and about Writers Discussed

Woody Allen

Getting Even (Vintage: New York, 1978)
Side Effects (New English Library: London, 1980)
Without Feathers (Sphere: London, 1972)
Secondary:
Bjorkman, Stig, *Woody Allen on Woody Allen* (Faber: London, 1994)
Lax, Eric, *Woody Allen, A Biography* (Vintage: London, 1991)

Paul Auster

Ground Work (Faber: London, 1996)
The Invention of Solitude (Faber: London, 1988)

Saul Bellow

The Actual (Viking: London, 1997)
Dangling Man (Penguin: London, 1971)
The Dean's December (Secker and Warburg: London, 1982)
Herzog (Penguin: London, 1965)
Humbolt's Gift (Penguin: London, 1976)
It All Adds Up (Penguin: London, 1990)
More Die of Heartbreak (Secker and Warburg: London, 1987)
Mosby's Memoirs and Other Stories (Penguin: London, 1971)

Mr. Sammler's Planet (Penguin: London, 1969)
Seize the Day (Penguin: London, 1966)
The Victim (Penguin: London, 1988)

SECONDARY:

Bradbury, Malcom, *Saul Bellow* (Methuen: London, 1982)
Clayton, John, *Saul Bellow: In Defence of Man* (Indiana University Press: Indiana, 1978)
Coles, Joanna, Interview with Bellow, *Guardian*, 10 September 1997, G2, pp. 2–3
Goldmann, L. H., Gloria L. Cronin and Ada Aharoni, *Saul Bellow: A Mosaic* (Peter Lang: New York, 1992)
Malin, Irving, *Saul Bellow and the Critics* (New York University Press: New York, 1967)
Nault, Marianne, *Saul Bellow: His Work and Critics* (Garland: New York, 1977)
Noreen, Robert G., *Saul Bellow: A Reference Guide* (G. K. Hall: Boston, 1978)
Sokoloff, B. A., *Saul Bellow: A Comprehensive Bibliography* (Folcroft Press: Penn., 1971.

Abraham Cahan

The Rise of David Levinsky (Penguin: London, 1993)

SECONDARY:

Chametsky, Jules, *From the Ghetto: The Fiction of Abraham Cahan* (University of Massachusetts: Amherst, 1977)
Stein, Leon, et al., *The Education of Abraham Cahan* (Jewish Publication Society of America: Philadelphia, 1969)

Jyl Lynn Felman

Hot Chicken Wings (Virago: London, 1996)

Leslie Fiedler

Fiedler on the Roof (David Godine: Boston, 1911)

Carolyn Forsché

The Angel of History (Bloodaxe: Newcastle, 1994)

Allen Ginsberg

Selected Poems 1947–1995 (Penguin: London, 1996)
Journals 1954–1958 (Viking: London, 1995)

SECONDARY:

Miles, Barry, *Ginsberg: A Biography* (Viking: London, 1989)

Erica Jong

Half Lives (Secker and Warburg: London, 1974)
Fear of Flying (Minerva: London, 1996)
Fear of Fifty (Vintage: New York, 1995)

Irena Klepfisz

Different Enclosures (Onlywomen Press: London, 1985)

Tony Kushner

Angels in America: Millennium Approaches (Nick Hern: London, 1992)
Angels in America: Perestroika (Nick Hern: London, 1992)

Meyer Liben

Justice Hunger (Rockliff: London, 1968)

Bernard Malamud

A New Life (Penguin: London, 1961)
Selected Stories (Penguin: London, 1985)

SECONDARY:

Abramson, Edward ,A. *Bernard Malamud Revisited* (Twayne: New York, 1993)
Kosofsy, Rita N., *Bernard Malamud: A Descriptive Bibliography* (Greenwood: New York, 1991)
Salzberg, Joel (ed.), *Critical Essays on Bernard Malamud* (G.K. Hall: Boston, 1987)

David Mamet

American Buffalo and *Duck Variations* in *Plays1* (Methuen: London, 1996)
Make-Believe Town (Faber: London, 1996)
Some Freaks (Faber: London, 1989)

SECONDARY:

Bragg, Melvyn, *South Bank Show: Interview with David Mamet* (ITV, 1992)
Carroll, Dennis, *David Mamet* (Macmillan: London, 1987)

Arthur Miller

After the Fall, Incident at Vichy and *The Price* in *Plays: Two* (Methuen: London, 1988)

Broken Glass (Methuen: London, 1994)
Danger: Memory! (Methuen: London, 1986)
Timebends (Methuen: London, 1987)

SECONDARY:

Bigsby, Christopher (ed.), *The Cambridge Guide to Arthur Miller* (Cambridge University Press: Cambridge, 1997)
Hayman, Ronald, *Arthur Miller* (Heinemann: London, 1970)
Martine, James J. (ed.), *Critical Essays on Arthur Miller* (G. K. Hall: Boston, 1979)
Nelson, Benjamin, *Arthur Miller: Portrait of a Playwright* (Peter Owen: London, 1970)

Tillie Olsen

Tell Me A Riddle (Virago: London, 1980)

SECONDARY:

Schultz, Lydia A., 'Flowing Against the Traditional Stream: Consciousness in Olsen's *Tell Me A Riddle*', Melus, vol. 22 no. 3 (Fall 1997) (University of Mass.: Amherst)

Cynthia Ozick

Portrait of the Artist as a Bad Character (Pimlico: London, 1996)
The Shawl (Vintage: New York, 1990)
What Henry James Knew (Vintage: London, 1993)

SECONDARY:

Blacher Cohn, Sarah, *Cynthia Ozick's Comic Art* (Indiana University Press: Indiana, 1994)
Kielsky, Vera Emma, *Inevitable Exiles: Cynthia Ozick's View of the Precariousness of Jewish Existence in a Gentile Society* (Peter Lang: New York, 1989)
Lowin, Joseph, *Cynthia Ozick* (Twayne: Boston, 1988)
Pinsker, Sanford, *The Uncompromising Fictions of Cynthia Ozick* (University of Missouri Press: Columbia, 1987)
Uffen, Ellen Serlen, *Strands of the Cable: The Place of the Past in American Jewish Women's Writing* (Peter Lang: New York, 1992)

Grace Paley

Begin Again: New and Collected Poems (Virago: London, 1992)
Enormous Changes at the Last Minute (Virago: London, 1994)
The Little Disturbances of Man (Virago: London, 1992)

SECONDARY:

Kaplan, Cora, interview with Grace Paley, in Mary Chamberlain (ed.), *Conversations Between Women Writers* (Virago: London, 1988), pp. 181–90

Chaim Potok

The Chosen (Penguin: London, 1966)
My Name is Asher Lev (Penguin: London, 1973)
The Promise (Penguin: London, 1971)

SECONDARY:

The World of Chaim Potok SAJL no. 4 (1985) (State of New York Press: Albany)

Adrienne Rich

Blood, Bread and Poetry Selected prose (Virago: London, 1986
Collected Early Poems 1950–1970 (Norton: New York and London, 1993)
The Fact of a Doorframe (Norton: New York, 1984)

SECONDARY:

Corson Carter, Nancy, 'Claiming the Bittersweet Matrix: Alice Walker, Sandra Cisneros and Adrienne Rich', *Critique* Vol. XXXV no. 4 (Summer 1994)
Guelpi, Albert, 'Adrienne Rich: The Poetics of Change', in Robert B. Shaw (ed.), *American Poetry since 1960: Some Critical Perspectives* (Carcanet: Manchester, 1973)

Henry Roth

Call it Sleep (Penguin: London, 1997)
A Diving Rock on the Hudson (Weidenfeld and Nicholson: London, 1995)
Requiem for Harlem (Weidenfeld and Nicholson: London, 1998)
A Star Shines On Mt. Morris Park (Weidenfeld and Nicholson: London, 1994)

SECONDARY:

See special issue of *SAJL*, vol. 5 no. 1 (Spring 1979)

Philip Roth

American Pastoral (Random House: London, 1997)
Goodbye, Columbus (London: Penguin, 1986)

The Great American Novel (Vintage: London, 1991)
Letting Go (London: Penguin, 1986)
Operation Shylock (Cape: London, 1993)
Portnoy's Complaint (Corgi: London, 1971)
The Professor of Desire (Penguin: London, 1977)
Zuckerman Unbound (Trilogy ed. London: Penguin, 1989

Non-fiction:

Reading Myself and Others (Cape: London, 1979)

SECONDARY:

Lee, Hermione, *Philip Roth* (Methuen: London, 1982)
Milbauer, A. Z. and D. G. Watson (eds), *Reading Philip Roth* (Macmillan: London, 1988)
Rodgers, B. F., *Philip Roth: A Bibliography* (Twayne: Boston, 1978)
Wade, Stephen, *The Imagination in Transit: The Fiction of Philip Roth* (Sheffield Academic Press: Sheffield, 1996)

Jerome Rothenberg

Esther K. Comes to America 1931 (Unicorn Press: New York, 1974)
Khurbn and Other Poems (New Directions: New York, 1983)
Poems for the Game of Silence (Dial: New York, 1971)

Muriel Rukeyser

Collected Poems (Yale University Press: 1979)

SECONDARY:

Louise Kertesz, *The Poetic Vision of Muriel Rukeyser* (Louisiana State University Press.: Baton Rouge and London, 1980)

Delmore Schwartz

In Dreams Begin Responsibilities (Secker and Warburg: London, 1978)
What is to be Given (Carcanet: Manchester, 1976)

Isaac Bashevis Singer

Collected Stories (Penguin: London, 1984)
Love and Exile (Cape: London, 1984)
In My Father's Court (Fawcett Crest: New York, 1962)

SECONDARY:

Kazin, Alfred, *Contemporaries* (Secker and Warburg: London, 1963) pp. 283–288
Sinclair, Clive, *The Brothers Singer* (Allison and Busby: London, 1983)

Lionel Trilling

The Middle of the Journey (Secker and Warburg: London, 1978)
Speaking of Literature (Oxford University Press: London, 1982)

Wendy Wasserstein

The Heidi Chronicles (Vintage: New York, 1991)

Anzia Yezierska

Hungry Hearts and Other Stories (Virago: London, 1987); Riva Krut, the editor, includes a valuable critical essay.
Gene Zeiger
Leaving Egypt (White Pine Press: New York, 1995)

2 Secondary Criticism and Literary Biography

Abramson, Edward A., *The Immigrant Experience in American Literature* (BAAS: London, 1982

Amis, Martin, *The Moronic Inferno* (Penguin: London, 1987)

Bailey, P. J., 'Why Not Tell the Truth?' The Autobiography of three fiction writers, *Critique*, 32: 4 (1991), pp. 211–23

Baym, Nina, 'How Theories of American Fiction Exclude Women Authors', in Elaine Showalter (ed.), *The New Feminist Criticism* (Virago: London, 1986), pp. 63–80

Bell, Pearl K., 'A Particular Kind of Joking' *Times Literary Supplement*, 10 October 1997.

Alan L., Berger 'Jewish Identity, Destiny, the Holocaust in Refugee Writing' *SAJL*, vol. 11 no. 1 (Spring, 1992)

Bermant, Chaim, *What's the Joke? A Study of Jewish Humour* (Weidenfeld and Nicholson: London, 1986)

Boyarin, Daniel and Jonathan Boyarin, 'Diaspora and Jewish Identity', *Critical Enquiry* (Summer 1993), pp. 693–725

Boyers, Robert, (ed.), *Contemporary Poetry in America: Essays and Interviews* (Schocken: New York, 1975)

Brenman-Gibson, Margaret, *Clifford Odets: American Playwright* (Atheneum: New York, 1981)

Burns, Jim, 'Isaac Rosenfeld', in *Penniless Press*, issue 4 (Spring 1997), pp. 23–30

Cheyette, Bryan, (ed.), *Between "Race" and "Culture". Representations of the Jew in English and American Literature* (Cambridge University Press: Cambridge and Stanford, 1996)

Davison, Peter, 'Tennessee Williams, Arthur Miller and Edward Albee', *American Literature* 9 (1984), pp. 553–65

Fried, Lewis (ed.), *Handbook of American Jewish Literature* (Greenwood: New York, 1988)

Fuchs, Daniel, 'Jewish Writers and critics', *Contemporary Literature*, vol. 15 no. 4, (Autumn 1974) (University of Wisconsin Press), pp. 562–79

Guttman, Allen, *The Jewish Writer in America* (Oxford University Press: New York, 1971)

Hapgood, Hutchins, *The Spirit of the Ghetto* (Schocken: New York, 1965)

Heller, Joseph, *Good as Gold* (Cape: London, 1979)

Hoffman, D., *The Harvard Guide to Contemporary American Writing* (Belknap Press: New York, 1979)

Howe, Irving, *The Immigrant Jews of New York* (Routledge: London, 1976)

Howe, Irving, 'The Suburbs of Babylon', *New Republic*, 140, 15 June 1959, p. 17

Jarrell, Randall, *The Complete Poems* (Faber: London, 1971)

Kahn, Lothar, *Mirrors of the Jewish Mind* (Yeseloff: New York, 1968)

Langer, Lawrence L., *The Age of Atrocity* (Beacon: Boston, 1978)

Lawrence, D. H., *Studies in Classic American Literature* (Penguin: London, 1978)

McConnell, Frank D., *Four Post-War American Novelists*: Bellow, Mailer, Barth and Pynchon (University of Chicago: Chicago and London, 1977)

Malin, Irving, (ed.), *Contemporary American Jewish Literature* (Indiana Univ. Press: Bloomington, 1973)

Meeter, G., *Philip Roth and Bernard Malamud: A Critical Essay* (Eerdmans: Grand Rapids, 1968)

Morrison, Toni, *Playing in the Dark* (Picador: London, 1992)

Nemerov, Howard, *Five American Poets* (Voice of America: Washington, 1969)

Odets, Clifford, *Six Plays* (Random House: New York, 1939)

Opdahl, R. K., 'The Nine Lives of Literary Realism', in Malcolm Bradbury and Kenneth Ro (eds) *Contemporary American Fiction* (Arnold: London, 1989), pp. 1–16

Pacernick, Gary, *Memory and Fire. Ten American-Jewish Poets* (Peter Lang: New York, 1989)

Pinsker, Sanford, *The Schlemiel as Metaphor: Studies in the Yiddish and American Jewish Novel* (Southern Illinois University: Prev: Illinois,, 1971)

Pinsker, Sanford *Jewish American Fiction 1917–87* (Twayne: New Jersey, 1992)

Rexroth, Kenneth, *American Poetry in the Twentieth Century* (Herder: New York, 1971)

Rose, Jacqueline, *The Haunting of Sylvia Plath* (Virago: London, 1991)

Shechner, Mark, *The Conversion of the Jews and Other Essays* (Macmillan: London, 1990)

Sherman, Bernard, *The Invention of the Jew in Jewish American Education Novels 1916–1964* (Yoselhoff: New Jersey, 1969)

Showalter, Elaine (ed.), *Modern American Women Writers* (Collier Macmillan: New York, 1991)

Solotaroff, Ted, and Nessa Rappoport (eds) *The Schocken Book of Contemporary Jewish Fiction* (Schocken: New York, 1992)

Soyer, Daniel *Jewish Immigrant Associations and American Identity in New York 1880–1939* (Harvard University Press: Harvard, 1997)

Steiner, George, *Language and Silence* (Faber: London, 1967)

Stepanchev, Stephen *American Poetry Since 1945* (Harper and Row: New York, 1965

Tanner, Tony, *City of Words: American Fiction 1950–70* (Cape: London, 1971)

Vago, Bela (ed.), *Jewish Assimilation in Modern Times* (Westview Press: Colorado, 1981)

Vendler, Helen, *Part of Nature, Part of Us: Modern American Poets* (Harvard: Camb. Mass., 1980)

Vidal, Gore, *Pink Triangle and Yellow Star: Essays 1976–82* (Granada: London, 1982)

Walsh, Richard, *Radical Theatre in Sixties and Seventies* (BAAS: Keele,1993)

Wesker, Arnold, *Distinctions* (Cape: London, 1985)

Wilson, Edmund, *A Piece of my Mind: Reflections at Sixty* (W. H. Allen: London, 1957)

3 General Background texts

Adorno, Adorno, *The Stars Down to Earth, and Other Essays on the Irrational in Culture* (Routledge: London, 1994)

Aleichem, Scholem, *The Best of Scholem Aleichem*, ed. Irving Howe and Ruth Wissa (Weidenfeld and Nicholson: London, 1979)

Alter, Robert (ed.), *The Selected Poetry of Dan Pagis* (University of California: Berkeley and London, 1989)

Beaver, Harold (ed.), *American Critical Essays: Twentieth Century* (Oxford University Press: London, 1959)

Berryman, John, *The Freedom of the Poet* (Farrar, Strauss and Giroux: New York, 1976)

Birmingham, Stephen, *The Rest of Us: The Rise of America's Eastern European Jews* (Futura: London, 1987)

Bradbury, Malcolm and Howard Temperley (eds), *Introduction to American Studies* (Longman: London and New York, 1989)

Breidlid Anders, et al., *American Culture* (Routledge: London and New York, 1996)

Bruce, Lenny, *How to Talk Dirty and Influence People* (Granada: London, 1975)

Bunschoten, Raoul *A Passage through Silence and Light* (Black Dog: London, 1997)

Cantor, Norman, *The Sacred Chain: A History of the Jews* (HarperCollins: London, 1995)

Chatwin, Bruce, *Utz* (Picador: London, 1988)

Cohn, Ruby, *New American Dramatists: 1960–1980* (Macmillan: London, 1982)

Cohn-Sherbok Lavinia and Dan Cohn-sherbok, *A Short Reader in Judaism* (Oneworld: Oxford, 1996)

Cooper, David (ed.), *The Dialectics of Liberation* (Pelican: London, 1968)

Cunliffe, Marcus, *American Literature Since 1900* (Sphere: London, 1975)

Dannatt, Adrian, *United States Holocaust Museum* (Phaidon: London, 1996)

Dinnerstein, Leonard et al., *Natives and Strangers: Ethnic Groups and the Building of America* (Oxford University Press: New York, 1979)

Fishman, Isidore, *Introduction to Judaism* (Vallentine Mitchell: London, 1966)

Fossum, Robert H. and John K. Roth, *The American Dream* (BAAS: London, 1988)

Glaser, Nathan, *American Judaism* (University of Chicago: Chicago, 1957)

Hoggart, Richard, *A Sort of Clowning: Life and Times 1940–59* (London: Chatto, 1990)

Horton, Rod W. and Herbert W. Edwards, *Backgrounds of American Literary Thought* (Prentice Hall: New Jersey, 1974)

Jenkins, Philip, *A History of the United States* (Macmillan: London, 1997)

Karpf, Anne, *The War After* (Minerva: London, 1997)

Kazin, Alfred, *Contemporaries* (Secker and Warburg: London, 1963)

Keenoy, Ray, Saskia Brown, *The Babel Guide to Jewish Fiction* (Boulevard: London, 1998

Lancaster, Brian, *The Elements of Judaism* (Element: Dorset, 1993)

Lee, Brian, *American Fiction 1865–1940* (Longman: London, 1993)

Lewis, Bernard, *Semites and Anti-Semites* (Weidenfeld and Nicholson, 1986)

Litvinoff, Emauel (ed.), *The Penguin Book of Jewish Short Stories* (Penguin: London, 1979)

Michaels, Anne *Fugitive Pieces* (Bloomsbury: London, 1997)

Moore, Geoffrey (ed.), *The Penguin Book of American Verse* (Penguin: London, 1983)

Neugroschel, Joachim (ed.), *Great Works of Jewish Fantasy* (Picador: London, 1976)

Ousby, Ian, *Fifty American Novels: A Reader's Guide* (Heinemann: London, 1979)

Plimpton, George et al., *Whither Mirth? 'The Paris Review'* no. 136 (Drue Heinz: New York, 1995)

Poleberg, Richard, *One Nation Divisible: Class, Race and Ethnicity in the US Since 1938* (Penguin: London, 1980)

Reising, Russell, *The Unusable Past: Theory and the Study of American Literature* (Methuen: London, 1986)

Rexroth, Kenneth, *American Poetry in the Twentieth Century* (Herder: New York, 1971)

Rosten, Leo, *The Joys of Yiddish* (Simon and Schuster: New York, 1976)

Sebald, W. G., *The Emigrants* (Harvill: London, 1993)

Sinfield, Alan, *Literature, Politics and Culture in Post-War Britain* (Athlone: London, 1997)

Smith, Stan, *A Sadly Contracted Hero:* The Comic Self in Post-war American Fiction (BAAS: London, 1981)

Styron, William, *The Quiet Dust and Other Writings* (Cape: London, 1983)

Wiesel, Elie, *All Rivers Run to the Sea* (Harper Collins: London, 1997)

Index

Yiddishkeit, 184
Yiddish literature, 31–2, 35

Zeiger, Gene, *Leaving Egypt*,
    113, 121–2

Zizek, Slavoj, 135
Zukovsky, Louis, 127
Zunser, Eliakim, 24